Small Works Supervision

Small Works Supervision

Jack T. Bowyer

Dip. Arch., FRIBA, FRSA, AIArb.

The Architectural Press Ltd: London

By the same author:
Guide to Domestic Building Surveys
A History of Building
(Crosby Lockwood)
With J. Trill:
Problems in Building Construction

ISBN 0 85139 564 3
First published 1975
© 1975 Jack T. Bowyer
Printed in Great Britain by
Diemer & Reynolds Ltd, Bedford.

Contents

6 Contents

Introduction

For every large contract placed there are many small works contracts of varying
size and complexity. Jobs may range from a simple small manufacturing unit
incorporating a production shed and administrative wing to the renovation
and rehabilitation of a large country house. The variety covered by small
works contracts is therefore immense and requires a high degree of adaptability,
exceptional competence and wide experience from those employed to supervise
these works. Supervision is in fact the greatest problem. Most trades are
present to varying degrees and while the work is usually less complex than in
large contracts, the speed at which it progresses and the close working
proximity of different tradesmen requires a very high degree of organising
ability if the contract is to progress satisfactorily and in proper sequence.
This book has been written to provide such a supervisor with a basic introduction to the art and craft of small works supervision. The problems of
man-management, which can only be learnt by experience, are of vital
importance if relations between site and supervisor are to remain friendly
and co-operative. Failure to follow effective techniques will be likely to cause
friction and dispute and the quality and tempo of the contract will suffer. To
enable the supervisor to carry out his work with competence and efficiency he
needs to have a wide range of knowledge of basic craft skills and details of
materials and workmanship, or to be in a position readily to put his hand on
the information required. He must be able to interpret the basic requirements
of British Standards Specifications and Codes of Practice and to be able to
relate these to the work in hand. Similarly, he needs to have more than a
passing knowledge of material testing and be able to carry out simple tests to
ensure the adequacy of supplied material.
Each chapter of *Guide to Small Works Supervision* deals with a separate trade,
usually with an explanatory introduction, and the information contained in
each trade chapter is given under separate specification clause headings. These
have been prepared from clauses in general use, modified as necessary to make
the required point. Each clause heading is provided, where appropriate, with
National Building Specification Clauses Codes to enable cross referencing with
that work. Following each clause heading information is given describing in
precise terms what are the particular requirements of the clause, in terms of
either workmanship or materials or both as appropriate. Details of sizes and
qualities of materials available, information as to the identification of grades

and qualities are provided and acceptable methods of storage and protection are given. Where appropriate, details of testing are described as well as specific requirements of the BS and CP. Much of the information is tabulated and sketches, diagrams and photographs to explain the text are provided.

This book can be used in two ways. Firstly as a guide to the small works supervisor, providing him with details of good trade practices, suitable materials, their identification, proper storage and testing together with a guide to the handling of men on the site which is a vital part of that building process known as supervision. Secondly the book will serve as a guide to the small works specifier, providing at his elbow in convenient form a compendium of specific information on items of recurrent use in small works contracts. He can refer to trade clauses during the preparation of his specification in the knowledge that he is dealing with basic specific requirements without spending valuable time sifting through a vast amount of information in attempting to find details to fit his requirements.

Asterisks in text thus:
*Indicate the commencement of a specification clause.

1 Preliminaries

Under the terms of the agreement between a building owner and his architect, it is the duty of the latter to inspect the works from time to time to ensure that they are carried out generally in accordance with the contract. He is not required to provide continual supervision; if that is required then a Clerk of Works will be appointed. In some instances, usually on very large or complex projects, a resident architect is provided, but in this case special arrangements are made both for his employment and remuneration outside the general services provided by the architect.

The Conditions of Contract between the building owner and contractor require certain site duties to be carried out by the architect or supervising officer, and these are generally described under Clause 5. One of the architect's duties is to check the setting out of the works at ground level to ensure that the building, at this point, is dimensionally in accordance with the contract drawings. Thereafter, it is the contractor's responsibility to check both the dimensions, the datum and finished ground-floor levels to ensure that these have been correctly related to existing and finished site levels. Any discrepancy in dimensions or levels at this time must be corrected at the contractor's expense if it is found that these are due to his error. The wisdom of including a note on each drawing instructing the contractor to check all dimensions and levels before carrying out any work will now be appreciated.

The datum point selected for each contract will vary, but it is advisable to choose some firm or dependable object such as a manhole cover in the road if an Ordnance Survey Bench Mark is not available in the vicinity. If it is necessary to transfer the datum to a point on the site, ensure that a stout wooden peg is used, placed where it is not likely to be disturbed and see that it is well concreted in as a further precaution.

Setting out should be checked with the foreman. It is not necessary to provide any tapes or other measuring aids as these will be provided by the contractor. The foreman and an assistant will lay the tapes against the profiles and lines to enable the supervising officer to see that the work is correctly dimensioned. At the same time he should check the diagonals and offsets to make sure that the building is square, and also the position of the building in relation to the side boundaries and building lines.

Any discrepancies discovered by the contractor in levels or dimensions during checking of the drawings must, under Clause 1, be notified to the architect in writing and instructions must be issued by the architect to the contractor for rectification of any error as soon as possible. In fact, it is advisable to deal with this problem immediately as the contractor will be completely held up on site and would be entitled to claim an extension of time for the delay. This may well prove to be an embarrassment when explaining the subsequent delayed completion date to the building owner!

Inspection

It is not easy to detect defects during an inspection, especially as work tends to be covered up from one inspection to the next and at the same time work proceeds through the inspection itself. This has led to many actions for alleged negligence against supervising architects and it was to safeguard to some extent their position, which had become almost intolerable, that the wording of the latest editions of the Conditions of Engagement between Architect and Building Owner has been so amended. This states categorically that 'he (the architect) shall not be responsible for any failure by the contractor to carry out and complete the work in accordance with the terms of the building contract between the client and the contractor'.

Site inspections should be a mixture of courtesy, firmness and tact. It is difficult to apportion priorities but in general the architect who employs all three will be respected and liked by the men and will, in general, be able to command a better standard of workmanship and co-operation than the architect who does not. While the Conditions of Contract gives the supervising officer or architect the right to enter the site and inspect the work at all reasonable times, he should always make it his first duty to report his presence to the foreman or agent so that the latter is aware that he is on the site. The foreman should always accompany, or offer to accompany, him on his inspection, so that he can answer any queries which may arise and be at hand to take any instructions which may be given. It is very bad manners to go on site and walk around the job without advising the foreman of your presence and this attitude will justifiably be resented.

Instruction Book

At the beginning of an inspection and as soon as he comes on the site, the supervising officer should ask to see the Instruction Book to see what queries have arisen since his last visit. If any queries need personal inspection on the spot they can be then fitted in in due course. An Instruction Book is a great boon. It saves endless correspondence, and eventually endless bickering and arguments as to what was meant and whether extra work was involved, intended or instructed. It also saves confirmatory written instructions as required under Clause 2.

Bloggs Bank Contract.   33
High St Limpton. - Job 8376

Q	A
47/ Please fix level of threshold to door D/4.	This is to be 51 mm above banking hall floor - level 12.74
48/. Detail required for extract fan mounting to staff lovatory Room 16.	Noted - detail will follow in 7 days.
49/. What is the selected colour for laminated plastic sheet to staff brew-up conter.	Lamin plast Colour no. 237 (blue grey)
50/. Sanitry fittings not delivered on 23/5 as promised.	Noted - are you chasing supplie /? yes!
51/. Can we have colour scheme for premises in four weeks please.	Colour schedule sent to Premises Dept for approval 16/5 - will chase.
52/- One pipe stud tested 22/5 and approved by	Noted.

Example of site instruction book

The Instruction Book is simply a tear-out triplicate book, usually quarto size, with a line drawn down the middle of the page – with questions posed by the contractor or foreman on the left-hand side against which answers are written in the right-hand column. These answers may be given by the supervising officer or they may be given by the sub-contractor concerned with the work involved about which a query has been made by the contactor. Queries by sub-contractors and replies by the contractor are made in the same way. To the answers quantities can be added and agreed, to provide a complete record of the work, agreed at the time it is carried out when all is clear in the minds of those involved. The supervising officer should sign each item and reply dealt with on each visit. When a page is completed he takes one copy for his own records, one copy is sent to the contractor's office and one copy stays on site. If a quantity surveyor is employed on the contract, this last copy can be shown to him on his valuation visits to enable him to keep in touch with and assess forthcoming variations. It should be made perfectly clear at the beginning of the contract that if the query is not in the Instruction Book, it will not be recognised at Final Account stage. The saving in administration costs to both supervising officer and contractor are so great as to make it a most valuable aid to running a contract. Having dealt with such immediate items, it is best to check on previous instructions to clear the position regarding these and chase up any signs of lethargy either on site or in the contractor's office. Here it may be policy to check the contractor's estimate of progress against his Progress Chart to see whether he is up to his programme and whether any delays in the supply of materials of sub-contractors' progress are likely to affect the work in the period leading to the next site visit. Any details or information required should be abstracted from the Site Instruction Book and any matters in connection with the progress or the lack of progress can be written in for record purposes. It should be appreciated that the supervising officer can make use of the Instruction Book for written instructions in accordance with Clause 2 in connection with many matters other than those concerned with the day to day running of the contract such as Clause 6 (opening up work for inspection and removal of defective work), Clause 11 (modification of design etc.) and other matters. For the purposes of Clause 2 this procedure is deemed to be sufficient and binding on the contractor.

Site Inspection
When carrying out an inspection it is necessary to remember that nothing can be insisted on which is not expressly included in the Contract without running the very great risk of incurring extra cost to the building owner. Having accepted this and bearing in mind local conditions which may provide temporary extenuating circumstances, the Conditions of Contract should be enforced with

firmness. If the site is untidy and littered with debris and there is a clause in the specification which requires the contractor to keep the site tidy and clear of all debris from site as it accumulates, the supervising officer should direct the debris to be removed and write his directive into the Instruction Book if his request is not complied with by the next visit. Few contractors care to risk a dispute over this sort of matter. If, however, the site is waterlogged due to excessive rain, it would be unreasonable to insist on the point. The Contractor may well be only too anxious to clear the debris away as soon as conditions permit. Discretion must be used in these matters.

The supervising officer should always start his inspection at ground level and work his way up a building by stairs or scaffold, completing his work by an inspection of the materials before returning to the site office. It is essential to follow a set route, taking in all parts of the building in sequence. This allows progress to be appreciated and queries raised at previous visits can be re-called and previous decisions and instructions compared with work in progress. The supervising officer should never allow himself to be diverted from his route to look at some point raised by the foreman. He should let this take its course and be picked up on route. Look out for evidence of bad practice as well as infringements of the specifications. In large contracts he should look out for signs of urination in dark corners where the distance to the latrine is too far for the lazy man. In due course when the plaster effloresces and blows at that point it will be too late to take action without disturbing the building owner.

Dealing with Site Personnel

At times during the inspection someone will raise a matter for discussion. It may be a trade foreman or it may be a sub-contractor. Let the man raise the point with the foreman. He will probably refer the matter to the supervising officer who can give his opinion or decision to the foreman and let him give the necessary instructions. This will maintain the foreman's position and authority and also enable the supervising officer to give a general answer without the necessity of going into trade technicalities which may well be outside either his experience or knowledge. If he is uncertain as to the practicability of his requirements he should not be afraid to say so. No tradesman or foreman will expect him to have a full and exact knowledge of all craft mysteries and technicalities. Most men will be only too pleased to explain these to an interested and appreciative audience and the supervising officer will learn more by listening to the experts than by reading a host of technical books. If he sees any work which is patently bad or not in accordance with the specification he should not draw the foreman's attention to it in front of his men. He should have a good look at it himself, decide exactly what is wrong and then as he moves away, advise the foreman that he is dissatisfied and give him the reasons for his dissatisfaction. He will generally find at his next visit that the work has been put right and the matter has been resolved without punitive measures. Probably the foreman was waiting to see if the supervising officer noticed and used his expressed dissatisfaction to put pressure on a sub-contractor to put the matter right. If, of course, nothing is done to correct the matter, the supervising officer should record the matter in writing and stand firm on his contractural rights. This way of dealing with things again preserves the foreman's position on site and this is very important as any falling off in his authority will adversely affect both workmanship and progress. On the other hand, a particularly good piece of work should receive its just praise. If the man responsible is near, he should hear any praise of his work, but again this should be directed to the foreman who will pass the praise on officially in due course. Sometimes he may tell the man immediately of the supervising officer's pleasure in his work who may then repeat his remarks to the man concerned. This is the right way to deal with this matter and the procedure should be followed at all times.

If a Clerk of Works is employed on site, the supervising officer will, of course, deal with such matters as praise or condemnation through him to the foreman. It is just as necessary to maintain the Clerk's authority on site as it is with the foreman and as condemnation is a reflection on his activities, this should be kept private from the contractor and the men on the site. When he arrives on a site where a Clerk of Works is employed, the supervising officer should visit him in his office first before seeing the contractor's representative. The Clerk will then be able to advise him of matters such as progress, difficulty and attitude which will enable him to judge the contractor's problems with some knowledge of the other side of the question. It is likely that after dealing with queries and problems with the contractor, he will inspect the works with the Clerk, the foreman attending to his own duties. This is quite usual and will allow him to discuss matters and agree policy without the foreman's presence intruding on the discussion. He may then leave the Clerk to instruct the foreman or contractor on matters raised during the inspection and to complete the Instruction Book regarding the practical matters affecting the works. Where these are likely to become a variation, they should be initialled before leaving the site.

At times it may be found that the foreman is absent from site and has left his ganger in charge. These men are usually highly skilled in the practical side of building and management and are fully competant to take any minor instructions the supervising officer may have to give during his site visit. The ganger should be treated exactly as the foreman but all matters discussed should be recorded in the Instruction Book, as gangers are essentially practical men and their appreciation of office and contract routine is often rather limited.

Materials and Workmanship

One of the duties of the architect or supervising officer is to ensure that the materials brought on site are in accordance with or equal to the specified requirements. In many cases it will be found that these requirements are those laid down by the relevant British Standard Specification or Code of Practice. In many cases, it must be admitted, these requirements are rock bottom minima and many contracts require much higher quality. Quite often in small contracts the requirements for materials are fully stated. In any event all materials must be supplied as 'marketable quality' or 'fit for the purpose', such quality or fitness as being generally accepted by custom and usage. Consequently the supervising officer must have a good working knowledge of what is generally acceptable and accepted in respect of common building materials and he should be familiar with their common defects and deficiencies which would render their use either unacceptable or even dangerous.

A second duty is to see that the workmanship employed is not only in accordance with the standards laid down in the specification but also the generally accepted trade practices which every good tradesman follows and which he was taught during his apprenticeship. It is even more important today to insist on these standards with the growing practice of employing 'jack-of-all-trades' technicians who have a smattering of expertise in all trades and have no real standards or dexterity in any. In the first place, the architect or supervising officer must be fully conversant with the standards of workmanship laid down in the specification and from these he will be able to extend his knowledge as his experience of craft practices increases. He must be prepared to ask why such practices are carried out and be keen to learn and absorb information on the subject. All craftsmen will be pleased to give him the full information he requires and to assist him in enlarging his knowledge in respect of their particular craft. While many of these will include the finer points of practice, there are many matters which he will need to know from the beginning and with which he should be fully conversant before he walks onto a building site.

2 Excavating

BSCP 101: 1972 Foundations and substructures for non-industrial buildings
of not more than four storeys
BSCP 2001: 1957 Site Investigations

*Excavate over the whole area of the works average 150 mm deep and wheel
and cart away excavated material from site to tip (wheel not exceeding
50 m and deposit on site in spoil heaps)
C11:1 1151, C11:4 4151, 4152, 4153
At the start of the contract the contractor will set up rough profiles around
the perimeter of the works to enable him to locate and define the area of
excavations. His next task will be to strip the defined area of all turf and top
soil which, if left under the building, would cause movement in the oversite
concrete due to the expansion of growing vegetable matter. This work is
usually carried out by a mechanical shovel which, in the hands of an experienced operator, can accurately grade the bottom of the excavations to
a predetermined level. The disposal of this material will be described in the
Specification. Usually this will require the material to be carted away and
consequently, as the topsoil is dug out it will be tipped direct into waiting
lorries. If the top soil is to be left on site for future garden works the position
of the spoil heap or tip should be located in such a position so that it will not
obstruct the works and will also be easily accessible for the landscaping contractor. Care must be taken to locate the spoil heap at a distance not exceeding
the distance specified otherwise a possible extra payment may be claimed.
*Excavate trenches for foundations to the widths and depths shown on the
drawings, level and prepare trench bottoms to receive concrete
C11: 1301, 1302
After stripping off the top soil the contractor will excavate trenches to the
widths and depths shown on the drawings. The bulk of this work will be carried
out by a tractor provided with a hydraulically operated backactor bucket
which scoops the material out and deposits it alongside the trench. Buckets
of varying widths are available to suit the dimensions of the trenches. While
a wider trench than that specified is acceptable, so long as the contractor does
not imply or infer an extra charge for the additional excavation and concrete,
a trench which is narrower than specified must be increased in width.
Great care must be taken over implications or inferences. A contractor may

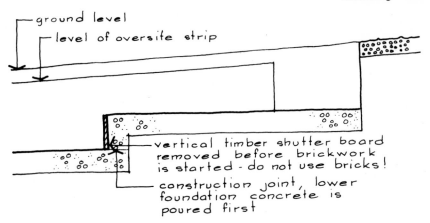

Change of level in trench bottoms

advise that he is having difficulty in obtaining a machine suitable for the work
and that only a larger size is available. This, contractually, is of little interest
to the supervisor who should beware of making any comment, otherwise he
may imply approval and be faced with a claim for extras.

Not all sites are by any means level. Changes of level or steps will occur in the
trench bottoms to avoid the foundations being either too near the surface and
thus liable to problems of frost heave or drying shrinkage, or the depth greater
than necessary and thus uneconomic. The vertical face of the step should be
so positioned as to enable the concrete forming the foundation at the upper
level to pass over the top of the lower foundation by a distance not less than
the thickness of the concrete.

Buildings are set out before the foundation trenches are dug by means of
profiles and lines from corner to corner parallel to the walls. The foundation
trenches must be excavated with the centre line of the wall lying very close to
the centre line of the foundation. A divergence of 25 mm is allowable but
should not be exceeded. If a greater divergence occurs, eccentric loading will
occur, exerting more pressure on one side of the foundation than the other.
In subsoils of uneven strength or high viscosity this might lead to the rotation
of the foundation and the possibility of structural failure. The contractor
should, therefore, indicate on his profiles the centre line of the wall. After the
trenches have been excavated, a line should be stretched between profiles
from the centre line positions and the position of the trench in relationship to
the centre line of the wall checked by measurement. If the wall, when built,
will not sit centrally on the foundation, the contractor should be asked to

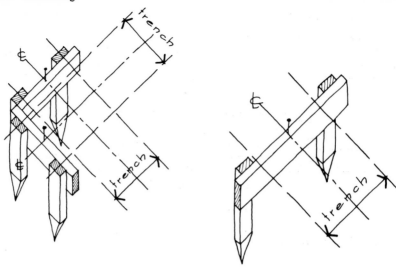

Profiles and centre lines

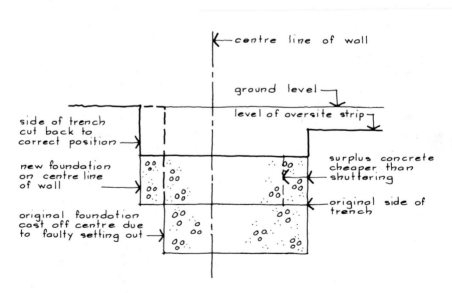

Foundation trench off centre line

extend the width of the trench as required. Any excess excavation and concrete will generally be at the contractor's cost.

If the concrete has been cast before the check is made and is found to be undersized or eccentric to the centre line of the wall, the contractor should be asked to re-excavate the trench above the surface of the in situ concrete and provide a foundation at the proper centre or to the correct size on top of the original, the work to be carried out to his sole cost. Approval should never be given to extending a concrete foundation by casting an extension on the side. The depth of the foundation should be checked by means of a level from a known datum. While it is rarely possible to exactly reproduce the requirements of the drawings on the site, these should not vary by more than 25 mm. Now is the time to agree any extras or savings on foundation works and note these in the Site Instruction Book. Later on, memories become dim on points of details and opening up foundations to verify matters is an expensive business.

The bottoms of all excavations are to be approved before any concrete is placed

C11: 3052, 3301

As soon as the excavations are completed, the contractor will ask for the bottoms to be approved so that he can commence concreting. In addition, the Building Control Officer or District Surveyor will also carry out an inspection as required under the Building Regulations. It is best for both the supervising officer and the official inspector to meet and carry out their inspection together. This will enable any extra work to be agreed and measured for extra payment if required. The responsibility for approving the foundation bottoms and for any subsequent settlement rests on both supervising officer and inspector and this should be borne in mind while the inspection is carried out. In this matter the contractor has no liability.

Firstly, the sides of the excavations should be examined to ensure that the exposed subsoil does not dip below the bottom of the trench, bearing in mind that the bottom is likely to have a thin covering of extraneous material laid over it, from the boots of labourers preparing or 'bottoming up' the trench.

If a dip occurs, it may be necessary for an instruction to be issued to take out the material (which may be either greater or lesser bearing quality than the rest of the trench) and the excavation filled in with concrete. This may be 1:12 as even concrete of this mix is usually stronger in restrained compression than normal subsoils.

Any dark streak in the trench wall will often indicate the presence of peat or partially decomposed vegetable matter. This will often occur on clay sites, and can be a cause of settlement in the foundations later on. The bottom of the trench should therefore be above any such layer and where the subsoil is

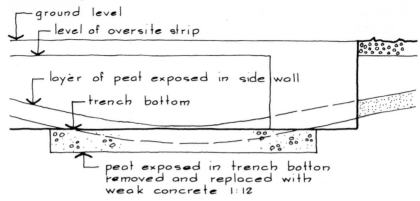

Dips in formation under foundations

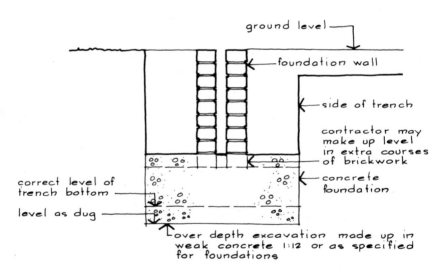

Backfilling over depth excavation

suspect, a small trial hole should be bored to ensure that no further weak patches are located close to the proposed foundations.

The condition aimed for should be a trench bottom of an even, solid and well consolidated natural strata, level and free from lumps and foreign matter and steps with straight and vertical faces. The sides should be straight and vertical. If the contractor in error excavates deeper than required, he should be allowed to back fill up to the required level either in weak concrete or concrete specified for the foundation at his discretion and sole cost.

Provide and insert in bottom of excavation mild steel rod pegs, the tops set level to top surface of concrete foundation

The depth of concrete should be indicated by means of mild steel rods projecting from the bottom of the trench. The use of timber pegs should be prohibited. If they are left in, as is usual, a dry rot situation could ensure. The steel rods should be measured to ensure that the correct depth of concrete is being provided.

Keep all excavations free from water by pumping, baling or as required
    C11: 5051, 5101, 5201. C11: 1304

The bottoms of all excavations must be dry and sound before concreting. A certain proportion of the concrete is 'killed' by contact with soil and this is greatly increased by laying concrete in mud and water. Consequently it is necessary to make sure that all excavations are properly drained and kept free from water by any means necessary. The exact methods are at the contractor's discrection and it would be unwise to give him any directions or instructions in this matter. If the trenches have been affected by water, it is likely that the bottom will have become soft and muddy, especially if men have been walking up and down when clearing the water. Consequently the trench will require rebottoming which means clearing out all the wet, soft and muddy material down to sound strata. Making up to the required levels by the use of weak concrete, increasing the thickness of specified foundation conrete or additional courses of brickwork should be at the contractor's discretion as he will be liable for the cost.

The contractor should not be allowed to pump ground water from the excavations into the drainage system due to danger of silting up. It is up to him to find a suitable natural outfall for the water to a ditch or watercourse.

Make up to required levels under concrete and pavings with approved hardcore, well consolidated, levelled and prepared to receive concrete
    C21: YP1.20. C21: 1051 1151

A bed of hardcore may be required to fill depressions or sloping oversite excavations and to raise the concrete after the removal of topsoil. The material should be chemically inert and not liable to expand on exposure to moisture. Ideally the proportion of fine material should be kept as low as possible as this will not only reduce the rise of ground moisture but also assist in accelerating the time taken for consolidation. Excess consolidation of fine material will cause the subsoil to be forced up into the voids in the hardcore. Where the surface of the site is wet it may be advisable to lay down 50 mm of clinker to serve as a base for the larger material and to bind the surface of the subsoil. Various materials are used as hardcore and depend on location as well as availability. Probably the best is still brick or tile rubble but this usually requires mixing and blinding with fine materials such as sand 'as dug' to fill the voids. Hogging is usually satisfactory, as is quarry waste or 'scappling'. Concrete waste is usually too large and requires a good deal of added fine material. PFA is good but expensive. Most of the other materials used incorporate a proportion of sulphates which are damaging to ordinary Portland Cement and concrete should be protected by a layer of stout polythene or bitum felt placed over the hardcore. Where brick hardcore incorporates some gypsum plaster similar protection should also be provided.

The material used must be of a maximum size less than the minimum thickness of the bed. With most materials this is no problem but with brick or concrete these should be broken to pass a 75 mm ring. This should not be done by placing the bricks in position and beating them with a sledge hammer. The breaking should be away from the bed and the broken brick or concrete placed in position. Otherwise damage to the foundation wall may ensue.

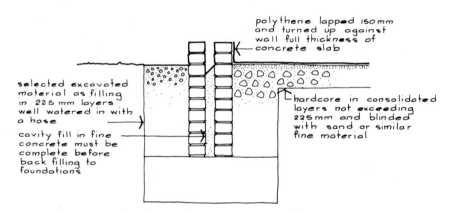

Hardcore around foundations

Hardcore should be placed in layers not exceeding 225 mm and each layer well consolidated by mechanical means before the next is laid. A vibrating roller or consolidator is probably the best machine but make sure that any cavity filling has been carried out or there is the possibility that pressure exerted on the hardcore may cause collapse of the cavity wall below damp course level. Where it is specified that hardcore should be finished with a layer of polythene sheet to receive concrete, this must be lapped at least 150 mm and is best turned up against walls to the full thickness of oversite concrete. The polythene, which acts as a d.p.c. also prevents cement from the concrete leaking into the blinding, can then be made continuous with the d.p.c.'s in the walls. This prevents rising damp circumventing the d.p.c. through the slab edge and at the same time provides separation between concrete and wall, allowing the two elements to settle slightly independently of each other.

Return, fill in and well consolidate selected excavated material (or hardcore) around footings up to the required levels

    C21: 1151

Ideally backfill around foundation walls under the oversite concrete should be in hardcore to reduce the risk of settlement which is possible if earth fill is used at this point. This settlement will result in cracks in the oversite concrete about 300 mm from the wall unless the slab is properly reinforced. Outside the building where no pavings occur earth fill is quite satisfactory.

Whichever fill is used it must be properly and adequately consolidated in layers not exceeding 150-225 mm thick with a proper rammer. If the fill is dry, it should be watered to assist consolidation.

Carry out all planking and strutting required

    C11: 1451

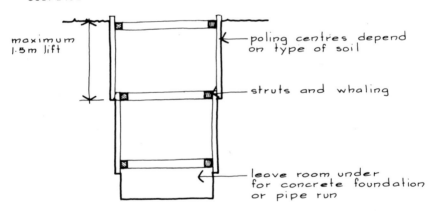

Typical planking and strutting to shallow trench

Excavations below a certain depth in all soils (except rock) and to all excavations in loose material, such as sand and loose shingle, require the sides to be strengthened by timbering or other supports. This is to prevent the sides of the excavation falling in which could be a danger to workmen as well as to the works under construction in the excavation.

The responsibility for the provision of any supporting work and its design is the contractor's, and he is liable if he disregards the requirements of the specification for any damage or mishap due to the collapse of trench walls, including injury or death of any workmen and the reinstatement of the works.

3 Concreting

BS 12: 1958   Portland cement
  Pt. 2 1971 Metric units
BS 882: 1965   Aggregates from natural sources for concrete
BS 1881: Pt 1:1970 Methods of testing concrete
BS 449: Pt 1:1970 Hot rolled steel bars for the reinforcement of concrete
BS 4483: 1969   Steel fabric for the reinforcement of concrete
CP 101: 1972   Foundations and sub-structures for non-industrial
  buildings of not more than four storeys
CP 102: 1963   Protection of buildings against water from ground
CP110 Pt. 1: 1972 The structural use of concrete
CP 114 Pt. 2 1969 Structural use of reinforced concrete in buildings

*Cement will be Portland of British manufacture complying with the BS 12:
  1958, delivered to site in the maker's original sealed bags and stored in a
  proper manner to avoid deterioration
  Y11:Yq.2.10.*

Cement for most contracts is supplied in the manufacturer's sealed bags although
on very large jobs it is delivered loose in bulk tankers, stored in silos on site and
from which it is drawn as required for use. In the latter case, cement is used in
the order in which it is delivered and there is little risk of staleness. Cement
delivered in bags should be used in the same way and this is ensured by system-
atic stacking and use. Cement must also be properly stored and kept in good
condition until used. Damp is its greatest enemy. Bags stored in the
open must be on a raised damp-proof platform and the whole properly protected by tarpaulins. Ideally, cement should be stored in a shed with a sound
concrete or boarded floor and a weatherproof roof.

The quality of British cement can be assumed and beyond checking that the
manufacturer is British, nothing further remains to be done with freshly
delivered cement. Cement which has deteriorated beyond its proper life span
will be caked and solid and should be rejected for use in any capacity in the
works.

*Sand (or fine aggregate) shall be clean river or pit sand complying in all respects
  with BS 882: 1965, well graded to pass a mesh 4.75 mm square with not
  more than 10 per cent to pass a mesh of 0.5 mm and equal to a sample to*

*Testing fine aggregate or sand for cleanliness. Left: using a 200 ml measuring
cylinder. Right: using a convenient bottle*

be deposited with and approved by the supervising officer
Y31:Yp1.10

Two kinds of sand are, in general, used for building purposes, one for mortar
and one for concreting. Sand for mortar is dealt with later. Sand for concrete
is generally washed by the suppliers to remove impurities which would cause
loss of strength in the concrete mix. These are generally loams and clays which
are easily washed out by mechanical means. A simple test to detect the com-
parative cleanliness of sand is to rub a little between the hands. If this leaves a
stain on the skin the sand may be too dirty and should be tested as follows:
Place 50 ml of 1% solution of common salt (1 teaspoonful to 1 pint of water)
in a 200 ml measuring cylinder. Add sand to the 100 ml mark and increase the
quantity of salt solution up to the 150 ml mark. Shake vigorously and allow
to settle for 3 hours. The silt in the sand will be deposited on top of this sand
and should not exceed 6% of the total depth of solid material. If this percentage is exceeded the sand should be rejected. A jam jar can serve the same
purpose as a measuring jar but without the same degree of accuracy.

Most suppliers will guarantee their product complies with the requirements of BS 882 and will certify to this effect. It is difficult to check grading with any accuracy without the requisite equipment. A good guide can be obtained by pouring the sample out onto a banker board or similar flat surface. Inspect the material for evenness of grading from the maximum size downwards. Too much fine 'flour' will be as undesirable as too great a proportion of large particles. The fine aggregate will fill the voids in the resultant mix and its ability to do this depends on even grading. The grains should be sharp and bright and damp to the touch. If all these conditions are present then it is very likely that the material offered complies fully or very closely with the specified requirements.

Coarse aggregate shall consist of natural gravel, crushed gravel or crushed stone complying in all respects with BS 882: 1965, well graded from the nominal maximum sizes specified.

All-in aggregate shall consist of natural gravel, crushed gravel or crushed stone, complying in all respects with BS 882: 1965, and shall consist of aggregate containing a proportion of material of all sizes well graded from the nominal maximum size down to 4.75 mm

  Y31:Yp1.10

Gravels, sands and crushed stone are all in common use as concrete aggregates. When mixed with cement and water these form concrete. The selection of aggregates is important as these form the bulk of the concrete mix. Aggregates must be clean and free from humus, vegetation and clay, all of which will prevent proper adhesion between the particles and the cement. An excess of fine dust or 'flour' lowers the strength of the concrete. All these should be borne in mind when examining sand offered for concreting work.

The maximum size of aggregate must be related to the purpose for which the concrete is required. In reinforced concrete it is necessary for all aggregate to pass between the separate reinforcing rods or between the rods and the sides of the shuttering. For this reason aggregate for this work should not exceed 19 mm in any one direction. For foundations, beds under drains and mass concrete 38 mm may well be entirely acceptable. Aggregate supplied graded should contain particles ranging from the largest to the smallest and graded quality should always be used for concreting. At the pit or quarry, grading is carried out mechanically using sieves which conform to BS 410. A simple method of checking evenness of grading is to place a bucketful of aggregate taken random from the inside of the pile onto a banker or similar flat

Facing page: testing coarse aggregate for even grading. Top: quartering sample taken from bulk. Centre: quartered sample. Bottom: two quarters set aside for reference and remainder ready for amalgamation and inspection

surface. Care must be taken to see that the sample is a fair one as all aggregates tend to segregate during delivery, the smaller particles falling to the bottom. When the load is shot on to site the large particles are delivered first with the fine material on top. Thus sampling from the interior will give the best average sample.

The aggregate on the banker should be carefully mixed with a trowel, flattened to 75 − 100 mm thick and divided into four quarters. Two opposite quarters should be stored for reference and the remainder remixed and spread out for examination. The sample should now contain material from the maximum size evenly graded down to fine course material. There should be very little 'flour' or fine dust and the sample should be clean to handle and free from deleterious materials described above. If the aggregate meets these conditions it should generally be satisfactory for use. It is as well to check later deliveries against the sample set aside to ensure that deliveries are consistent in quality.

The storage of aggregates on site is important to prevent accidental mixing of different grades and the inclusion of impurities. Aggregates should be tipped onto a hard dry surface and if this is not available, an area of weak concrete should be laid for storage. Divisions should be provided to keep apart the various grades.

Slump test for concrete. Facing page, top: standard slump cone with compacting rod. Left: compaction of concrete in cone. Right: measuring slump of test concrete. This page, below: types of slump

*Water for concreting should be clean, pure main water, properly stored in
   clean tanks kept for the purpose or drawn direct from the main as required
   Y11:Yw4.10. Yw4.11*

Water fit for drinking purposes and drawn direct from the main is generally
perfectly satisfactory for concreting. When water is delivered to the mixer by
hose from a standpipe no problems arise, but when storage is from a cistern
care must be taken to see that no impurities or organic solids are introduced
which would affect the strength of the concrete. This could come about by
washing shovels, picks and other earth-moving tools in water stored for concreting. Separate facilities should be provided for this latter activity.

Where mains water supply is not available, local river or well supplies which
comply with the requirements of BS 3148 are perfectly satisfactory. There are
testing establishments which will carry out the necessary testing or the public
analyst will usually carry out the tests on payment of a fee. Water is usually
drawn in special glass containers and the testing laboratory should be first
consulted to find out its specific requirements.

*The amount of water shall be sufficient only to give a good workable mix but
   in no case shall the slump measured in accordance with BS 1881: Pt 1: 1970
   exceed that permitted
   Y31: 66056 7151*

The strength of concrete depends mainly on the relative properties of the water
and cement it initially contains, the greater the proportion of water the weaker
the concrete. It is therefore important to see that the volume of water used is
just sufficient to provide suitable workability to enable efficient compaction of
the concrete when placed in position. Aggregates with sharp edges and rough
surfaces need more water than smooth round aggregates to produce a workable
mix. The usual method used to measure workability is the slump test. This
helps to control the consistency of concrete providing the same proportion of
ingredients are used throughout the contract. The supervising officer should ask
for frequent slump tests throughout concreting and always when a new batch
of aggregate is started.

A standard 'slump cone' is of sheet steel, 300 mm high, 200 m across the base
and 100 mm at the top, both top and bottom being open. The cone is placed
on a clean, level surface and filled in four successive layers with fresh concrete
from the pour in progress, each layer being well compacted by rodding at least
25 times with a mild steel rod. The top is smoothed off and the steel cone is
lifted off the wet concrete. Complete or partial collapse of the concrete will
take place. Very wet concrete will collapse completely, very dry hardly at all.
The amount of settlement or 'slump' is measured by placing the rod across the
top of the cone and measuring down to the top of the concrete.

Three kinds of slump are encountered. Natural or true slump occurs when the concrete merely sinks, keeping more or less its true shape. Sheer slump occurs when the mound of concrete falls over sideways. Both types of slump can occur with the same mix, usually sheer indicating faulty preparation for the test, which should be carried out again. Collapsed slumps indicates a very wet mix. The following is a guide to permissible slumps for concrete for different purposes:

Pavings and vibrated mass concrete work High strength vibrated concrete	25 mm
Hard compacted mass concrete Normal r.c. work with vibration	25 - 50 mm
Hard compacted normal r.c. slabs, beams, columns and heavily r.c. work with vibration	50 - 100 mm
Heavily reinforced work without vibration and where compaction is difficult	100 - 150 mm

Materials for concrete shall be measured in approved gauge boxes on a clean boarded platform. Due allowance shall be made for the moisture content of the aggregates. Unless otherwise approved, mixing will be carried out using an approved mechanical batch mixer, and will continue until the materials are uniformly distributed throughout the mass which shall be of consistent colour and texture
Y31: 3051 3102 3201 3401 3402 3451 3501 3502 3503 3701
E31: 4101

Different concrete mixes require different proportions of constituent materials, often of different nominal maximum size. Care must be taken in measuring or batching aggregates if consecutive batches are to be uniform in consistency and, therefore, strength. The following quantities of aggregate for each 50 kg cement are required for mixes stated and the coarse and all-in aggregate shall be of the nominal maximum sizes stated:

Nominal mix	Fine aggregate m^3	Coarse Aggregate m^3	All-in Aggregate m^3	Nominal maximum size in mm
1:12			0.425	38
1:7			0.247	38
1:2:4	0.070	0.140		19
1:1½:3	0.053	0.106		19

Cement should always be weighed, as the weight by volume varies considerably depending on the way the box is filled. Gauge boxes for aggregate should be deep and narrow as boxes of this shape can be filled more accurately than wide, shallow boxes. The filling should always be carried out on a clean platform, preferably boarded, which can be hosed and swept down regularly to remove spilt material or mud from the site. In mixes specified by volume, the sand is assumed to be dry. In practice, sand is very seldom in this condition and its volume of a given weight varies with its moisture content. Equal weights of dry and saturated sand occupy the same volume but the same weight of damp sand can occupy up to 40% greater volume. This is known as 'bulking'. Allowance must therefore be made in practice to bulking or the concrete may contain too little fine aggregate. The problem does not occur with coarse aggregate, and coarse sands bulk less than fine. A rough guide to the extra sand required is to increase the volume of material by 25% when damp. A more accurate method is to fill a 200 ml measuring cylinder up to 100 ml mark with sand, dropped in lightly and levelled without compaction. Water is then slowly added up to about 100 ml in volume, the sand and water being stirred with a rod to ensure it becomes thoroughly saturated and free from contained air. The difference in levels between damp and saturated sands will be the percentage bulking.

Mechanical mixers are highly efficient aids to concrete manufacture so long as they are used properly and simple rules are observed. The first batch of concrete of the day's production should be rejected as this will probably contain excess coarse aggregate with the cement and fine material remaining on the drum and paddles. A first run of cement and fine aggregate will usually deal with this problem. After all materials and water have been added to the drum, the concrete should be mixed for at least two minutes, preferably three with a large mixer. For uniform consistency of mix the time of mixing should be kept constant throughout. Mixers must be kept clean and in good mechanical order. The drum and paddles must be cleaned after each run and it is usual for the drum to be charged with coarse aggregate and plenty of water and run for 15 minutes or so until it is perfectly clean.

In urban areas, the tendency now is for concrete to be prepared in central batching plants and delivered to site by road in specially constructed vehicles. Two systems are employed for this method. 'Ready-mixed' concrete is generally mixed in a central container and conveyed wet to the site in revolving containers which keep it agitated to prevent segregation. 'Truck-mixed' concrete contains aggregate and sand batched dry with water in a separate container. This is introduced either during the journey or on arrival on site. By this latter method concrete in dry bulk can be delivered to a greater distance than wet when the problems of initial set have to be faced. Very high-quality materials and strength can be obtained by these methods where these are required on small sites and which would be difficult to obtain by site mixing. Each batch of concrete should be supplied with a certificate giving actual weights of aggregate, cement and water used, to guarantee that the concrete is in accordance with the specification. These should be retained by the Supervising Officer for future reference if required.

There are occasions when, on all sites, small quantities of concrete are required at frequent intervals. As it is usually uneconomic to provide these by mechanical means, hand mixing has to be resorted to as required. The cement, fine and coarse aggregates should be carefully measured in their correct proportions (increasing the cement content by 10%) on a clean hard surface or banker platform (not on tarmac or concrete paving) to prevent dirt and sand being shovelled up with the concrete. Hand mixing should be carried out on this platform, the materials being turned at least twice dry and twice wet with sufficient water only being added through a rose to make the mix workable and the colour of the wet concrete uniform and consistent throughout.

When weather is frosty it is essential to ensure that aggregates are well covered with hessian or tarpaulins to keep frost off the material. The use of uncovered material in such a situation is inadmissable. The minimum temperature during which concreting can take place without pre-heating water and/or aggregates is 5°C and the temperature of the concrete at the point of discharge must not be less than 4°C. This cannot be achieved with frost covered aggregate. The temperature of protected aggregates will rise to the required temperature sooner than unprotected material. Any concrete damaged by frost, and showing signs of disintegration on the surface and edges, must be broken out immediately and replaced.

Concrete shall be transported and placed in position as soon as possible after mixing and in any case within 30 minutes in a manner to prevent segregation and loss of ingredients

E31: 1051 1101

E31: 3301 3353 3401 3551 3553 3554

Wherever concrete is required, it must be placed within 30 minutes of mixing to prevent initial set taking place before it is in position. It is therefore necessary to move it rapidly from mixer to final position so that it arrives in the best possible condition. Three main defects must be guarded against: premature drying out; the segregation of ingredients and consolidation.

Whether the concrete is delivered by ready-mix lorry, dumper or barrow these problems occur. Drying out can occur in hot weather or in a strong wind and concrete should be covered with wet sacking if it has to travel any distance. Segregation occurs along the journey as large particles sink to the bottom leaving water and fine material at the top. Consolidation occurs in very dry mixes and is caused by jolting during transportation.

All barrow and dumper runs should be as smooth as possible and concrete should be discharged at or immediately adjacent to the point of placing. Dropping from a height encourages segregation and chutes should be used when problems such as deep trenches are encountered. If possible ready-mix lorries should discharge direct from their chutes into the placing position.

Foundation concrete will probably be a simple mass concrete mix with a slump between 25 and 50 mm. Unless special requirements are specified the concrete will be well 'trodden in' by the concreting gang to provide good compaction and then smoothed off with the back of a spade to the level required and indicated by the mild steel levelling pegs referred to in Chapter 00. These should always be left in place and concreted in.

Where steps occur in the foundation the top section of concrete should oversail the bottom by at least the thickness of the foundation and a proper sawn shutter face provided. A few loose bricks piled on the lower level of concrete is not satisfactory. Any areas where the excavations have been taken deeper than necessary can be filled with weak concrete (1:12 - 38 mm) mix but in practice it is usual to concrete these in as the foundations are poured to save time and trouble.

While the concrete is still green and slightly soft, the foreman may mark out the corners of the building in its top surface on areas floated smooth for the purpose, ready for the bricklayers to set out their bottom course, but otherwise on no account should any work or traffic be permitted on the foundation concrete for at least 48 hours after pouring to give the concrete time to harden sufficiently.

In general, the drier the mix the stronger the concrete, so long as it can be properly compacted. Vibrators give proper compaction to dry or heavily reinforced mixes which cannot be properly compacted by hand. When mixes are too wet, vibrators will cause excess fine material and water to rise to the surface forming a layer of weak concrete short of coarse aggregate. The use of the vibrator to move concrete in the shutter will cause similar segregation and should be avoided. Where hand compaction is used a sharp pointed 13 mm mild steel bar makes a useful tool, well working the concrete around the reinforcement while the concrete is poured from the top, to compact the full thickness of the concrete. Consolidation is usually complete when all air bubbles have stopped appearing on the surface.

Freshly placed concrete shall be protected by approved means to prevent loss of water and shall be kept constantly damp for a minimum period of four days after concreting or longer if so directed
  E31: 5052 5101 5102 5151 5201

Concrete must be 'cured' or kept moist for a period after placing so that the water it contains can complete the chemical action taking place as the concrete hardens. If concrete dries out too quickly surface cracks will appear which may affect its effective life. Water curing is the best method and is carried out by covering the concrete with wet hessian or sand and keeping these wet by spraying or covering with waterproof paper or polythene. These materials will, if kept close to the surface, retain the moisture already in the concrete. Curing should start as soon as the concrete is hard enough not to be marked by traffic or the covering and, with ordinary Portland cement, should be carried out for a minimum of four but preferably seven days. In winter this period should be doubled discounting any days on which frost occurs. With the use of rapid hardening cement the normal minimum curing period should be 3 days. In cold or frosty weather the method of protection employed must not include water. In these circumstances polythene or building paper are likely to be the best materials to employ.

Construction and daywork joints shall be arranged and provided in approved positions. Before any new concrete is placed on old work, the face shall be well cleaned down to remove all cement laitence, well wetted and covered with a thin layer of equal portions of cement and sand to give a good bond between old and new concrete

E31: 2051 2151 2201

E41: 2051 2052

E41: 3051

Construction joints can be very unsightly unless they are pre-planned. Most walls and columns require these joints, in walls at about 1 m apart vertically, although columns can usually be cast full height up to the soffit of the beams. In either case stubs of concrete are usually provided at the bottom, 100 mm high, called 'kickers', which can be accurately set and dimensioned and used to set out the shuttering for the rest of the lift.

Shutter hands should therefore bear the height of lift as well as any surface features very much in mind when preparing sections of shuttering. While a continuous pour of 1 m is quite in order with mechanical pouring, concrete placed by hand should not exceed 150 mm thick.

At the end of a run of concreting or a day's work, the concrete should be stopped off against a vertical and securely fixed temporary shutter stop, preferably notched over the reinforcement and provided with a batten on face to provide a joggled joint. This board should be removed as soon as the concrete has hardened sufficiently or at the most within 24 hours of casting. The faces should be washed off with a hose to expose the aggregate, or the laitance chipped off if the concrete has been allowed to harden too much. Before concreting recommences, the surface should be well wetted and grouted to ensure bond between new and old.

The position of daywork joints is important. Large areas of concrete should be laid in alternate bays so that shrinkage is taken up fully before the space between slabs is filled in. Suspended beams and slabs should be cast continuously but where daywork joints are unavoidable. They should occur at one third span in all cases and care taken to provide vertical stop boards as described above. With slabs the maximum area for a single pour should not exceed 50 m^2 with a maximum length of 10 m. This refers to ground-floor slabs. Suspended slabs, as stated, should be cast together with edge beams etc. in a single day. These days a consulting engineer will be involved where large suspended slabs are to be cast and he will indicate where the daywork joints are to be made — these will not necessarily be at one third span points.

Include the Provisional Sum of £X.00p for testing concrete cubes. Preliminary test cubes shall be taken from the specified concrete mixes as follows:

For each grade of concrete six cubes shall be taken, three tested at seven and three at 28 days. At each age test no cube strength shall fall below $1\frac{1}{3}$ times the specified works test cube strength. Compression tests to comply with BS 1881: Part 4

Y31: 6102 6151 6201

Y31: 7051 7101 7351 7352

With most concrete structures the strength of the concrete is of importance, especially in reinforced work. Test cubes are therefore taken so that the strength of the concrete can be measured. The cubes usually measure 150 mm in all directions but 100 mm are sometimes used for the smaller aggregates (19 mm and under). The steel moulds must be clean and the concrete a fair sample of that going into the work and taken from the point of delivery or placing. Details of the time, temperature, weather conditions and batch number (if any) should be recorded together with the exact location of the remainder of the concrete batch in the structure. The supervising officer should personally see the moulds filled, hand compacted or vibrated, the top smoothed over and reference number and date inscribed in the smooth cement on the top surface.

The cubes, three of which should be taken for each test, should be left in the moulds for 24 hours before being removed and placed either in sealed polythene bags or immersed in water to cure. On no account should test cubes be subjected to freezing temperatures or left out in the sun.

Concrete cubes may be specified to be tested at 24 hours, 7 or 28 days and should hold up to the full minimum strengths specified for the particular period. Arrangements can be made either by the supervising officer or by the contractor. In either case, the cubes should be carefully packed for transportation to the testing laboratory to keep them damp and prevent damage and the cubes should arrive at least 24 hours before the test. The results of the test should be sent to the supervising officer with a copy to the contractor. When low results are

---

Facing page: testing concrete cubes. Top left: standard 150mm steel mould with ms compacting rod. Top right: mould being filled and hand compacted. Centre left: hydraulic testing machine with test cube in position. Centre right: concrete cube under test. Bottom: satisfactory cube at end of test

obtained, instructions must be given to improve the quality of the concrete mix and, if necessary, the poor batch must be broken out and replaced. Low results are of more concern in tension members such as beams and suspended slabs than in compression members such as foundations. Each case must be considered on its merits. The most common cause of low test results are incorrect batching due to excess water, the use of unsuitable aggregate or contamination.

Leave or form all mortices and grooves in concrete for fixing bolts, bottom tracks of sliding doors and water bars
  E11: 1501 1502

Labours required for fixing other elements are best carried out during casting rather than the expensive and labourious method of cutting away afterwards. This is especially true when the concrete is to be left fair face and appearance is important. With regard to the water bars, balusters and similar items, these should have slightly undercut sides to provide a good grouting key and expanded polystyrene is probably the best material. This can be burnt out successfully to clear the hole when required. Neat cement can be used very effectively as a grout but the best material is undoubtedly run lead which not only sets the metal in the concrete but allows a certain resilience to movement. Also it sets in less time allowing temporary supports to be removed more quickly, in the case of balustrades clearing access to the stairs.

Foundations to receive structural steelwork will have mortices for holding down bolts formed during pouring. This is preferable to casting bolts in situ as it allows freedom for adjustment if slight discrepancies or creep occurs in the steel frames. Of the various types of former probably a tapered box of expanded metal lath gives a greater degree of adhesian to the grout when this is poured around the holding down bolt.

Steel reinforcing rods will comply with BS 449:Pt1:1970, and fabric rein-forcement with BS 4483: 1969. All steel will be free from loose rust, scale, dirt, oil or other deleterious matter and securely fixed in position to avoid displacement during pouring of the concrete.

All reinforcement should be placed strictly in accordance with the drawings, bars bound together with No. 16 swg (1.6 mm) pliable iron wire or other approved binding and so fixed as to allow proper cover to be provided by means of approved spacers
  E21: 1051
  E21: 3101 3201 3351 3502

The success of a concrete structure depends a lot on the correct placing of the reinforcement. Insufficient cover will allow the steel to rust and blow the concrete face. If the bars are moved during the placing of the concrete the structure may well fail under load.

All reinforcement must be rigidly fixed to prevent movement or displacement during concreting or vibration. This is usually achieved by wiring each intersection with stout galvanised wire or purpose-made clips. Steel fabric, used in conjunction with bar reinforcement, should be securely fixed to each bar in a similar way. Where fabric only is employed, as in oversite concrete, each sheet should be lapped at least 150 mm and wired at each intersection of the cross members of the mesh. Where light steel fabric is used to reinforce the concrete casing to a structural steel member, the fabric should be lapped in a similar way. With steel beams fabric is only required to the soffit and half the depth, suspended with stout galvanised wire hangers over the top flange at 600 mm centres.

The provision of a minimum concrete cover to steel is necessary for a number of reasons, all practical, which are not relevant here. It is sufficient to ensure that the reinforcement is fabricated and assembled to provide the specified cover when it is placed in the shutter box. If it is not, it is necessary to check the dimensions of shutter and reinforcement to see which is at fault and give instructions for the fault to be remedied. To ensure proper bottom cover it is normal practice to set the steel up on spacers. These may be small concrete blocks with fixing wires cast in, bent mild steel rods or plastic units. They should be set at sufficiently close centres to lift the reinforcement clear of the shutter to the correct height throughout and be securely fixed to the steel to prevent displacement. The thoroughly bad practice of hooking up the fabric

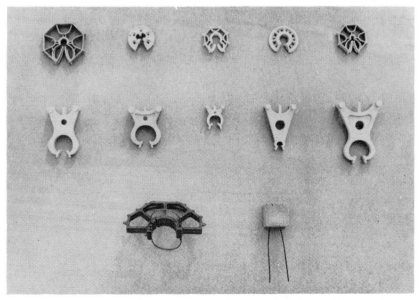

Types of spacers in general use to ensure required cover to reinforcing steel.

during concreting to get some concrete under the reinforcement should not be tolerated under any circumstances. The position of steel in a slab is critical and must be placed accurately in the correct position in the slab.

It is necessary to anchor round mild steel reinforcing rods in concrete to prevent loss of frictional grip and consequential failure. This can be provided effectively by hooking the ends of the rods, the radius of the hook being twice the diameter (D) of the bar (2D) which should be extended a further 4D to provide sufficient anchorage. Another method, often used when bars are spliced together, is to allow a length of bar equal to 30D to provide anchorage. This latter method is not practicable in isolated lintols but can be used in continuous beams over a number of supports. When reinforcement is left projecting for further extension this length (30D) should be left projecting for future splicing.

All formwork will be of sufficient strength to carry the loads imposed upon it during construction without distortion or undue deflection. No formwork or struts shall be removed until the concrete is of sufficient strength. All formwork shall be cleaned out before concreting takes place and properly treated to avoid adhesion

E11: 1051 1151 1251 1351

E11: 2051

E11: 3051 3151 3202

It should, in theory, be unnecessary to direct that formwork should be of sufficient strength to carry the weight of wet concrete poured into it. Shutters are, however, often of insufficient strength, accidents do occur, and props are often inserted to keep the shutter in place. Where a shutter or formwork is required for concrete which is to be vibrated, this should be of stouter construction than normal, otherwise displacement may occur and fine material leak out through the joints leaving behind cellular concrete.

Where a shutter abuts face brickwork it is important that no grout damages the brickwork. The use of a mastic seal to the joints is worthwhile considering to minimise the risk. Shuttering should not be struck for at least 7 days after pouring and the soffit supported for at least 28 days. Where long spans of beams or lintols occur, with clear voids under, have the shutter wedged up slightly in the middle to reduce the optical illusion of sagging which occurs in dead flat beams or lintols.

Care must be taken to remove all sawdust and chippings from the shutter as well as any mud or rubbish immediately before the concrete is poured. The interior surface of the shutter should be cleaned and either thoroughly wetted or treated with an approved mould oil or release agent. This latter material must not come into contact with the reinforcement or it will cause loss of adhesion. Mould oil is generally only effective for about 24 hours and if the shutter is not filled within this period a further coat should be applied before concreting.

4 Bricklaying

BS 187: Pt. 2: 1970	*Sand lime bricks*
BS 1180: 1972	*Concrete bricks*
BS 3921: Pt. 2: 1969	*Clay bricks*
CP 111 Pt. 2 1970	*Structural recommendations for leadbearing walls,*
Metric Units	
CP 121: Pt. 1: 1973	*Brickwork*
CP 122: 1952	*Walls and partitions of blocks and slabs*

*Bricks shall be hard, sound, square and clean. Clay bricks shall be well burnt and in respect of size shall comply with BS 3921: 1969
Fg. 2. 10 - Fg. 2.26 (Inc.) Fg. 2.40. Fg. 2.43
Sand lime bricks and concrete bricks will comply with BS 187: 1970 and 1180: 1972 respectively
F11: Ff1.10 Ff1.13-Ff1.21 (incl.)

The requirements and standards specified for bricks vary with the type and use to which the brick is to be put. For instance, while you would be quite justified in condemning stock facings with damaged arrises due to bad handling, such a defect would not be serious in common bricks which were to be plastered. Certain defects are, however, common to all clay bricks and where they are observed the bricks should be condemned.

'Underburnts' are soft bricks which easily scratch under the thumbnail and have fragile arrises which break off under pressure.

'Overburnts' on the other hand, although apparently hard, are usually friable or brittle and break easily when struck against a sound brick.

Both these defects may show cracking or pitting of the surface. Any facings which show unburnt nodules of clay or lime, gravel or stones or have areas of partial vitrification should be thrown out as these defects are likely to lead to rapid disintegration of the whole brick.

*Separate samples of each type of brick taken at random shall be deposited with and approved by the architect before being used and subsequent deliveries shall equal the random sample
F11: FAO.01. FaO.02

All bricks should have true faces and beds and be free from twisting. Where pressed bricks are being used see that their arrises are keen and sharp. All bricks should approximate closely to standard dimensions and, except where multi

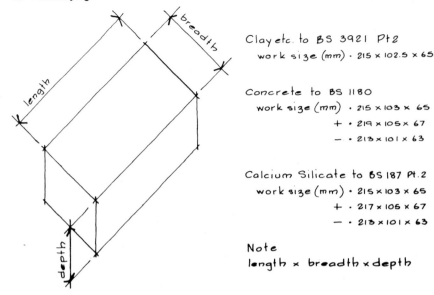

Clay etc. to BS 3921 Pt 2
work size (mm) · 215 × 102.5 × 65

Concrete to BS 1180
work size (mm) · 215 × 103 × 65
+ · 219 × 105 × 67
− · 213 × 101 × 63

Calcium Silicate to BS 187 Pt.2
work size (mm) · 215 × 103 × 65
+ · 217 × 105 × 67
− · 213 × 101 × 63

Note
length × breadth × depth

Dimensions of bricks and allowable tolerances

facings are concerned, the colour should be uniform throughout, with a uniformly burnt internal texture. All bricks should have a clear metallic ring when either struck together or with a trowel. As a brick will spend much of its life repelling water, it follows that it should have a limited absorption, not exceeding 20% of its weight.

To check absorption of a brick, select a newly delivered sample, thoroughly dry it in an oven, weigh it, and totally immerse it in cold water for exactly 24 hours. Re-weigh after ensuring that all surface water has drained away. The difference between the two weights is the amount of water absorbed.

You should arrange to inspect the first load of bricks on delivery with the foreman and agree any defects which you are not prepared to allow and which do not conform to the specification. Have samples of these defects set aside for reference in case of dispute at a later date.

*Care should be taken in handling bricks and no damaged facings shall be used
   in the works
   F11: FaO.05. FaO.06*

Never on any account allow bricks to be shot on to a site. Always insist that they are properly unloaded either by hand or on pallets and properly stacked. Facings should be stacked on hard standing to prevent discolouration of the bottom layers from water and mud on the site.

*All brickwork shall be set out and built to the respective dimensions, thick-
nesses and heights as shown on the drawings*   –
     F11. 2451 F11. 3051

The use of good quality bricks is no guarantee of good brickwork. The final
result will depend on the skill, care and attention given to his work by the
bricklayer. The supervising architect should have some knowledge of craft
practice as well as accepted standards of workmanship. When brickwork is set
out from the foundation, insist that all openings and features are set out at
this point so that the bond can be set to accommodate these when the brickwork reaches the right level. Watch carefully to see that no half bats are used
to make out and condemn any work which incorporates these. A closer set to
the corners is the right way to deal with this situation. If you see that these rules
are followed the bond will be maintained throughout the work.

All perpends should be neatly kept, that is all vertical joints should occur one
above the other in alternate courses. The corners and arrises should be plumb
and upright and a good bricklayer will select bricks for these positions to ensure
perfection.

*Face brickwork shall be kept perfectly clean and no rubbing down of
brickwork will be allowed*
     F11. 1251 F11.4

All brickwork should be kept neat and clean, especially facework. This can only
be assured by the bricklayer laying and spreading the mortar in a workmanlike
manner, just sufficient being used to bed the bricks properly. The surplus
squeezed out of the bed joint should be removed by holding the blade of the

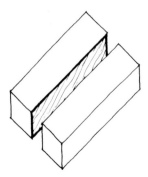

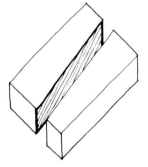

Queen closer
(usually placed next to the
quoin header to provide
lap)

King Closer
(used in reveal construction
to provide full brick width
on bed)

Closers cut from whole single bricks

trowel at right angles to the face of the brick and pushing it in a forward movement of the wrist. A sharp tap on the brick with the trowel should be sufficient to bed it properly. Excessive tapping indicates too much mortar and too little skill. Smeared facework will always result from failure to follow this procedure. Always insist that scaffold boards next the wall face are turned back each night, and in wet weather, to reduce the risk of splashing the brick face from mortar droppings or mud left on the scaffold.

*No brickwork will be carried out in frosty weather except with the express
    written approval of the architect
    F11: 1151 etc.*

The use of frost proof additives is now fairly common, their main objective being to raise and maintain the temperature of the water in the mix until set has been reached. Care must be taken in face work to ensure that any additive does not affect the colour of the mortar and cause stratification of the work. In any case the top of all work must be properly covered by scaffold boards, polythene or similar forms of protection when there is danger of frost.

*Brickwork generally shall be built in English (Flemish etc.) bond, with
    half brick walls in stretcher bond
    F11.3*

English bond · used for 225 mm thick walls but can generally be built fair on one side only

Double Flemish bond · used for 225 mm thick walls providing a very deorative pattern with dark headers

Flemish Garden Wall bond · used for 225 mm and double skins cavity walls in good class work

Stretcher bond · used for 112 mm walls or skins in cheap work · closer shown with broken joint where necessary

Common brick bonding to quoins

Much of the strength of a wall lies in the bonding of individual units. It is essential that all cross joints be confined to one course alone and not extend into the course above or below. The proper arrangement should best form what is known as quarter bond, when every perpendicular cross joint showing on the face of the wall is a minimum of 112 mm apart. This will ensure that the weight of the wall is spread evenly over the whole of the foundation. Various bonds are used in traditional brickwork, mostly derived from English and Flemish bonds. You should have a thorough knowledge of the proper application of correct bonding and insist that the correct methods are used on site.

*Partitions should be properly bonded to one another and to brick walls
*   F11.3*

The bonding of different materials, one to another, is also important to provide a homogeneous structure and prevent differential cracking due to varying degrees of shrinkage. This is most noticeable when light-weight blocks are bonded to brickwork. By covering the joints with plasterer's scrim or a good

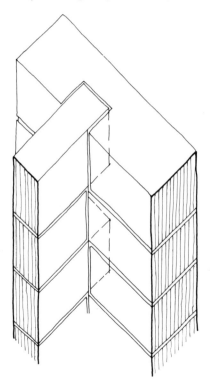

Blockbonding partitions

width of expanded metal before plastering this problem can be minimised. Sometimes the bricklayer will omit block bonding where partitions are joined to structural walls and rely on strips of brick reinforcement built into the joints. This is normally sufficient for strength and to reduce cracking but to make quite sure, the finishing coat of plaster should be provided with a quirk in the internal angle to localised cracking which may occur as the structure dries out.

Build the partitions shown on the drawings of approved light-weight blocks (or concrete – moler – breeze etc.)

F11. 2401 et seq. F11.3

The two main classes of building block used in building are of dense concrete or light-weight aggregates. Blocks should be thoroughly dry before use or they will dry out after the wall is built and shrinkage cracks will ensue. On delivery to site, blocks should be stacked on a dry surface, timber sleepers or a layer of old blocks to keep them off the surface of the ground. Blocks should be stood on edge and, if left in the open, covered with a tarpaulin to keep off the rain. Blocks must be handled with care and in fair face work all blocks with chipped arrises and corners should be discarded.

Blocks of all kinds should be laid true to line and plumbed on the face of each course. They must also be bonded together at wall junctions as well as in walls. The mortar joints should be solidly flushed up and the top of the wall protected over night and at times of heavy rain. You should ensure that the mortar specified and used is always weaker than the block itself so that any cracking takes place in the joint and not through the block. All ties in block cavity work should be placed clear of the vertical joint and pointing in fair face work should be neatly carried out without smearing the face of the block.

Rake out all joints in brick or blockwork where plastered or rendered

F11. 4451

In some blocks with a high surface suction the joint may be flushed up, but

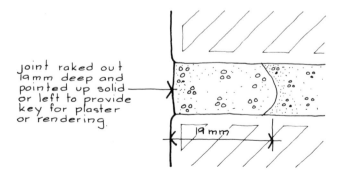

joint raked out
19 mm deep and
pointed up solid
or left to provide
key for plaster
or rendering.

19 mm

Raking our joints in brick or blockwork

where the face has low suction, and always in external work, the joint should be raked out 19 mm to provide a good key for plastering or rendered finishes.

Internal blockwork may be constructed in frosty weather subject to proper precautions being taken to protect the work

F11.1151

Blockwork in cold or frosty weather should be avoided if at all possible but if there is no alternative you should direct that warm water is used for mixing the mortar, that all materials are free from ice and that the work is protected for some days by covering with sacks or tarpaulins to prevent freezing.

Never allow bricks and blocks to be mixed in the same wall face. Sometimes bricklayers will make out around lintols and make courses under timber joists with bricks in a predominantly block wall. Have no hesitation in condemning this as the result will be unsightly shrinkage cracks and loose plaster.

Mortar shall be mixed on a proper boarded platform, turned twice dry and twice wet, or by means of an approved mixer. Ingredients shall be properly measured in gauge boxes and the quantities should be sufficient for one day's use. Knocking up on the following day will not be permitted

Y11. 1301

Y11. 3052 3151

A brick building is as strong as its mortar, although too strong a mix will cause more trouble than a relatively weak mix. The aim should be to provide a mortar slightly weaker than the material used for the wall. Any shrinkage or settlement cracks will then occur in the mortar joints and not fracture the material itself. This precaution makes remedial work less expensive to carry out.

Very clean sands are unsuitable for mortars as they give too harsh a mix. The best results are obtained with a sand containing clay or silt up to 10% by decantation. The method of assessing or determining the purity of sand for mortar is the same as for concrete. A rough and ready method is to rub a little sand between the hands. If a slight stain is left on the skin the sand is probably suitable.

Water shall be clean and free from acids, vegetable matter etc., and obtained from the main supply

Y11: Yw4.10

Yw4.11

Water should always be added from a rose and direct from the main supply. Mortar can be made on a steel or wood banker or a small mixer but never on pavings or the ground. Cement should be added to sand, both gauged by volume and the water added while the mix is turned over.

Weak mortars for facework usually have non-hydraulic lime incorporated in them but modern practice tends to use either a plasticiser (which, taking the place of lime, renders the mortar 'fatty' or easy to use), or special cements which obviate the need for lime. Plasticisers which dissolve in the mixing water are preferable to powders added to the mix as the correct quantity can more easily be added to the predetermined volume of water required for the prepared mix. Mortar must be used on the same day as it is prepared and care must be taken at the end of the day's work to clear all old 'pug' off the scaffold bankers and barrows and the whole, including mixing banker, mixer, and batch boxes, cleaned and hosed down ready for the next day's work. The use of any old mortar, kept moist overnight in a barrow, under an old sack, must not be allowed.

Include in the tender for the construction of a small panel of facing brickwork not exceeding one metre in area as a sample for bond and pointing
    F11. 1051

On most contracts, the colour of the mortar for pointing facework is important and this must be uniform throughout the whole of the facework. Variations are unsightly, and many buildings otherwise of merit are spoilt due to lack of care in matching the pointing. If the work is to be pointed on completion, you should insist on the contractor bulking the sand against an approved sample. Have several samples made up and the sample panel erected and pointed in the different examples to see the effect of the different colours of mortar produced against the brick. Let the samples dry out for a week or two before making your choice as the colour of mortar varies considerably between the wet and dry state and most wet mortars look the same. Supervise the preparation of sample mortars and once you have made your choice see that the work is carried out to the

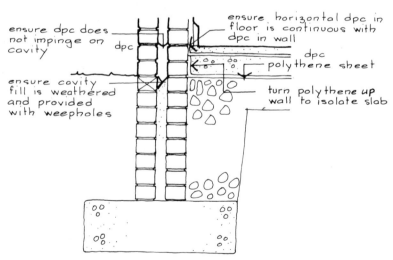

Detail of junction of dpcs in external cavity wall and solid floor

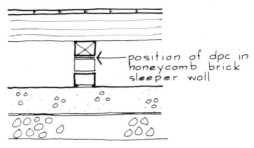

position of dpc in honeycomb brick sleeper wall

Dpc in brick sleeper wall

sample. If it varies, have the work taken down and done again until it is right.
*Provide and build into cavity every 990 mm horizontally and every 450 mm
vertically approved galvanised wall ties*
    F11: Xt6.10 Xt6.15 Xt6.20 Xt6.31
Wall ties are provided to integrate the two leaves of the cavity wall into a single
homogeneous mass. At certain places in the wall extra ties are necessary to take
up extra stresses, at external corners and at the reveals of windows. Ties should
be provided one above each other every 225 mm in height. With butterfly
pattern ties always see that the twisted tang in the middle points down to shed
any water which finds its way on to and may run across the tie.
Provide and build into every wall and partition an approved damp proof course
    F11:6
Care must be taken to ensure that the d.p.c. fulfils its proper function. You
must see that the joins are properly lapped at least 100 mm and that the lengths
of d.p.c. do not incorporate any tears or other defects. The d.p.c. should be
the full width of the wall and not project into the cavity where it may well be
a means of collecting mortar droppings. Choose a d.p.c. which does not bleed
under heat or load and see that this is placed flush with the face of the wall
and not set behind a mortar pointing. All partitions built off site concrete
should have a similar d.p.c. but sleeper walls should have the d.p.c. placed under
the timber wall plate as sometimes water will collect on top of the over-site and
may well bridge the d.p.c. if at that level. With solid floor construction ensure
that continuity is provided between the d.p.c. in the wall and that provided in
the floor, otherwise bridging may occur and rising damp in the wall ensue.
Clean all cavities from mortar droppings and keep wall ties clean
    F11: 5051 5151 5301
Despite all care taken, mortar droppings will fall into the cavity. One method
of preventing this is to place a batten over the wall ties in the cavity to collect
droppings and raise this and clean it off every 450 mm lift. This method is un-
popular with bricklayers as it slows down their work. In any event make sure

that sand courses are left over windowheads and above the cavity fill so that
the droppings can be scraped out and the cavity left clean. Before this takes
place any mortar on the ties should be knocked off with a batten poked down
the cavity. A lot of trouble in this connection is caused by the cavity filling. The
regulation requirement brings this too high in relation to the average d.p.c. and
so it is very necessary to ensure that all mortar droppings are removed from the
base of the cavity to maintain the minimum distance of 150 mm between top
of fill and d.p.c. Make sure also that the top of the fill splays out to throw any
water penetrating the cavity to the other face of the wall to enable it to escape
through the weepholes provided.

Build in all frames and trays over openings

    F11: 7501

    F11: 6251

While it is not always either necessary or politic to build frames and linings
into internal brick walls, as they are constructed (although they should always
be built in externally) it is necessary for these to be built into block partitions.
In any event hardwood pallets and nails are not sufficient fixings and proper
sheradised cramps or similar should always be used, screwed to the back of
frame or lining and built solid into the wall. Where frames are set into prepared
openings care should be taken to leave out sand courses to receive the cramps.
Trays over openings should always project at least 50 mm clear of the solid
work to the reveal and the ends turned back to throw any water back on to
the tray where it can find its way out through the weepholes provided. Otherwise water could dribble down under the tray and cause a wet patch in the top
corner of the opening.

5 Roofing

BS 747 Pt. 2: 1968   *Roofing felts – metric units*
BSCP 144 Pt. 3: 1970   *Roof coverings – built up bitumen felt*
BRS Digest 8   *Built up felt roofings*
BRS Digest 110   *Construction*
BRS Digest 144   *Asphalt and built up felt roofings – durability*
The Felt Roofing Contractors Advisory Board: Built-up Roofing

All roofs must be considered as a unified structural element composed of a number of components, the failure of any one of which will endanger the adequacy of the whole. The effect of temperature changes, moisture content in construction or arising from internal condensation, dead, imposed and wind loadings will all have an effect on the roof. All must be considered and related to all works carried out in weatherproofing the structure.

The underlying structure must be designed to take into account the provisions of BSCP 3 [in connection with loading] and BSCP 144 Pt. 3 (Roof coverings: built up bitumen felt). Provision must be made for the correct and secure fixing of the various components to the underlying structure with allowance for possible movement and allowable deflection. Concrete roofs must be provided with methods for draining stormwater or water from construction before the weatherproof covering is applied. Failure will delay drying out the structure with possible future problems associated with entrapped moisture.

Efficient natural drainage is important, a minimum fall of 1 in 60 over the whole roof including valleys and gutters is essential. Dead flat roofs create more difficult conditions for the roofing and it is essential that glass fibre or asbestos based roofing felts are used here. All work to the sub-structure, abutments, verges, eaves, projections through the roof and outlets should be completed before the sub-contractor starts work on site. Any work which has to be carried out to any part of the structure necessitating traffic or access over the finished roof must be carefully controlled and adequate protection provided before the work is commenced.

The storage and stacking of materials is important. Rolls of felt should be stood on end on a clean boarded or concrete standing and the bitumen neatly piled on a similar clean platform. Chippings for the roof finish should be discharged onto a clean concrete platform and retained within boarded or similar sides to preclude any spillage and the risk of inclusion of deleterious matter such as mud.

*Provide and install to whole surface of roof a vapour barrier consisting of
(felt laid in hot bitumen - 500 g polythene)*
L31: Ln2.10
Ln6.10
Ln6.20

The type and positioning of the vapour barrier will depend on the construction
of the supporting deck. Often insulation is combined with the vapour barrier
in an integral unit. These materials supplied in sheet form are usually of semi-
rigid foamed plastic construction and should be used as the manufacturer's
directions.

Aerated concrete structural slabs can be satisfactory without the provision of
a vapour barrier. Normal concrete, however, must be provided with one and
this is usually combined with insulation, the vapour barrier being placed under
the insulation. It is not, however, practical to provide a vapour barrier under
an insulating screed. In this instance the provision of a battened or suspended
ceiling finished and backed with a vapour check should be used. Extra insulation
can be provided to roofs with insulating screeds. This should be formed from an
inorganic insulating material laid on a vapour barrier of felt in hot bitumen.

A similar method is used for concrete roofs with normal cement/sand screeds,
but the thickness of insulation is usually increased as screeds of this nature
have, unlike proper lightweight insulating screeds, little insulative value. Timber
roof decks require a slightly different procedure. The insulation should be laid
over a layer of felt laid in hot bitumen as a vapour barrier and the roof covering

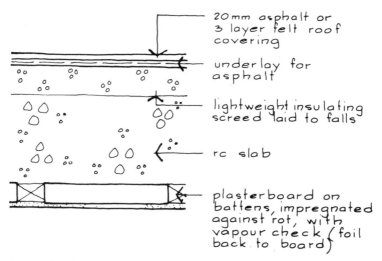

20mm asphalt or
3 layer felt roof
covering

underlay for
asphalt

lightweight insulating
screed laid to falls

rc slab

plasterboard on
battens, impregnated
against rot, with
vapour check (foil
back to board)

Vapour barrier for rc slab with lightweight screed

applied over the insulation. Care must be taken to ensure that the free ends of the insulation are sealed to prevent any moisture entering the material. In addition a vapour check should be provided between the ceiling finish and the timber supporting joists to obviate the risk of moisture rising into the structure from the room below. The roof cavity can be sealed or ventilated but as condensation will be higher on ceiling vapour checks with ventilated roof cavities the workmanship and care in properly fixing the check must be of a higher quality. When large slabs of high moisture movement characteristics, [e.g. strawboard,

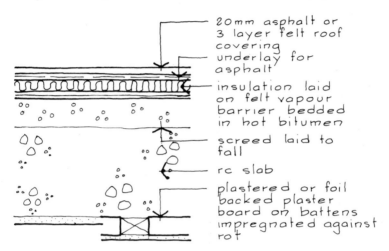

20 mm asphalt or 3 layer felt roof covering
underlay for asphalt
insulation laid on felt vapour barrier bedded in hot bitumen
screed laid to fall
rc slab
plastered or foil backed plaster board on battens impregnated against rot

Vapour barrier for rc slab with normal screed

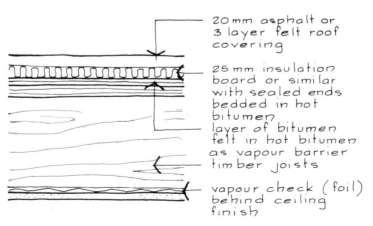

20 mm asphalt or 3 layer felt roof covering

25 mm insulation board or similar with sealed ends bedded in hot bitumen
layer of bitumen felt in hot bitumen as vapour barrier
timber joists

vapour check (foil) behind ceiling finish

Vapour barrier for timber roof deck

chipboard] are used for decking, it is advisable for a strip of vapour barrier material to be bonded to one side of the joint prior to bonding the vapour barrier itself to permit small movements to occur without tearing the main barrier.

Provide and lay to roof structure ....
all in accordance with the requirements of the roofing sub-contractor and prepare to receive built-up roofing
P13
R55
R51: Ri4.30
R51: 2751 2851
H41: 3051, et seq.

The provision and preparation of various materials to receive built-up roofing is important as the care taken will be reflected in the eventual life of the roof covering. Unless the work is carried out properly the roofing sub-contractor may either refuse to lay his material or to accept liability for subsequent failure.

Screed Generally concrete and screeded surfaces must be free from steps, gaps or irregularities and finished from a wood float. The material must be properly cured, free from frost damage and no reinforcement or fixing clips should project above the surface. Screeds should be laid in areas not exceeding 15 m^2, not less than 25 mm thick on solid concrete and composed of cement/sand 1:4. Lightweight screeds must have a 13 mm thick cement/sand 1:4 applied immediately following the laying of the aggregate. Where a strong bond is required on an exposed site, a bitumen primer should be applied to concrete or screeded roof surfaces before the first layer of felt.

Woodwool slabs must be type B, not less than 51 mm thick and sufficiently strong to carry the weight of the roof felters. The upper surface, if not pre-screeded or felted, must be finished with a minimum of 10 mm cement/sand 1:4 screed. Pre-screed or felted slabs should have their joints taped with a strip of felt bonded to the slab with bitumen compound to prevent the bitumen passing through the joints. Channel reinforcement slabs must be provided with extra insulation to avoid the formation of cold bridges which will cause condensation on the underside. Dry sheet insulation applied to the whole of the upper surface over a layer of hot bonded bitumen roofing will both overcome the problems of cold bridging, assist in combating movement, provide a vapour barrier and increase insulation. Any roof space below must be ventilated by 300 mm^2 per 300 mm run of eaves.

Plywood for decking must be exterior grade WBP (weather and boil proof) to BS 1455, the grade appearing in the stamped mark on the face of the plywood. The boards should be nailed with suitable sheradised wire nails at 150 mm centres to all supporting timbers with extra at the perimeter if the site is exposed. The nails should be at least 38 mm longer than the thickness of the plywood. All free edges must be supported and at vertical abutments at 50 x 50 mm splayed sawn fir angle fillet must be fixed to the deck to provide an air space between wall and structure. Vapour barrier and insulation must be provided and the roof space must be ventilated to open air as described before for wood wool slabs.

Metal decking is usually designed to receive an overlying vapour barrier and dry sheet insulation as described before for wood wool slabs.

Timber boarded decks should be formed from well seasoned material, tongued and grooved and minimum nominal thickness of 25 mm. The timber should preferably be treated by a proprietary impregnation against infestation and rot. The boards must be fixed in a manner similar to boarded floors (see Floor Finishes). An overplying vapour barrier and insulation and ventilation of the roof void to open air must be provided as described for wood wool slabs.

The built up roofing will be three layers self finish bitumen felt as BS 747, 1968, laid with 50 mm side laps and 75 mm end laps, staggered, the layers bonded together in hot bitumen (laid on and bonded to insulation previously specified). The whole of the work will be in accordance with BSCP 144 Pt 3: 1970. The layers of felt will comply with the following specification:

L22:L

L22:2

L22:3

L22:4

For flat roofs, three layer specifications are generally used. Sloping roofs may be provided with two layers only, except when additional durability is required. BSCP 144 Part 3. table A2 provides a schedule of types and weights of roofing felts of which the following are recommended.

	BS 747 Ref.no.	Type of felt	Nom.wt. kg/$10m^2$
Underlays	1 B	Fine sand surfaced bitumen felt	17.0
	1 C	Self finished bitumen felt	13.0
	2 B	Fine sand surfaced bitumen asbestos felt	16.0
	2 C	Self finished bitumen asbestos felt	13.0
	3 B	Fine sand surfaced bitumen glass fibre felt	18.0
	3 G	Venting base layer bitumen glass fibre felt	32.0
Exposed	1 E	Fibre based mineral surfaced bitumen felt	36.0
layers	2 E	Asbestos based mineral surfaced bitumen felt	36.0
	3 E	Glass fibre based mineral surfaced bitumen felt	27.0

It should be noted that built-up roofing felt types 1 B and 1 C and asbestos types 2 B and 2 C are in their particular types equivalent and interchangeable. Felt based materials (1 B, 1 C and 1 E) are used extensively in low-cost specifications. They have lower dimensional stability and their use is not recommended on low pitched decks or over screeded concrete slabs.

Asbestos-based materials (2 B, 2 C and 2 E) are relatively inert and provide an improved fire resistance on combustible decks. On timber boarded decks the first layer should always be asbestos-based roofing. Specifications employing all asbestos-based materials provide high quality roofing with good dimensional stability.

Glass fibre based materials (3 B, 3 G and 3 E) are increasingly used in good quality work. Being of all mineral composition they have a high degree of dimensional stability, are rotproof and non-absorbent.

The satisfactory performance of built-up roofing is often related to its method of attachment to the roof. The first layer is fixed according to the nature of the decking as follows:

Nailing at 150 mm centres is recommended for normal timber boarded roofs with extra nails at the perimeters in positions of high exposure.

Partial bonding by spot or strip bonding at intervals depending on the degree of exposure for prescreeded or prefelted wood wool or plywood decking. This technique can be employed also for the fixing of vapour barriers to decking under dry insulation. Partial bonding prevents the formation of blisters between the deck and the waterproofing by water vapour and allows a certain degree of movement in the roofing deck. A proprietory venting base layer (3 g) will also give similar protection.

Full bonding is provided in areas of high exposure to concrete and screeded roofs and to decks including metal decking where dry insulation material is incorporated in the roof design. It is necessary to apply a coat of bitumen primer over screeded and concrete surfaces, which should be allowed to dry and be free of all volatiles before the first layer of roofing is applied.

Movement joints in the structure provide serious problems unless they are properly allowed for in the built up roofing work. Minor movement joints, e.g. daywork construction joints, can be isolated by a strip of heavy roofing

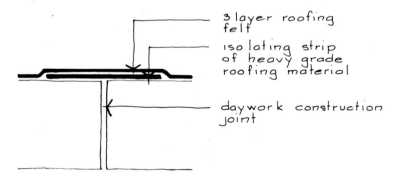

Detail of movement joint for felt roofing over daywork construction joint

material laid over the joint and either partially bonded or left loose and the roof covering laid over the strip without interruption. Where a change in construction is encountered and moderate movement due to differential expansion and construction is likely the joint covering can be a hessian based damp course material fixed over a 13 mm plastic pipe with the roof covering applied over the whole in the usual way. Where expansion joints are provided in the structure and considerable movement is anticipated, vertical upstands should be provided in the substructure with the roofing being taken to the top of one side, and to oversail a metal flashing fixed to the other side. This provides a weathered dissociation on either side of the expansion joint.

Built-up felt roofing is generally laid with the fall of the roof in hot bitumen

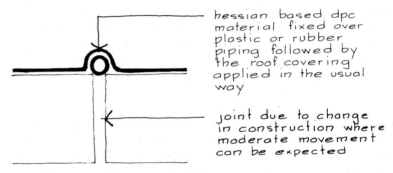

hessian based dpc material fixed over plastic or rubber piping followed by the roof covering applied in the usual way

joint due to change in construction where moderate movement can be expected

Detail of movement joint for felt roofing at change of construction

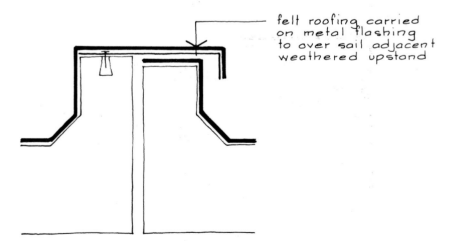

felt roofing carried on metal flashing to over sail adjacent weathered upstand

Detail of major movement joint for felt roofing

and laps as indicated must be provided to ensure waterproof joints. Abutments should be provided with angle fillets (essential with timber boarded decks) or in lieu an additional strip of roofing felt provided as reinforcement in the angle. D.p.c.'s must be at least 150 mm above the surface of the roofing with a metal flashing built in as the work proceeds. The use of hessian based or similar d.p.c.'s as flashings is not suitable.

Where gutters are incorporated in the roof deck the roof covering and gutter lining should form a continuous membrane. Angle filters or angle reinforcing strips should be provided and d.p.c. and flashing as generally described for abutments.

Eaves and verges can be provided with a welted drip a minimum of 50 mm deep nailed to a 38 x 25 mm (minimum) impregnated sawn (or wrot) timber batten. The welted felt strip is returned onto the roof surface and lapped to the built-up roofing layers. Alternatively the built-up roofing material may be dressed over a check fillet, a metal trim screwed into position and a separate roofing strip bonded to the trim or weatherproofing. Bonding of bitumen to aluminium trim is facilitated by the application of a thin cement grout over the bonding area of metal.

Vent shafts and similar projections through roof structure and weathering should be collared and the roof covering made good to the collar and protected by a separate weathering hood. This will allow the pipe to move without endangering the weatherproofing of the roof. Projections through the weathering should be provided with similar weathering hoods to allow the felt to be dressed as under.

Surface water outlets should preferably be set below the general roof surface

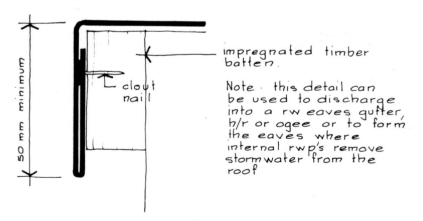

Detail of felt dressed and welted eaves

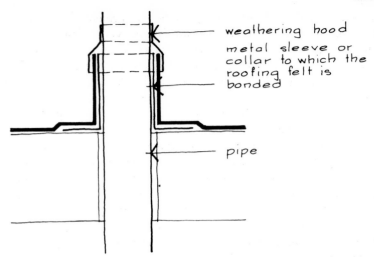

weathering hood

metal sleeve or collar to which the roofing felt is bonded

pipe

Detail of protection around pipes penetrating felt roof surface

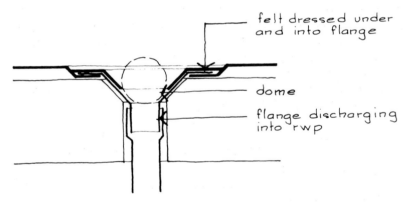

felt dressed under and into flange

dome

flange discharging into rwp

Detail of rainwater outlets in felt roofing

and provided with a suitable flange to allow a bonded lap with the built up roofing of at least 100 mm. The bottom layer should be set under the flange, the second cut to it and the third dressed down into the outlet.

Provide and lay to the whole surface of the roof 10 mm white spar chippings laid shoulder to shoulder and bedded in bitumen dressing compound L22: 8051 8101

Spar, durite or granite chippings as specified should be applied to the finished roof as soon as possible after the last coat is laid or, if necessary, after all other building operations are completed. Builders traffic over a chipping finished room may well damage the built-up layers and in any case, cement, abrasion or paint spills will certainly spoil the appearance. The whole horizontal surface of the built-up roofing is covered with a good application of bitumen and the chippings are cast onto it to form a dense even finish with no bare places. Care must be taken to keep outlets free for 300 mm immediately around the outlet and the dome placed in position before casting to prevent chippings passing through the outlet and building up to cause a possible future blockage at the foot of the pipe. The soles of all guttering incorporated in the roof deck should be kept free from chippings to faciliate drainage. Some roofers roll the chippings in, some brush them thoroughly. All loose chips surplus to requirements should be removed, otherwise they are likely to fly off in a high wind.

Provide and bed in hot bitumen to the top layer of built-up roofing where shown on the drawings 300 x 300 x 8 mm approved asbestos cement flat roofing tiles, laid straight joint to falls provided. Perform all cutting and fitting required
L22: 8051 8151

Where any access is required in excess of occasional maintenance, these tiles should be provided. In addition to their use as a protective pedestrian decking, they also provide a reflective surface to reduce the absorbtion of solar heat in the same way as spar chips. The tiles should be close butted and neatly cut to free edges and abutments and around outlets.

Provide and fix to timber purlins Messrs ....
corrugated (profiled) asbestos cement roofing sheets in accordance with the manufacturer's recommendations with ...... mm side laps and ...... mm end laps
N33:N

Particular manufacturers have their own requirements as to the profiles of their products as well as sheet sizes. Their literature must be consulted for these. In addition, the centres of supports are determined by the strength of the material and the depth of the profile or corrugation. Recommended purlin spaces for standard sheets are as follows:

Profile	Purlin centres (mm)	Side lap (mm)	End lap (mm)
Standard 3 corrugated sheets	925	102	150
Major 6 corrugated sheets	1375	70	150

Minimum pitches to sheets are as follows:

Minimum pitches to sheets	Pitch [degrees]
Standard 3 corrugated sheets	22.5
Major 6 corrugated sheets	22.5

With end laps sealed the above pitches can be reduced to 15°. An unsealed end lap of 305 mm will also be weatherproof down to 15°.

On delivery to site sheets should be carried horizontally by two men and stacked flat on bearers, two for sheets up to 1525 mm and three for sheets over this length. Asbestos cement sheets should not be stacked over 1220 mm high. The two top sheets should be pulled out to provide weather protection and the whole weighted down or tied. Coloured sheets must be covered up and protected.

Sheets should be cut with a hand saw and fixing holes drilled, not punched. Side laps should nest over the corrugation and where end laps are sealed mastic should be applied 25 mm from the top of the underlapping sheet. Laps should be made facing away from the prevailing wind. It is necessary to mitre one corner of each sheet at the bottom corner by an amount equal to the diagonal of the end and side laps to effect neat setting.

The sheets should be fixed with galvanised mushroom headed gimlet pointed screws with galvanised diamond washers complete with bitumen sealing washer to the timber purlin. Plastic sealing washers may be used instead of the above. Fixings should be on the top of the corrugation, three to each width as follows:

Profile	Detail and length of screws
Standard 3 corrugated sheets	7 x 80 mm
Major 6 corrugated sheets	7 x 100 m

Various accessories are available for both profiles, e.g. eaves filler pieces, standard, tapered and gable barge boards to finish off the free edges of the roof.

6 Asphalting

Asphalt tanking:	BS 1162, 1418, 1410: 1966	Natural rock asphalt aggregate
	B 988, 1097, 1076, 1451: 1966	Limestone aggregate
	BSCP 102: 1963	Protection of buildings against water from the ground
Asphalt roofing:	BS 747: Pt 2: 1968	Black sheathing felt
	BS 1369: 1947	Expanded metal lathing
	BSCP 144 Pt. 2: 1966	Roof coverings: mastic asphalt

Asphalt shall comply with BS ...... and the whole of the work shall be carried out by an approved specialist sub-contractor in accordance with the provisions of the relevant British Standard Codes of Practice

All mastic asphalts offered in this country (UK) comply with the relevant British Standard Specifications. These asphalts vary with the use to which the material is to be put but the basic materials remain identical. These comprise either natural lake asphalt or bitumens derived from crude oil residues, fine aggregates composed of natural rock asphalts or finely crushed limestone and coarse aggregate of various types.

BSCP 102 requires certain basic precautions to be taken in the structure to prevent any possibility of failure in respect of the asphalters' work. These are (a) that construction joints should be kept to a minimum and where unavoidable water bars should be incorporated to minimise any risk ot water penetration of the structure

(b) movement joints cannot in any circumstances be allowed. These matters should be carefully considered at design stage and followed throughout the work to remove the principal cause of failure of waterproof asphalt tanking.

Lay over concrete bed forming bottom to pits for stanchion bases a horizontal damp proof course of asphalt in three layers to a total thickness of 30 mm and to brick sides similar 19 mm thick. Properly make good junctions between lining to pits and horizontal d.p.c. to the floor and run two coat angle fillets to all internal angles

P41:2

P41:3

*Protect asphalt immediately each section of work is complete by the applic-
cation of concrete loading coats and continue pumping until such loading coats
are thoroughly set*
    P41:4
Concrete bases to receive horizontal tanking must be designed to carry the
loads placed upon them as well as give adequate support to the asphalt. In
addition the concrete must be of sufficient strength to safely and adequately
withstand any upward pressures caused by pressure of ground water which
may be present. Where ground water pressure is suspected or discovered a
reinforced concrete loading coat is placed over the asphalt tanking to ensure
that the pressures are restrained and the asphalt membrane is not ruptured.
The surface of the concrete must be free from all water before asphalting
commences and as soon as the work is completed the asphalt must be protected from all damage by a minimum of 50 mm fine concrete screed or the
final loading coat whichever is required.
Vertical asphalt tanking must be supported on a wall of sufficient strength to
withstand hydrostatic pressures and be protected by a skin of brick or block
walling built clear of the asphalt membrane and flushed or grouted up with
mortar as the work proceeds. Alternatively, asphalt can be applied to an in situ
concrete wall, concrete from a sawn shutter providing an adequate key. On
smooth concrete walls from a ply or sheet steel shutter a splatter coat of
cement and sand (1:2) or a coat of bitumen based primer may be applied to
the concrete to provide the necessary adhesion. The joints in brick walls
should be raked out 19 mm to effect a sufficient key for the asphalt.
*Lay over the whole area of the basement floor on concrete bed previously
    specified in Clause ....., a horizontal d.p.c. of asphalt in three layers to a
    total thickness of 30 mm*
    P41: 3201
The principle to be followed is to provide a continuous waterproof membrane
of mastic asphalt to the horizontal base concrete, fully continuous with the
vertical asphalt applied to the basement walls. External application of the
vertical membrane is preferable but not essential so long as the supporting
wall and the protection afforded to the asphalt are adequate.
On horizontal surfaces and inclined surfaces not exceeding 30°, three coats
of asphalt of a total thickness not exceeding 30 mm should be provided.
*Provide to the outer face of the basement wall a vertical damp proof course
    of asphalt in three layers to a total thickness of 20 mm, carried up at least
    150 mm above ground level and sealed to the horizontal damp proof course
    provided in the walls*
    P41: 3251

On vertical and inclined surfaces over 30 degrees three coats of asphalt not exceeding 19 mm should be provided and extended at least 150 mm above ground level.

Warm, clean and properly make good junctions between horizontal and vertical asphalt membranes with two coat angle fillets at all internal angles
P41: 3351

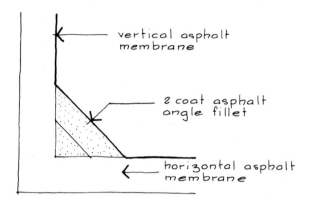

Detail of two-coat asphalt angle fillet

Joints in successive coats should be staggered 150 mm for horizontal and 75 mm for vertical work and internal angles should be provided with an angle fillet worked in two coats and at least 50 mm wide.

Lay to all concrete flat roofs on and including approved black sheathing felt underlay, asphalt in accordance with BS ...... the work carried out by an approved specialist sub-contractor in accordance with the provisions of the relevant British Standard Codes of Practice
P43: Ys4:10 Ys4:15
P43: 1051 1101
P43: Ln2:10

The asphalt will be laid in two layers to a total thickness of 20 mm with laps not less than 150 mm and the final layer properly finished by rubbing with sharp sand
P43: 3101 3201
P43: 4051

Structural movement caused by thermal, moisture and physical factors cannot be wholly excluded from a roof structure. Care must be taken to ensure that the weatherproof membrane can take up these movements and retain its effectiveness.

Asphalt roofing requires an isolating membrane to be laid over the structural base before the first layer of asphalt is applied to prevent any slight movement being reflected in the finished roof. Black sheathing felt to BS 747 Clause 4A is normally used for this purpose as an underlay to the asphalt.

Asphalt is an expensive material. Any falls required should be built up in the screed or by setting the sub-structure to the required inclination. 1 in 80 or 36 mm in 3 m is generally suitable.

Provide to all vertical abutments a two coat skirting minimum height of 150 mm above the highest portion of the flat roof with top splayed (and turned 25 mm into groove in wall) and with two coat angle fillet at junction with flat roof

    P43: 3551

Care must be taken to ensure the minimum height of skirting as it is at this point that so much damp penetration occurs. It is also here that structural movement can cause splitting of the asphalt at the junction of the skirting and the flat roof. When a lead cover flashing is provided to protect the top edge of the asphalt skirting this should be dressed down the face 75 mm. When skirtings are required for asphalt laid over timber flat roofs, it is usual

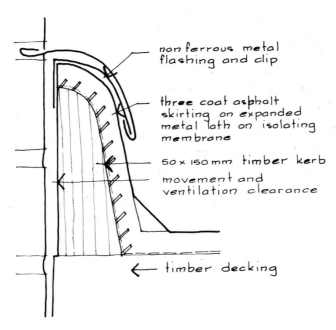

non ferrous metal flashing and clip

three coat asphalt skirting on expanded metal lath on isolating membrane

50 x 150 mm timber kerb

movement and ventilation clearance

← timber decking

Detail of asphalt skirting to junction of brick wall and timber decking

to provide a 50 x 150 mm splayed fir fillet securely spiked to the timber roof and clear of the abutment wall and for the asphalt to be dressed up this support. This will prevent differential movement between timber and wall from fracturing the asphalt at the angle. A metal flashing should be employed to protect the top edge of the skirting and a two coat angle fillet provided at the bottom. Concrete rooflight curbs should have asphalt skirtings carried up over the top to ensure a completely weathertight seal. Timber curbs should be provided with expanded metal lathing stapled to the timber at 150 mm centres to support the vertical face of the asphalt.

In all cases the sheathing felt should be carried up the vertical abutments to the height required for the asphalt to maintain structural isolation. On old brickwork it is usually necessary to dub out the wall in cement and sand (1:3) to provide a smooth and level base to receive the asphalt skirting.

Properly make good asphalt flat around rain water outlets and dress asphalt into luting flanges
   P43: 3601

A proper asphalt to iron joint must be provided or leakage will occur. The luting flange seals the junction satisfactorily. Care should also be taken to see that the top level of the grating is level with or slightly below the top surface of the asphalt. Otherwise ponding of storm water will occur.

Provide and bed in hot bitumen 300 x 300 x 8 mm approved asbestos cement flat roofing tiles, laid straight joint to falls
   P43: 4251

These tiles provide not only a protective pedestrian decking to asphalt flats but also an external reflective surface to reduce the absorbtion of solar heat. The tiles are best set 9 - 12 mm apart to induce water runways and the tiles should be neatly cut to abutments and around outlets.

Finish open edges of flat roofs with (solid water check roll and) apron 100 (150) mm deep, with undercut drip at bottom edge
This detail will require a 25 mm sawn batten to support the asphalt drip. This should be 50 x 25 mm for a 100 mm deep drip and 100 x 25 mm for a 150 mm deep drip. This batten should be impregnated against rot before fixing by an approved process as it is a favourite target for wet rot.

7 Tiling and Slating

BSCP 142: Pt 2: 1972   Slating and tiling

Tiles:
BS 402   Clay plain roofing tiles and fittings Pt. 2, 1970: Metric units
BS 473, 550   Concrete roofing tiles and fittings, Pt. 2, 1971: Metric units
BS 4471: Pt 2: 1971   Wood battens and concrete batterns for slating and tiling

Slates:
BS 680   Roofing slates Pt. 2: 1971: Metric units
BS 690   Asbestos cement slates and sheets Pt. 1 : 1963

Felt:
BS 747   Roofing felts Pt. 2 : 1968: Metric units

All tiles and slates are delicate and require careful transport, handling and storage. Most break easily when subjected to shock and all are easily chipped. Some have surfaces which, while perfectly serviceable on a roof, are easily damaged by contact with other materials.

Tiles and slates may be delivered loose or palleted and care must be taken to inspect these on delivery to see that the consignment is sound and perfect. A consignment of chipped tiles should be rejected as they will not be acceptable if placed in the roof in this condition.

Slates and tiles generally should be off loaded and stacked on their long edges onto a clean dry concrete or boarded platform. Asbestos cement slates, which are bundled, should be stored flat under cover in open stacks to facilitate air movement. This will prevent dampness causing efflorescence on the rear of the slates staining the surface of adjoining slates. Once stacked, they should be protected against excessive wet, frost and dirt by sheeting over with polythene or tarpaulins until they are loaded onto the roof.

Work commences with the fixing of a sarking felt over the whole area of the roof to be covered with slates or tiles. This is only temporarily fixed being followed by the tiling battens which, being well nailed to the rafters, properly secure the felt to the roof structure. Slates and tiles are moved to position on a roof in suitable numbers which are inserted between the battens to suit the areas of roof to be covered. This provides material readily at hand for the tiler. The tiles are set out on a gauge from one end, commencing at the eaves and working towards the valleys, hips and ridge. Work generally commences at the left hand side working towards the right.

Provide to all pitched tiled or slated roofs .... untearable sarking felt conforming to BS 747 Pt. 2: 1968, with 75 mm horizontal and 150 mm vertical laps

N11: Ln2.10

N11: 1051 1052 1101 1151

All tiled or slated roofs should be provided with sarking felt placed over the rafters for the following reasons:

To improve insulation by reducing draughts in the roof void

To keep the roof void free from wind blown dust and dirt

To remove moisture or driven rain penetrating the roof covering due to low pitch or high exposure

To assist the vapour and thermal insulation of roofs sarking felt can be obtained which incorporate aluminium foil on one face which acts as a reflector. Building paper with a similar finish can also be used satisfactorily. Many tiling systems rely to a considerable extent on the waterproof quality of sarking felt as the laps provided are not weatherproof in conditions of high wind and rain. Felts to BS 747 are provided with a woven hessian base which is virtually untearable. The felt is laid parallel to the ridge, commencing from the eaves. Care must be taken to ensure that sufficient felt overlaps the fascia to prevent any water penetrating the tiling from either lodging behind the fascia, where it can cause wet rot or dribbling down the face and dripping off the bottom edge. A projection of 50 mm should ensure discharge into the eaves gutter. Each width of felt should overlap the one below by 75 mm and end laps should be 150 mm and placed over a rafter. At the ridge the felt should be dressed up 50 mm above the top of the ridge board.

Valleys and hips need special treatment. Here a full width of felt should be laid under the felt at valleys and over the hips. Care should be taken to avoid perforations for vent pipes through the felt at low areas and valleys. Water can penetrate at these points if this is not observed.

Felt between rafters will sag slightly due to self weight. This is no disadvantage as it will allow penetrating water to be channelled under the tiling battens. Nailing with 32 x 2.5 mm aluminium clout head nails should be at 300 mm centres to each rafter to hold the felt in place prior to fixing battens. This is a temporary measure only as the felt is securely held by the battens.

Provide to all pitched tiled (slated) roofs .... mm sawn fir battens impregnated in accordance with BSCP 98: 1964 and nailed to rafters with non-ferrous nails to ...... mm gauge

N11: Hil.15

N11. 1301 1351 1352

All battens are of rift sawn softwood, in lengths not less than 1220 mm and each should be supported on at least three rafters. The size of battens used varies with the load imposed by the covering coupled with the spacing of the rafters, the following being recommended sizes in:

Roofing material	Spacing of Rafters	
	460 mm	610 mm
Slates natural (sized)	40 x 20	40 x 25
(random)	50 x 25	50 x 25
asbestos cement	40 x 20	40 x 25
reconstructed stone	40 x 20	
double lap concrete	40 x 25	40 x 30
Tiles plain	25 x 20	30 x 25
single lap	40 x 20	40 x 25
double roman	40 x 20	40 x 25
pantiles	40 x 20	40 x 25

Where counterbattens are required their size should not be less than 40 x 6 mm. There are a number of preservative treatments for timber, the best incorporating vacuum and pressure impregnation. The battens should be sawn to size before treatment and as some preservatives are colourless, a certificate should be requested to confirm that the material has been impregnated in accordance with BSCP 98: 1964.

Nails for fixing battens should be galvanised and from 30 to 45 mm longer than the thickness of the batten. The battening gauge size for different tiles and slates is as follows:

	Size of tile or slate in mm	Gauge of battens in mm
Plain clay tiling	265 x 165	100
Plain concrete tiling		100
Pantile interlocking	380 x 230	305
Double Roman interlocking	420 x 330	343
Interlocking	380 x 230	305
Bold roll	380 x 230	305
Double pantile	420 x 330	343
English pantile	420 x 280	343
Interlocking slate	432 x 380	355
	610 x 356	265 (25°)
Natural slate – Welch	610 x 305	265 (25°)
	508 x 254	214 (25°)
	508 x 254	220 (30°)
Reconstructed stone slate	458 x 305	190 (25°)
	458 x 458	190 ($17\frac{1}{2}^{\circ}$)
	712 x 458	306 (20°)
	712 x 458	294 (15°)
Asbestos cement slates	610 x 356	255 (25°)
	610 x 305	255 (25°)
	508 x 254	205 (25°)
	508 x 254	205 (30°)

Provide and lay to the whole of the roofs .... plain clay roofing tiles size 265 x 165 mm conforming to BS 402, Pt. 2: 1970, laid to a lap of 63 mm in accordance with BSCP 142
N22: Ng2.15
N22:1
N22:2

The specification for concrete plain tiles, natural and asbestos cement slates generally follows that for plain clay tiling. Tiles should be carefully stacked on a clean, level platform on edge and protected from mud and dirt. The fixing principles are similar and only vary in details and dimensions.

Plain clay roofing tiles manufactured to BS 402 are made in a standard size with special tiles for eaves and ridge (usually 165 mm long), tile and half for making out to verges and a range of standard fittings for valleys, hips and ridge. Each tile is provided with either two separate or one continuous projection or nib along the top edge not less than 20 mm with a projection of at least 7 mm which allows the tile to move freely on the batten and two holes for nailing in exposed positions. Three main categories of tiles are available, hand-made, machine-made and machine-made sand faced. Machine-made tiles have a hard, smooth, greasy non-porous surface in contrast to the textured surface of the other categories, the latter, in the main, having a better resistance to lamination or flaking in frost due to their porosity and open texture. All tiles should be supplied free from chips, cracks and laminations and conforming to the colours specified. The thickness should fall between 10 and 15 mm. The minimum pitch of the roof should not be below 40°.

Plain concrete roofing tiles manufactured to BS 473, 550, are manufactured to the same size as clay plain tiles but are not liable to lamination or damage by frost. Their texture resembles a 'sand faced' finish but the colours are hard and regular and do not have the softness of the sand faced clay article. Nibs and nailing provisions are as clay and the fittings provided to match are suitable for the same purposes. Tiles should be free from chips and cracks and the colours should conform to the specification. The minimum pitch for concrete tiles is 35°.

Single lap tiles of clay and concrete are of many and various patterns, colours and profiles and are ordered by number. They allow the pitch of the roof to be drastically reduced and thus tend to rely on the sarking felt to ensure complete weather tightness. Simple roofs without valleys and hips are best for these tiles as cutting can be difficult and often the detailing of roof angles is clumsy. The use of a plain tile course at eaves will provide a slight tilt but some patterns provide a special tile for this purpose, often with blocked ends, visually more acceptable than cement pointing. Special verge tiles are available to ensure that both verges are identical. Overhangs should, in the case of eaves and verge, not exceed 50 mm. Nailing is required at verges and the tiles should be bedded in cement mortar. Tiles should be free from chips and cracks and the colours should conform to the specification.

Natural slating to BS 680 can be carried out using materials from a wide variety of sources. Sizes are either random for laying in diminishing courses or to certain accepted sizes.

Welch slates are produced in three main grades, best, seconds and thirds, but each quarry operates its own system of grading and advice must be taken on appropriate quality applicable to the specified conditions. Slates are sold by the thousand or by the ton. Due to the cost of carriage the difference in price between the best and thirds is minimal at any distance from the quarry. Standard sizes available are:

Length & Breadth (mm)	Thickness (mm)	
610 x 355)	Best or firsts	4.0
460 x 230)	seconds	6.0
405 x 255)	thirds	7.5
510 x 225 (tons)		8.0 plus

Each slate should be provided with two holes not less than 25 mm from the edge of the slate, made from the bed to the back of the slate, thus forming a small countersink to receive the 'fixing nail'. This indicates if the slate has been correctly fixed.

Colours range from dark grey-blue to blue and blue-green depending on the quarry. Slates are laid with a double lap as plain tiling with a standard lap. With random slating the carpenter has to fix the battens after the slater has graded his slates for size and decided the individual spacing of each course. Eaves are provided with a double slate eaves course, verges with either a double course or an undercloak of short narrow slates all bedded in cement mortar. Ridges and hips are finished either by a half round or a two piece blue vitrified clay ridge, piece bedded and pointed as for tiled roofs. Mitred hips and valleys with lead soakers are rarely used today due to lack of skilled slaters. Abutments are similar to tiled roofs and employ soakers.

Reconstructed stone slating is usually regularly coursed but can be obtained in random widths, providing an interesting surface pattern. Colours are usually varied for interest and the surface is irregular. The slates are usually hung by two 38 mm aluminium nails over the batten except for pitches over 40° where the slates are nailed to the batten. Special top and eaves courses are provided and verges are made with slate and half, not half slates, except with 450 x 450 mm slates where halves are satisfactory. Verge slates are bedded in cement and sand mortar 1:3 and nailed to the batten with 50 mm oversail. Special hip, valley and ridge tiles are manufactured and bedding follows the procedures for plain clay tiles. Although these slates are not cambered the rough texture prevents capillary problems. Abutments are similar to tiled roofs and employ soakers.

Asbestos cement slates manufactured to BS 690 are regularly coursed and obtained in grey or blue, simulating natural material, and are sold by the ton. The sizes supplied are related to recommended roof pitches and generally the more exposed situations will require small slates at steeper pitch. The following will give a guide to size and pitch:

Size of slate (mm)	Name	Thickness (mm)	Min.-Rafter Pitch
610 x 356	Princess	4.0	25° (with 100 mm lap)
610 x 305	Duchess	4.0	25° (ditto)
508 x 254	Countess	4.0	25° (ditto)
508 x 254	Countess	4.0	30° (with 75 mm lap)

With sites of high exposure or when roof pitches are below 25° the manufacturers shall be consulted.

Eaves should project as for plain clay tiling and two under-courses of slate provided obtained by cutting the full length slate into two unequal lengths, the longer being used for the second course. Sprocketted eaves are not recommended. Verges should be made out using slate and half, not cut widths less than 150 mm which in any case require slates below to be site drilled and rivetted to the substructure. Overhang should not exceed 50 mm, the verge slates being bedded in mortar with a slight inward tilt from the edge. Ridges should have the top course head nailed to the batten and one piece ridge tiles of 915 mm effective length secured to the apex timbers with 50 mm x 16 s.g. roofing screws with plastic sealing washers, the socket in the ridge tile sealed and pointed with an alkali resisting mastic. Valleys are formed from lead or similar material and the slates cut to rake leaving 100 mm clear width of gutter. Hip tiles are not made but ridge tiles may be used where the pitch is appropriate. Abutments are similar to tiled roofs and employ soakers.

Asbestos cement slates are laid straight cover and each centre fixed with two 32 x 30 mm copper nails with a copper disc rivet at the tail to prevent the slates becoming dislodged in heavy weather. Slates should be held firmly the nails not being tightly driven but to allow for some movement. A slight gap should be provided next to the rivet between the two underslates.

To ensure the weather tightness of any roofing tile or slate, each course must cover the other by a certain distance. These distances, called laps, vary with different materials, as follows:

Material	Size	Recommended lap
Plain clay tiles	265 x 165	70 mm (see below)*
Plain concrete tiles	ditto	ditto
Single lap tiles	Varies with individual manufacturers	
Slate - Welsh	Varies	75 mm at 35° pitch (increase by 6mm for each 5° reduction)
Asbestos cement slates	Varies	100 mm at 25° pitch
Reconstructed stone	Varies	75 mm at 30° pitch
		Varies from 75 mm at 25° to 125 mm at 150° pitch

With situations of high exposure the lap should be increased to 75 or even 90 mm.

In view of the possible variations in length of roofing units it is preferable to specify the lap rather than gauge for fixing.

Every fourth course of plain tiles shall have each tile nailed with two 38 x 2.5 mm aluminium nails. In addition each two end tiles of every course adjacent to valleys, hips, abutments and verges together with all tiles in the top two courses next the ridge shall be nailed in a similar fashion N22: 2101 2201

Various materials can be used for roofing nails but ferrous should always be avoided. The following alternatives are available:

Aluminium – 38, 51, 63 mm x 2.5, 3.0, 4.0 mm diameter

Copper wire – ditto

Composition – 38, 51, 63 mm by weight per thousand

Cut copper – ditto

Details of nailing techniques for other roofing material may be found under a previous clause.

The eaves will be formed with a proper tile undercourse set to project 50 mm over the fascia with tiles to match the exposed roof tiling. All undercourse tiles will be twice nailed as specified before N22: 2151

All undercourses should be of materials and colours to match main roof surfaces. Without exception they require nailing and care must be taken to see that both the felt and eaves tiles properly project the required distance to ensure that stormwater is completely discharged into the gutter.

Verges shall be formed with an undercloak formed from plain tiles to match the exposed roof tiling set to project 50 mm beyond the face of the brick-work and bedded in cement mortar 1:3. The verge tiles are to be tilted to throw stormwater back from the edge of the roof and the whole bedded as described before, the mortar being cut back 6 mm to produce a neat finish. Bonding shall be carried out with tile and one half tiles and no cut tiles will be permitted N22: 2301

Verges are generally formed with an undercloak except for very thin laminates such as natural slate, some single lap tiling systems and asbestos cement slates. In any event all verges must be securely tied down to prevent their lifting and tilted to prevent stormwater draining off the edge. Particular requirements of materials may be found under a previous clause.

Cover the ridges with approved clay hog back (half round) ridge tiles carefully bedded and pointed in cement mortar (1:3). Fix only lead saddles at junctions of ridges and chimney stacks (vertical abutments). Fill in the free ends of ridge tiles with small slips of cut tile (bottle end) and point up neatly in cement mortar
N22: 2401

Ridges are exposed to severe weather conditions and must not only be properly secured to the roof but must be effectively weatherproof. Joints must be solidly bedded and neatly pointed up as well as the junction between the main tile surfaces and the ridge tile. Free edges are filled in solid with mortar which is decorated with tile slips or bottle ends. When this pattern of ridge is used for single lap tiles with bold contours, tile slips are usually inserted in the wide mortar joint between the ridge tile and the lower part of the single lap tile to improve the appearance. With dark coloured tiles, coloured cement used in the pointing will greatly improve the appearance of the whole roof. Concrete tile manufacturers generally supply this with the tiles and the tiler should be directed to use it. Particular requirements of materials may be found under a previous clause.

Lead saddles are laid under the ridge tile as described in Chapter 10.

Cover the hips with approved clay bonnet (half round) hip tiles carefully bedded and pointed in cement mortar (1:3). Each hip tile will be nailed to the hip rafter with a 63 x 4.0 mm aluminium nail
N22: 2451/2453
N22: Xt6.50. Xt6.31

With ridges, hips are very much exposed to the weather. Bonnet hip tiles must be supplied to bond to course with the plain tile areas of the roof, carefully nailed, and the bedding and pointing carefully carried out. Half round hip tiles are fixed in a similar way to ridge tiles but to avoid their dislodgment and the possibility of their cascading off the roof wrot iron hip irons should be provided at the foot of each hip to hold the whole run in position. These irons should be galvanised and secured to the top surface of the hip rafter with stout sheradised wood screws. Particular requirements of materials may be found under a previous clause.

Valleys will be formed from purpose made clay valley tiles laid dry and to course with matching main roof tiling
N22: 2501

Valley tiles should be provided to bond to adjacent tiled areas, match in colour and texture, suit the dihedral angle of the roof and laid in position. Adjacent tiles should be twice nailed as they hold the valley tile in position. On completion the tile should be firmly held without rocking.

Swept, laced and mitred valleys are now very rarely provided due to high cost and the shortage of skilled labour. Lead valleys are described in Chapter 10. Particular requirements of materials may be found under a previous clause.

Carry out all cutting and fitting required, fix only all lead soakers provided to abutments, remove all chipped or broken tiles, replace with whole and leave roofs perfect and weather-tight on completion
  N22: 2551

Cutting and fitting of tiles is necessary for practically all roofs. Care must be taken to ensure that no slips are incorporated and cuts are produced from tile and half. Each tile against a vertical abutment must be provided with a soaker as described in Chapter 10, fixed to the back of the batten by means of a copper nail to stop it slipping. Chipped or broken tiles should be lifted out and replaced with sound and any defective pointing made good.

8 Carpentry and Joinery

Timber is the most useful material available to the building industry, but when it is used without proper appreciation of its limitations, problems and possible failure can occur. Timber as a natural material incorporates built in hazards which the supervisor must ensure are no greater than can reasonably be accepted. Natural defects in timber may be structural, due either to the nature of the material itself, undue stress or damage during growth or to stains or decay caused by external influences such as fungal attack. Structural defects may be so serious as to render the timber unfit for conversion. Knots, which are dead branches surrounded by later growth, may be a source of weakness and for structural purposes very knotty timber is of little use. A defect known as 'upsett' where the fibres are partially broken across the log causes serious weakness. Shakes or cracks along the length of the timber also produce weakness. Where structural timbers are concerned permitted limits are defined in BSCP 112, the measurement of characteristics affecting strength being defined in BS 1860, Pt. 1. Large dead loose knots which will, in the course of time, shrink and fall out and expose the timber to weakness at this point should be avoided.

Wane, a defect of conversion which allows a portion of the exterior of the peeled log to form one or more arrises of the member, is not only unsightly but causes loss of cross sectional area and consequential loss of strength. The amount of wane is expressed as a fraction of the width of the surface on which it occurs and BSCP 112 lays down permissible limits for this defect.

Shakes should not occur in converted timber except as small surface intrusions, usually filled in the case of softwoods with resinous matter. Any timber with shakes should be excluded from structural work.

Blue stain, often found in the sapwood of softwoods and caused by a fungi, causes no deterioration in the strength of timber and should only be excluded when a natural finish is proposed for joinery.

Modern methods of seasoning precludes the likelihood of infestation introduced from new timber. Small pinholes will occasionally be found in such timbers as mahogany, originating from borers in naturally growing timber. The possibility of active beetle being present is remote although the pinhole will be unsightly in polished work.

The treatment of timber and timber products delivered to site is important, not only to prevent damage but also to preserve the specified moisture content. Storage and protection is dealt with in detail later in this chapter. All timber to be painted should be delivered to site properly protected with the specified primer on all faces, not just those faces which are to receive a painted finish. Special care must be taken to prime end grain as it is here that maximum moisture absorbtion will take place. Joinery which is to have a clear finish should be delivered with the bedding faces primed and exposed surfaces sealed to minimise the risk of plaster stains.

Structural timbers and those to be fixed in positions of high decay risk are often treated against fungal attack and beetle infestation. With joinery the preservation is often colourless and it is difficult to check whether the timber has been treated, especially when the material is primed. A certificate of impregnation from the joinery supplier should always be requested. Carcassing timbers are usually dyed by the process as follows: Tanalith — yellow brown stain; Protim — green stain; Celcure — clear crystalline.

As with joinery timbers a certificate of impregnation should be requested from the merchant.

Defective installation accounts for most timber maintenance in buildings. Seasoned timber in a dry, well ventilated position, is unlikely to be affected by disease and, when impregnated by a satisfactory preservative, can be guaranteed against such defects as infestation and fungal attack. Decay is the decomposition of wood tissue due to the action of fungi. This attack is usually accompanied by discolouration, brittleness and an unusual smell. Awareness of situations where timber is open to attack will help ensure that it is installed in a manner which will eliminate, as far as possible, any possibility of future decay. Moisture is a necessary conditon for fungal growth and there are many reasons why timber in a building may have a moisture content in excess of 20% and consequently be ripe for attack. Rain penetration through external walls, rising damp, water vapour rising in an enclosed space under a timber floor, rain or snow penetration through a roof.

In practice fungal decay occurs chiefly in suspended timber ground floors and adjacent joinery, external doors and windows, timber fascias and soffits and the following three points should be watched with great care:

(1) With regard to suspended timber ground floors, care must be taken to ensure that the timber wall plates are properly bedded onto continuous d.p.c.'s and where these are of strip form, properly lapped at least 100 mm. The ends of joists should be cut back at least 25 mm from the face of the outer wall and sufficient air bricks provided and situated above the d.p.c. for free passage of air to all compartments under the floor. At least one 225 x 75 mm air brick should be provided to each 3 m run of external wall and the flue sealed around in slate or asbestos sheet in cement mortar, or a proprietory flue used. In addition internal partitions and sleeper walls should be of honeycomb construction to permit free flow of air below the floor. Structural cross walls should be provided with ventilation openings in agreement with the structural engineer.

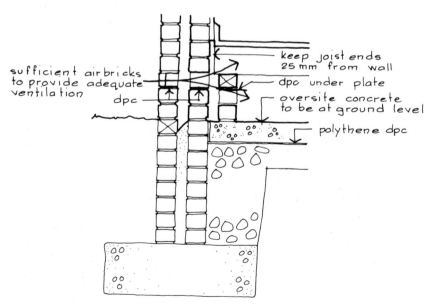

Detail of suspended timber ground floor

(2) Modern joinery is very prone to decay due to poor quality timber, bad detailing, the inadequacies of jointing and gluing and the almost universal omission of a d.p.c. under the cill. The use of white lead as a jointing compound, proper weathered surfaces and sensibly dimensioned throatings to cills, all safe-guard against decay. When fixing horns are cut away the newly sawn ends should be well primed immediately before the work is built into the wall. A strip of bituminous d.p.c. tacked to the underside of the cill will protect this from damp rising out of the wall underneath. The backs of frames are best protected by a 225 mm width of similar d.p.c. tacked to the back of the frame about 12 mm from the front face and returned into the cavity. This will provide protection to the frame at its weakest point and fulfil the role of vertical d.p.c. The joint between wall and frame should be pointed in mastic

(3) Fascias, soffits and weatherboarded surfaces should be primed *all* faces before being fixed and all header joints, cut ends and mitres put together in white lead. In addition all boarding fixed to a solid backing should be fixed to grounds previously treated with a preservative and with a layer of building paper between grounds and wall. Make sure that air circulates between the grounds by stopping these off or cross grooving at intervals as decay will usually strike

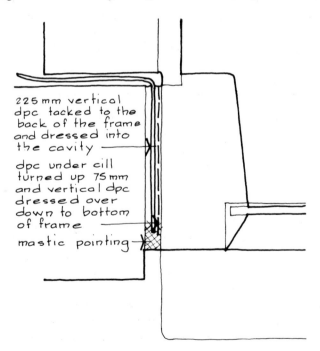

225 mm vertical
dpc tacked to the
back of the frame
and dressed into
the cavity

dpc under cill
turned up 75 mm
and vertical dpc
dressed over
down to bottom
of frame

mastic pointing

Protection of bedding surfaces of external joinery

from the back through condensation. Sarking felt should project 50 mm over the top edge of the fascia to ensure water blown under the tiles and collected by the felt will discharge into the gutter and not be trapped behind the fascia and cause rot at this point.

Softwood for structural work will comply in all respects with BSCP 112, The Structural Use of Timber, the measurement of characteristics affecting strength being measured in accordance with BS 4978: 1973 H21:Hi0.46. Hi0.52

The requirements of the Code of Practice and British Standard are complex but can be divided into the following categories:

(1) Species of timber of general availability which include the following allowable under the Building Regulations D14 (b) Schedule 6: Douglas fir, western hemlock (commercial and unmixed) pitch pine, redwood, whitewood, larch (European and Japanese) Scots pine.

(2) Stress grading which provides for preferred sizes and geometrical properties of timber for structural purposes and defines the qualities of timber to enable it to comply with the structural grades to which reference is made.
The grades for timber stress graded in the U.K. are as follows:

Visual stress graded	Machine stress graded
GS (General Structural Grade)	MGS (Machine General Structural)
SS (Special Structural Grade)	MSS (Machine Special Structural)

All stress graded timbers shall be marked on at least one face, edge or end as follows:
Visual Stress Graded: grader's identifying mark/grade of the piece.
Machine Stress Graded: licence no. of grading machine/grade of the piece/ BSI Kite Mark/BS 4978.

(3) Moisture content which requires that the timber be seasoned as far as practical to a moisture content which is appropriate to its structural location. European softwood is generally dried to a moisture content below 23% before shipment to the U.K. but North American softwood is generally unseasoned but shipped dipped in a fungal inhibitor. Wood is less prone to decay if its moisture content is below 25% and is reasonably immune below 20%. As timber shrinks during drying, the moisture content should be very close to the optimum if shrinkage in the final position will have an adverse effect on the structure. The requirements of BSCP 112 in this respect are as follows:

Position in building	Average m/c to be obtained in dried out structure	Average m/c at time of erection
Timber for prefabrication	16	17 - 22
Timber for site framing) and sheathing)	16	22
Rafters, roof boarding,) tiling battens etc)	15	22
Ground floor joists	18	22
Upper floor joists	15	22

Methods for assessing measurable characteristics and the moisture content of softwood to enable the strength of individual members to be computed are briefly as follows:

(a) Tolerances on sawn sizes are as follows:

Nominal dimension (mm)	Max. Variation (mm)	
	Minus	Plus
25.5 to 51	1.5	3.0
51 to 152.5	3.0	6.5
152 to 305	6.5	6.5
Over 305	6.5	12.5

(b) Surfacing reduction is the same between American and European stock timber as follows:

Nominal dimension (mm)	Reduction (mm)
25.5 to 76	3.0
76 to 305	6.5

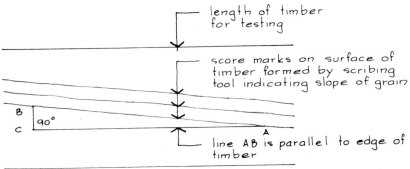

length of timber for testing

score marks on surface of timber formed by scribing tool indicating slope of grain

90°

line AB is parallel to edge of timber

the proportion of BC to AB is the slope of the grain

Determination of slope of grain in timber

Size of fissure   *Size of fissure*   *Determination of number of growth*
is A   *is B + C*   *rings*

(c) Maximum slope of grain permitted varies with the grade as follows:

Grade	Maximum slope of grain
GS	1 in 6
SS	1 in 10

Slope of grain is not covered in machine stress graded timber.

(d) Maximum size of fissures measured as B+C or A is as follows:

Grade		Maximum size of fissure (fraction of the member thickness)
GS	either	$\frac{1}{2}$
	or	exceeding $\frac{1}{2}$ but less than 1 not exceeding 900 mm on $\frac{1}{4}$ length of piece
	or	1 not exceeding 600 mm in length
	or	1.5 at the end of the piece
SS	either	less than $\frac{1}{2}$ unlimited in number
	or	exceeding $\frac{1}{2}$ but less than 1 not exceeding 600 mm or $\frac{1}{4}$ length of piece
	or	exceeding 1 permitted at ends only, length not exceeding width of piece

The fissure is measured with an 0.2 mm thick feeler gauge.

(e) Minimum number of growth rings for each 25 mm of growth, commencing from 25 mm from the pith when present or the longest possible line normal to growth rings passing through the centre of the piece and 75 mm long. If this is unobtainable the measurement to be taken on the longest line possible to normal growth

Grade	Rate of growth (per 25 mm)
GS	4
SS	4

(f) Wane is measured as the sum of the wane at the two arrises and is expressed as a fraction of the dimension of the surface on which it occurs. The maximum permitted is as follows:

Grade		Maximum permitted wane
GS	either	$\frac{1}{3}$
	or	$\frac{1}{2}$ not exceeding 300 mm in length not nearer than 300 mm from the end of the piece
SS		$\frac{1}{4}$

(g) Knots are found in all timbers and are of several types. Knots are assessed by the knot area ratio which is taken as the ratio of the sum of their projected cross-sectional areas to the cross-sectional area of the piece. Knots less than 5 mm diameter are ignored and no distinction is made between knot holes, live or dead knots. Knot area ratios for grades are as follows:

Grade	Maximum knot area ratio
GS	$\frac{1}{2}$
	$\frac{1}{3}$ with margin condition
	$\frac{1}{3}$ with square cross section
SS	$\frac{1}{3}$
	$\frac{1}{5}$ with margin condition
	$\frac{1}{5}$ with square cross section

In cases of dispute the methods for resolving this to determine the knot are area ratio is as follows:

1 Choose that section in the piece where the knot area ratio produces the lowest grade due to the intersection of a knot or growth of knots

2 Take into account all knots exceeding 5 mm diameter in calculating the knot area ratio of both margin areas and the whole piece. Make a full size drawing of the chosen section and mark margin areas. Mark points on the side of the rectangle representing any surface knots. These points represent the widest projection of the knot on that face or edge.

3 Calculate the knot area ratio of the margin in two ways according to whether or not the pith occurs within the cross-section or not:

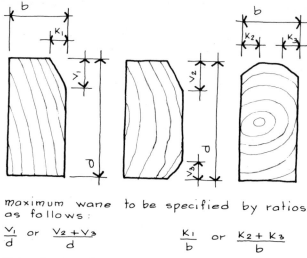

maximum wane to be specified by ratios
as follows :

$$\frac{V_1}{d} \quad or \quad \frac{V_2 + V_3}{d} \qquad\qquad \frac{K_1}{b} \quad or \quad \frac{K_2 + K_3}{b}$$

Determination of maximum permitted wane

(a) if the pith is within the cross section of the piece, the limits of the knots should be joined to a point representing the estimated position of the pith. Measure the area within these lines which represent knots for the whole cross-section and for the area lying within either margin.

(b) where the pith lies outside the cross-section mark its estimated position in relation to growth rings and join to the face limits of the knots, assuming that each is a cone with its apex at the pith. Measure the area enclosed, corresponding to the estimated position of the knots, for both cross-section and margin areas.

4   In both cases 3 (a) and 3 (b) express:

(a) the total area of knots within each margin area as a proportion of the whole to decide whether a margin condition exists

(b) the total area of knots within the cross-sectional area of the piece as a proportion of the corss-sectional area to determine the knot area ratio of the section

Timber for carcassing work shall hold to the full basic size, and where prepared for joinery reductions by processing shall conform to BS 4471: Pt. 1: 1969.

H21:2151

The basic sizes of sawn softwood vary with the moisture content at the time of measurement. Generally sizing relates of a moisture content of 20%, 1% being allowed in either dimension for each 5% reduction in moisture content.

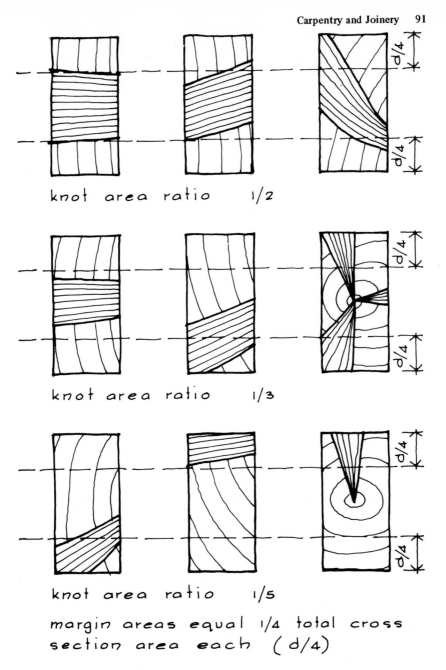

knot area ratio   1/2

knot area ratio   1/3

knot area ratio   1/5

margin areas equal 1/4 total cross
section area each (d/4)

Typical knot area ratios

Permissible deviations are allowed on quantities not exceeding 10% of the whole in any one parcel of timber and this is regulated as follows:

Thickness and Width (at 20% m/c)	Permissible deviation
Under 100 mm	− 1 mm and + 3 mm
Over 100 mm	− 2 mm and + 6 mm

The following are the basic sizes of sawn softwood:

Thickness (mm)	Width (mm)								
	75	100	125	150	175	200	225	250	300
16	o	o	o	o					
19	o	o	o	o					
22	o	o	o	o					
25	o	o	o	o	o	o	o	o	o
32	o	o	o	o	o	o	o	o	o
36	o	o	o	o					
38	o	o	o	o	o	o	o		
40	o	o	o	o	o	o	o		
44	o	o	o	o	o	o	o	o	o
50	o	o	o	o	o	o	o	o	o
63		o	o	o	o	o	o		
75		o	o	o	o	o	o	o	o
100		o		o		o		o	o
150				o		o			
200						o			
250								o	
300									o

Basic lengths of sawn softwood are provided and no minus deviation is permissible.

Dimensions in metres	1.80	2.10	3.00	4.20	5.10	6.00
		2.40	3.30	4.50	5.40	6.30
		2.70	3.60	4.80	5.70	
			3.90			

The preparation of softwoods to accurate finished sizes for joinery involves the reduction in size of the material. As the original size of the sawn material is not precise only average figures can be established by calculation and experience.

Purpose	For sawn sizes of widths or thickness (mm)				
	15-22	22-35	35-100	100-150	Over 150
Finished constructional timber	3	3	3	5	5
Flooring (ex. tongue)	3	4	4	6	6
Matching) Planed all faces)	4	4	4	6	6
Trim	5	5	7	7	9
Joinery etc.	7	7	9	11	13

*Softwood for carcassing and joinery will be treated with water-borne copper/
chrome/arsenic compositions in accordance with BS 4072: 1966.
H21:Hi0.20
H24:2151
H41, H42 & H43: Hi0.50
The treatment of timbers which are at maximum risk from decay or infestation
and the rejection of other timber is exposing the latter to eventual attack. Care
must be taken however, to ensure that small items which are used for fixings
and support are all treated otherwise precautions are circumvented. The treatment covered by BS 4072 covers the impregnation of the timber by the full-
cell vacuum and pressure impregnation process or the Lowry empty-cell pressure
impregnation process. The preservative used consists of mixtures of copper
sulphate, sodium or potasium dichromate and hydrated arsenic pentoxide.
The situation and exposure to hazard of the timber for treatment will require
varying degrees of salt retention. The following are applicable in this instance
and must be regarded as minimal:

Class	Description	Hazard	Example	Average net dry salt retention (min.) Kg/m^3
1	Interior timbers	Fungal decay and insect attack	Carcassing tim-bers and struc-tural joinery	4.0
2	Interior timbers	ditto	Dry rot repairs	5.3
3	Exterior timbers	Severe fungal decay and/or insect attack	Window & door frames & cills Shop fascias & signs	5.3
4	Exterior timbers in ground	ditto	Fence & gate posts	5.3

*The contractor is responsible for ensuring that the moisture content of timber
for carpenter's work and joinery is appropriate to the conditions to which
the material is to be employed
H21: Hi0.01
H24: Hi0.01
Practically all timber used in building today is kiln dried. When dried timber
is exposed again to the atmosphere it absorbs moisture and expands and this
continues until the surface of the wood can be protected against further absorbtion. As no surface protection can be absolutely sure of sealing the surface
it is necessary to use timber, particularly for internal joinery, at a moisture
content which is as near as possible to the moisture content for the average
humidity likely to be experienced. When central heating is installed the moisture
content of the timber must be lower than if intermittent heating only is to be
employed but care must be taken to have some heat in the building at least

before the doors and second fixings are installed, otherwise the moisture content will increase, taking up moisture from the higher humidity of the cold building. At the same time, the introduction of a full heating temperature must be avoided as excessive shrinkage causing cracking and splitting will occur. The heat should be applied gradually from a minimum to the maximum of a period to ensure the minimum distortion. External joinery which has one face exposed to higher humidity is best prepared from timber with a higher moisture content than internal, joinery. BS 1186 Pt. 1 makes recommendations for various situations which are generally satisfactory:

	Min. M/C %	Max. M/C %
Internal joinery with continuous heating	10	12
Internal joinery with intermittent heating	14	17
Internal doors with intermittent heating	12	15
External joinery	17	20
External doors	15	18

It is of little use specifying and obtaining timber of the correct moisture content if the material is allowed to revert before it is incorporated into the building. Joinery should always be primed in the shop which will, to some extent, protect the timber from saturation. In any event joinery should not be delivered to site until the work is ready to receive it and should be properly covered and protected in transit as well as on site. Here it should be stacked clear of the ground and well sheeted over. The moisture content should be checked on arrival on site and when built in by means of a moisture meter.

Timber for carpenter's work should be at a moisture content of about 22% when delivered to site. the timber should be stacked clear of the ground and sheeted over to minimise absorbtion as much as possible. Owing to methods of construction, absorbtion is likely to increase sharply in wet weather. By good planning it should be possible to have the roof weatherproofed by a layer of felt or the sarking felt as soon as the structure is completed which will help to keep the timber to a reasonable moisture content. This will soon return to equilibrium moisture content for average humidity if the windows are left unglazed for a week or two.

Species of timber should be selected bearing in mind the position they are to occupy in the building. This applies to hardwoods as well as softwoods.

Unless specified specifically by name timber should be selected from species suitable for both the work and the position in the structure it is to occupy. H24: Hi0.52

The selection of timber for joinery should be undertaken with care and sound advice is contained in BS 1186 Pt. 1. A summary of suitable species for specific situations is as follows:

External joinery	Suitable species	
	Hardwood	Softwood
Window cills	Afromosia, Agba, Guarea,	Cedar (western red)
	Gurgan, Iroko, Keruing	Pitch pine
	Meranti, European oak,	
	Teak, Utile, Yang	
Door thresholds	Ditto	Pitch pine
Window & door frames,	Ditto	Cedar, Douglas fir,
sashes and casements		Redwood
Doors	Ditto	Cedar, Douglas fir, Hemlock,
		Yellow pine, Redwood
Internal joinery		
Door frames and linings,	Afromosia, Agba, Ash,	Cedar, Douglas fir, Hemlock,
	Beech, Elm, Guarea, Idigbo,	Parana pine, pitch pine,
	Iroko, Mahogany Makare,	Yellow pine, white pine,
	Meranti, Oak, Obeche,	Redwood, Whitewood
	Ramin, Sapele, Utile	
Stairs	Afromosia, Agba, Ash,	Cedar (yellow), Douglas
	Beech, Guarea, Idigbo,	fir, Hemlock, Parana pine,
	Iroko, Mahogany, Makare,	Redwood, Whitewood
	Meranti, Oak, Sapele,	
	Sycamore, Utile	

Other more exotic and expensive timbers are suitable but not in general use due to the small quantities generally available from local stock.

All plywood will be Grade 1 – 2 BR and conform in all respects with BS 1455: 1972, and bonding between veneers will be as defined in BS 1203: 1963 H24:Ri4.10

Plywood is a most useful material for use in joinery, being composed of a number of veneers, the grain of each being at right angles to the next and the whole glued together to form a rigid sheet material. The number of veneers employed varies with the overall thickness and some of those in common use are as follows:

Thickness (mm)	Number of plies
4	3
6	3
9	3 or 5
12	5

Plywood above 12 mm in thickness is rarely an economic material to use in terms of cost. The size of sheet available varies with manufacturers but sizes available from stock to the above thicknesses are:

Length (mm) – 2440 – 1830

Width (mm) – 1220

Plywood is graded according to the quality of the face veneers and by the bonding material used. As grading varies between the producer countries reference to BS 1455 will ensure that the distributor is fully aware of the grade required and will supply accordingly. Grades of veneers covered by this standard are as follows:

Grade 1 veneer – formed from one or two pieces of firm and smoothly cut veneer. When two pieces are used they should be reasonably matched for colour and jointed approximately at the centre of the board. No knots, worm or beetle holes, splits, glue stains, dote, filling or inlays of any kind are permitted and end jointing is not permissible.

Grade 2 veneer should have a solid surface free from open defects. Veneers need not be matched for colour or equal width, a few sound knots are permissible as is slight discolouration, glue stains and isolated pinholes not along the plane of the veneer. Occasional splits not exceeding 0.8 mm in width and 10% of the length of the panel or slightly open joints may be suitably filled. Solid hard and level inserts of the same veneer may be provided to repair the face but no end joints are permissible.

Grade 3 veneer admits wood defects including worm holes precluded from Grades 1 and 2 so long as they do not impair the serviceability of the plywood and may include rough cutting, overlaps, gaps or splits but no end jointing.

It will be seen therefore that the following uses may be specified for particular grades:

Grade 1 Natural faced work to be polished or clear sealed: as a high class base for painted finishes

Grade 2 As a base for painted finishes of good quality: for interior work for fittings

Grade 3 For interior backing work where the surface is hidden.

The core of the plywood may contain defects so long as they do not impair the strength of the material or deform the facing veneers.

Four kinds of bonding agent are used in the manufacture of plywood, depending on the resistance to external influences the material is required to withstand.

Type WBP (weather and boil proof) provides a joint which is highly resistant to the weather, micro-organisms, cold and boiling water, steam and dry heat. The adhesive is of the phenolic range.

Type BR (boil resistant) provides good resistance to weather and boiling water, will resist cold water for many years and is highly resistant to attack by micro-organisms.

Type MR (moisture resistant) is only moderately weather resistant and will fail after only a few years. While resistant to cold water for a long period it fails to withstand boiling water but resists attack by micro-organisms.

Type NT (interior) is resistant to cold water but not to micro-organisms.

The first three bonding agents are defined by BS 1203 but the fourth is not. Generally, the use of the types can be defined as follows:

Exterior use   type WBP either painted or in the clear

Interior use   Where exposed to conditions where heat and damp is likely type BR

Where exposed to conditions which are both dry and warm – type MR

Temporary work type NT

Apart from the requirements listed above, the bond between the plies must be continuous and adequate over the whole area of the board and any delamination or blistering is unacceptable. The moisture content should not exceed 8 to 12% and the length or width should not be less than the specified size or exceed it by more than 3 mm in either direction.

To assist in checking the quality of the board offered, all plywood manufactured to BS 1455 is required to be marked near an edge on the back with the following information:

Manufacturer's name or mark/Country of manufacture/BS 1455/Grade for face and back (e.g. 1 – 2)/Bonding (i.e. WBP, BR, MR or INT)/Nominal thickness of board.

Sheets should be stored flat, supported clear of the floor over the whole underside, in a dry warm store.

All hardboard will be ..... mm thick standard grade Masonite (or other trade name) to conform to BS 1142 Pt. 2, 1971

H24: Rj1.10. 11 15

Hardboards are used in great quantity in standard stock joinery fittings and for facing cheap flush doors. The material is manufactured from ligno-cellulose fibres felted together and subjected to high pressure. They vary in colour from light to dark brown with one smooth and one textured backing face. Three grades are produced, standard, super and tempered, the first usually employed where wear is unlikely or the surface is to be painted and the last used externally. The size and thickness of sheets generally available from stock is as follows:

Length (mm) – 915 – 1220 – 2440

Width (mm) – 610 – 1220

Thickness (mm) – 3.2 – 4.8

Sheets should be stored flat, supported clear of the floor over the whole underside in a dry warm store.

All resin bonded wood chipboard will conform in all respects with BS 2604 Pt. 2 and supplied by Messrs.................... or other equal and approved manufacturer.

H24: Rj7.10. 20

The use of chipboards is growing in the building industry, not only for fittings but also for flooring, both as a base for applied finishes and as a naturally exposed sealed product. The material is manufactured in several ways and two grades (medium and high density) but primarily consists of wood chips bonded under pressure with resin glues. While one manufacturer will supply a board 1220 mm wide of any transportable length, the generally available sizes from stock are as follows:

Length (mm)   2440
Width (mm)   1220
Thickness (mm)   12 – 18

As the board is formed from natural materials it is prone to moisture movement which, unlike timber, is equal in each direction. Care must be taken to allow for this in fixing as close butt joints can lead to trouble. While simple tongue and groove lap and dowel joints are suitable sophisticated joints are rarely satis‣ factory due to the nature of the material.

Two finishes are obtainable, sanded and unsanded, depending on the location of the material and whether it is to receive an applied finish. Thin veneers require the sanded surface to obviate the possibility of surface unevenness, while plastic laminates can be satisfactorily bonded to the unsanded grade. The moisture content of the board should not exceed 6 – 14% and the length and width not exceed the normal size by more than 8 mm and 4 mm respectively.

To assist in checking the quality of the board offered, all resin bonded wood chipboard manufactured to BS 2604 Pt: 2M is marked with the following particulars:

BS 2604/Name, trade name or trade mark of manufacturer/If extruded the word 'extruded'/If for flooring use, the word 'flooring'/The date of manufacture or a date identification mark.

Boards should be stored flat, supported clear of the floor over the whole underside, in a warm dry store.

Blockboard will be Grade 1/2 MR and conform in all respects with BS 3444: 1972

     H24: Ri4.31. 35

Blockboard (and laminboard) are used in quantity for good quality joinery and consist of a core formed from strips of softwood covered on both sides by fairly thick veneers, either in one or two plies. The width of the strips for blockboard is about 25 mm wide, those for laminboard being about 9 mm and usually of hardwood. The latter material is therefore more expensive due to the greater labour content. The size of board available from stock is as follows:

Length (mm)   2440
Width (mm)   1220
Thickness (mm)   12 – 15 – 19

Blockboard is graded according to the quality of the face veneers and by the bonding material used. The following grades are covered by BS 3444:

Grade S — specially selected between purchaser and manufacturer

Grade 1 — one or more pieces of firm, smooth cut veneer matched for colour and well jointed. The pieces should be equal in width (up to 10% tolerance) and not less than 250 mm wide. Slight discolouration and occasional closed splits are allowable but not beetle or worm holes, knots, splits, dote, glue stains or end joints.

Grade 2 — to have a solid surface free from open defects, with veneers of varying width and not necessarily matched for colour. Otherwise the veneer is similar to Grade 2 veneer for plywood.

Generally Grade 1 is the exposed face (unless Grade S is required for a special purpose) and Grade 2 is suitable for backing or where a painted finish is envisaged.

Cores must consist wholly of timber of the same species, which may contain sound knots. The direction of growth rings relative to the face of the core is not very important although quarter sawn material is preferable.

Three kinds of bonding agent are used in the manufacture of blockboard and their properties are the same as those used for plywood. The agents used are:

Type BR/Type MR/Type INT

and their type and location is as described for plywood. Other requirements in respect of bond and surface are also generally as for plywood. The size of the board shall not be less than specified or exceed this by more than 6 mm and the surface both sides will be sanded or scraped. The moisture content shall not exceed 8 — 12% and the board shall be free from bow, twist and warp.

To assist in checking the quality of the board offered, all blockboards manufactured to BS 3444 are marked on an edge or on the back near an edge with the following particulars:

Manufacturers name or mark/Country of manufacture/BS 3444/Grade for face and back (i.e. 1/2 or 2/2)/Bonding (i.e. BR, MR or INT)/Specified thickness of board.

Boards should be stored flat, supported clear of the floor over the whole underside, in a dry, warm store.

Frame up and construct the roof to the pitch shown, as indicated on the drawings and of the timber sizes indicated. The roof timbers are to be framed together in the best possible manner, all joints properly formed and securely nailed, strapped or bolted together

H21:3151 4401

Roof timbers are cut and formed on the ground before being fixed in position to form the roof structure. Consequently certain basic requirements are needed for the geometry involved and these are Span and Pitch.

The span of the roof is the distance between the wall plates and in order to construct a satisfactory roof the plates must be bedded dead level and parallel.

Unless this is provided the roof will be unsatisfactory. Certain timbers should be in single lengths, some can be jointed. Generally plates, purlins, ridge boards and ceiling joists can, with certain reservations, be jointed in their lengths, but rafters or spars, hip and valley rafters should be in single lengths. Lap joints should always occur over a partition support or the roof provided with a binder and hangers at every joist to support the ceiling timbers. The strength of a traditional timber roof is mainly in its jointing and care must be taken to ensure this is carried out in a satisfactory manner as follows:

(a) Ceiling joists where jointed should lap at least 900 mm and be well nailed and the ends clenched. The best method of jointing joists to rafters is with a dovetail halved joint which should always be used when the joist is raised above the plate level to act as a collar. Today the joint is usually well nailed and clenched although sometimes connectors may be used for wide spans over 6 m

(b) Wallplates are usually jointed by simple halved joints

(c) Purlins should be jointed over struts by means of a lapped joint. Where joints occur at points between bearings a splayed scarf joint should be used

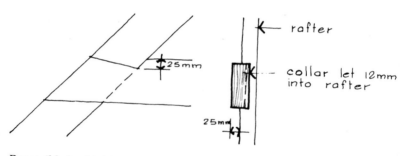

Dovetail halved joint

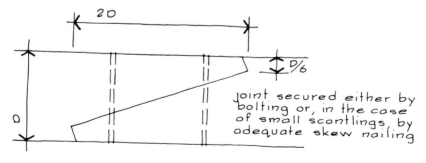

Splayed scarf joint

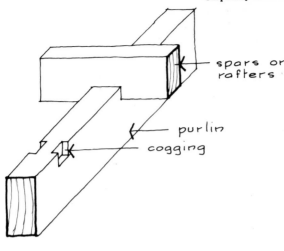

spars or
rafters

purlin

cogging

Cogged joint

(d) Rafters should be cut at the top end to fit snugly against the ridge board, and be birdsmouthed over the plate at the foot. When the ceiling joists are raised above the plate as collars the rafters should be cogged over the purlin to prevent them slipping

(e) Ridge boards are jointed by scarf joints to keep the boards in line to receive the rafters

Form first floor of ...... mm fir joists at ..... mm centres with 50 x 38 mm fir herringbone strutting where shown on the drawings. Provide and fix fir trimmer joists to stack and staircase size ...... mm all securely tusk tenoned together

H21: 4501

The size and spacing of timber joists for domestic construction is laid down in the Building Regulations and Building Acts and is relative to the clear span between supports. Suitable timber is free from large dead knots, appreciable wane or shakes and the timber should be straight and square cut.

Support for the ends of the joists must be carefully considered to provide not only structural stability but also rigidity. Where wall plates are provided, these must be bedded dead level and the joists toe nailed into the plates. Unless the joists have been wholly impregnated, the ends should be well soaked in preservative or wrapped in building paper to preserve them from decay when built into external cavity walls. The minimum bearing which should be permitted must not be less than 75 mm. The space between joists should be filled in solid with brick or block as appropriate.

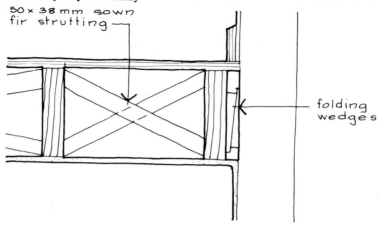

50 × 38 mm sawn
fir strutting

folding
wedges

Detail of herringbone strutting

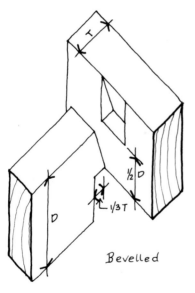

Bevelled

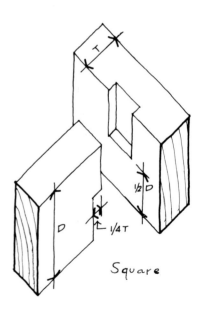

Square

Half depth joints

Timber joisted floors should be strutted at centres of about 2 mm to render the floors as rigid as possible. This will reduce both stress on the supporting walls and, by cutting down vibration, the likelihood of cracks in the plastered ceiling below. The usual form of strutting is known as herringbone and formed by nailing 50 x 38 mm sawn fir to form a series of crossing diagonals in a straight line across the joist framework in the centre of the floor. Where the battens butt the sides of the joist the surface should be fully in contact and securely nailed to the joist. Care must be taken to ensure that folding wedges are inserted between the end joist and the wall to complete the bracing. Otherwise, as the timber shrinks, the strutting will become progressively less effective. Where openings or projections impinge on the floor structure trimmers are provided to carry the ends of the joists. These are housed into the trimmers by half depth joints either bevelled or square housed. A more efficient but more expensive joint is the dovetailed housed joint. Rule of thumb methods require trimmers to be 13 mm thicker than normal joists and this works well in practice. Trimmer joists which carry the joist ends are housed into trimmed joists by means of tusk tenon joints. With the advent of metal connectors these satisfactory traditional methods are being supplanted by sheradised steel plates secured by nailing.

*All notching or cutting away of joists shall be agreed with the architect before any work is put in hand

H21: 2201

All holes for conduit or pipes must be centred on the neutral axis of the joist and must not exceed one third its depth. Notches must be formed from straight cuts to drilled holes. Where loading conditions warrant it double joists should be provided, nailed together, to support the load where the joists are weakened.

*Timber for joinery shall be entirely free from decay and insect attack and comply in all respects with the requirements of BS 1186 Pt. 1. Appendix C.

H24: Hi0.50

BS 1186 Pt. 1. provides for four classes of timber for exposed surfaces of joinery, the classes providing for different standards depending on the quality of work envisaged. When an article of joinery is specified as being of a particular class, the standards apply only to the exposed surfaces and the requirements for concealed and semi-concealed surfaces apply to such surfaces in all joinery.

The following is a convenience summary of the requirements of Appendix C :

Feature	Class 1S	Class 1	Class 2	Class 3	Concealed or semi-concealed surfaces
Knots	As Class 1	Pinholes up to 6mm.	(up to 25) one half (25 – 50) 13 (50 – 100) one quarter (over 100) 25	(up to 40) one half (40 – 60) 20 (60 – 150) one third (over 150) 50	(up to 45) two thirds (45 – 60) 30 (60 – 100) one half (over 100) 50
Checks and shakes	W – 0.3	As 1S	1.5 (filled if over 0.5)	As 2	Any width
	L – 300	As 1S	300	As 2	Not continuous for whole length $\frac{1}{2}$
	D – $\frac{1}{4}$	As 1S	1/4	As 2	
Pitch pockets	Not permitted	Must be cut & filled	As 1	As 1	Permitted
Plugs & inserts	Not permitted	With not to be more than 6mm. greater than max. permitted knot size.			
Joints & laminations	None is so stated	Not unduly conspicuous	As 1	As 1	No requisite specified
Rate of growth	Not fewer than 8 growth rings per 25 mm at any point on cross section.				
Slope of grain	Not greater than 1 in 10 softwoods or 1 in 8 in hardwoods.				
Species of and grain	Some on all surfaces	No requirements specified.			
Boxed heart	Permitted in softwoods only if no shake on exposed surfaces.				
Pith	Not permitted	Permitted if hard	As 1	As 1	Permitted
Pinholes	Not permitted	Permitted if filled	As 1	As 1	Permitted

Methods of determining the measurement of characteristics is contained in BS 1860 Part 1 and is discussed elsewhere in this chapter.

The joinery shall be put together with all necessary tenoning, morticing, grooving, tonguing, rebating, housing and all other labours necessary for carrying out the work in a proper and workmanlike manner, including for the construction of all linings and framings and their fixing into the building. The joiner shall supply all plates, screws, nails, and other items required for the proper execution of the work.

H24: 3151 et. seq.

The quality of workmanship for joinery is difficult to specify in detail and much must depend on the standards of the workshop and the quality of work as a whole. Some check can be made by the inspection of joinery during its manufacture, but this requires a knowledge of the craft usually far beyond that of the average supervisor. Consequently, in many cases, joinery of quality is covered by a Prime Cost Sum, enabling the Architect to nominate a firm for the work in whom he has confidence borne of previous experience. For the run-of-mill work, however, this procedure is often impracticable. What then are the standards which should be expected for good commercial standard joinery.

(a) Generally the faces of jointed members should be flush and in close contact throughout their length. Moulding on the edges of adjoining members should be in alignment. Tenons should be a push fit in the groove and with a gap of not more than 1.5 mm between the end of the tongue and the bottom of the groove. Where the end grain of a tenon combed or halves joint shows on the face it shall be flush

(b) Dowels grooved for glue, are to be a drive fit to within 6 mm at each end when assembled

(c) Mortice and tenons shall be parallel and a push fit with wedges the same width and taper as the mortice and a tight fit for three quarters of the tenon. All mating surfaces shall be coated with adhesive for at least the root half of the length of the tenon

(d) Combed joints shall be generally as for mortice and tenon but *all* mating surfaces should be coated with adhesive

(e) Halved joints cut to half the thickness of members forming the joint shall have all surfaces flush with one another where exposed to view, meeting surfaces smooth and in close contact for gluing

(f) Dovetail joints shall have all mating surfaces in close contact for all surfaces to be glued

(g) Housed joints are to be square with the face of the member housed, of equal width and accurately fitted using an oval or lost head nail or countersunk screw fixing

(h) Rebated joints shall have the shoulder square with the face of the rebated member, flush with the same, properly fitted with all mating surfaces spread with adhesive and properly countersunk screwed or nailed with an oval or lost head nail

(j) Tongued and grooved joints at angles shall have the thickness of the tongue not exceeding two fifths of the thickness of the grooved member, and the tongue length not exceeding one and a half times its thickness. The shoulder will be square, shoulders fit accurately, mating surfaces smooth and true and spread with adhesive to ensure proper adhesion. Stopped shoulders should be a close fit to the abutting surface

(k) Movement joints

When ply panels are set in grooves these latter shall be not less than 9 mm deep, the panel cut 3 mm shy in length and width and fit closely to the sides of the groove

Solid panels fitted to grooves will generally be as for ply but allowance should be made by the joiner for any moisture movement which may be anticipated Flush panels fitted flush shall not have the framework unduly weakened by the formation of the groove, be properly flush and not fixed in such a way as to prevent free expansion and contraction. In practice the bottom edge of the panel oversails the frame at this point to provide allowance for movement

(l) Doors and sashes shall be set into the rebates with the following allowances all round:

For painted work   — 1.5 to 2.5 mm
For natural finished work — 1.0 mm

(m) Sliding drawers must be fitted with runners, guides and kickers to prevent undue play in either direction. Permitted allowances for width and height of drawer fronts are as follows:

Width of drawer front in opening (any dimensions) — 1.5 mm
Height of drawer front in opening — over 130 mm high — 3.0 mm
                                    under 130 mm high — 1.5 mm

(n) The adhesive used for jointing may be any of those recommended in BS 1186 Pt. 2 but for external painted white lead using pinned dowel joints is still the best jointing adhesive. Otherwise the following may be used:
Animal glue to BS 745.
Synthetic resin adhesives to BS 1203 and BS 1204 (close contact or gap filling) Cold setting caesin for wood to BS 1444.
When discolouration of the surface is a consideration as in polished or natural finished work, care must be taken in the selection of adhesives. The joinery manufacturer should be asked for advice in this matter

(o) Laminated timber may be employed so long as the timber is not less than 8 mm or greater than 50 mm thick. End joints must be made with finger joints, properly mated and in close contact for gluing.

The surface finish of all joinery should be such as that if the final decoration be a matt paint, any imperfections in manufacture will not be apparent. Gloss paint will expose such imperfections and consequently a better finish should be specified at the time of tendering so that the contractor is left in no doubt of the quality of workmanship required.

The staircase is to be constructed of wrot deal, all rebated and grooved together, glued and blocked, with each tread screwed to the riser with three long steel screws

Most timber staircases for domestic work are prepared and fabricated in bulk by specialist manufacturers who provide a range of sizes suitable for most applications. These staircases are consequently cheap and in the main they are satisfactory. One problem which occasionally arises is when the floor-to-floor height in a building is not standard and consequently a standard size staircase when fitted will either tip forward or backward depending on the difference between its total rise and the floor-to-floor height, be blocked up to take the extra height on the bottom riser or have the top or bottom riser reduced to suit. All these makeshift devices are unsatisfactory and the stair should be condemned and one with the proper rise provided for the work.

The staircase should be inspected to see that the timbers are of the correct thickness and are put together in a proper workmanlike manner. Risers and treads should be housed together, glued and provided with at least three blocks glued under the nosing and a similar number of long steel countersunk screws provided to strengthen the internal angle of tread and riser. The use of nails is unsatisfactory as they tend to work loose and in time, squeak. Treads and risers should be let into routered grooves in the strings and securely glued with long

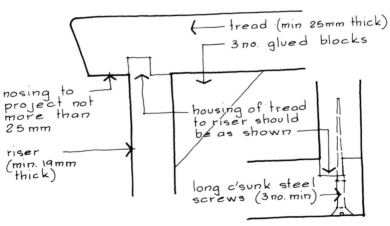

Details of domestic timber staircase

wedges driven home underneath and blocks glued to the sides for additional strength. Nosings to the treads should be rounded to reduce carpet wear and project a maximum of 25 mm to avoid the danger of the toe catching on the projection when mounting the stairs.

Stairs more than 914 mm in width will require a bearer or rough carriage to provide additional strength, either securely spiked to the floor joists (if these coincide) or birds mouthed over a batten securely nailed to the boarding at the foot of the flight. At the top the bearer should be birdsmouthed to the landing trimmer or an additional cross bearer called a pitching piece. The bearer should touch the bottom edges of the steps (notching being unnecessary) direct support being provided by rough brackets formed from 25 mm sawn timber nailed alternatively on either side of the bearer with their upper edges tight against the treads.

Balusters should be securely housed into the top of the string and the underside of the handrail. All handrails and balustrades should be very firmly fixed to ensure complete safety to persons using the stair.

Door and window frames are to be built in as the work proceeds. All internal door frames and linings are to be secured with 3 no. sheradised steel fixing cramps to each reveal at intervals not exceeding 675 mm vertically.

(3)21: Xt6.91. Xt6.92

(3)21:2 et. seq.

Fixed joinery such as window and door frames should be built in as the work proceeds to provide a more secure fixing and to obviate any tolerance defects which might accure. A gap in excess of 6 mm around a frame is difficult to fill completely and any less will not accept sufficient mastic to provide a proper seal. Fixing is usually effected by cutting back projecting horns provided at the ends of head and cill to suit the position of the frame in the reveal and building the brick or blockwork around the remaining projection. Care should be taken to see that the cut face of the horn is well re-primed before the frame is built in and the vertical d.p.c. to the reveal should pass in front of the horn to provide additional protection.

Internal door openings are usually formed and the linings and frames fixed to the prepared openings immediately before plastering commences. The reason is to prevent damage to the arrises of the timber by the passage of barrows and material while the structure is being erected. Fixings have to be provided to the jambs and these can be of several types as follows:

(a) Timber slips (pallets) about 9 mm thick and 75 mm square built into joints as the work is carried out

(b) Sheradised steel cramps made from thin steel strip, one end bent at right angles with the two holes for fixing to the back of the frame with screws and the long tail jagged at the edges to provide a key when built into the mortar joint of the wall. Where these cramps are to be fixed the joints are usually filled with sand which is replaced with mortar rammed in around the tail of the cramp when the frame is fixed

(c) Sheradised steel wire holderbats which are provided with one end pointed and threaded for screwing into the back of the frame and the rest formed into a loop which is built into the brick joint as above

All fixings are provided at intervals of nine courses of brickwork (three courses of blockwork) and in standard doors three fixings are provided to each jamb.

9 Ironmongery

Ironmongery is usually selected from samples or patterns, very rarely now by competitive tenders. The variety of items offered and finishes obtainable are very diverse and in most cases selection is made not only on price but also on particular appearance, finish and ease of fixing. The cost of site fixing can, in many cases, exceed the initial cost of the item. Doors become thinner, rails and stiles become narrower and it becomes increasingly difficult to find locks and door furniture which can be incorporated in the component and at the same time operate satisfactorily and without difficulty. In no other sphere of building can there be any greater false economy than the use of cheap locks and ironmongery. Cost is almost always related to durability. Style can vary, selection being made from suitable and appropriate patterns.

Include the P.C. Sum of £   for the supply and delivery to site of selected ironmongery by a nominated supplier. Add for agreeing details of handing, taking delivery and profit.

(3)21:Xt7.01

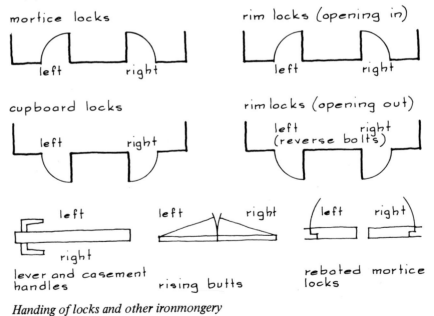

Handing of locks and other ironmongery

Selection of ironmongery should be completed early in the contract so that
any adjustments to joinery can be carried out to suit fixing requirements.
Handing of items is best dealt with by the contractor as there is some con-
fusion as to the best way to describe the way a door swings and consequently
he can use any method he likes to secure the correct items. Most lever handles
are reversible, like knob sets, and can thus suit either hand. Single items or
half sets must be so described as door furniture is supplied in pairs. Window
casement fasteners on the other hand are, like most other items, supplied
singly.

Hinges are of many types to suit particular requirements and situations. Butt
hinges are usual on wood casement doors, sold in pairs, exclusive of screws. It
is necessary to provide three hinges for most doors other than light flush internal
patterns and these are described as 'one and a half pairs'. Brass or bronzed
finishes are often specified for natural finish doors and these are best of cast
pattern as pressed hinges are rarely strong enough for the load. Steel pins and
washers are usual. Hinges for fire doors must have metal washers as plastic are
unacceptable. Hinges for external doors are best of cast iron but these are
difficult to obtain and sheradised steel have often to be accepted for painted
finishes. Hinges for external doors are usually 100 mm deep while 75 mm are
usual for internal doors.

Spring pivots can be used for single or double swing doors providing a spring
mechanism situated in a box set into the floor and a pivot at the head which
keeps the door upright and stable. The appropriate pattern must be ordered for
the situation and a check action specified if required.

Helical spring hinges which provide a similar action, are also obtainable but as
they provide no check a separate check spring will be required to stop the door
banging in the rebate. These need extra strong linings and fixings as they tend
to quickly work loose in practice.

Overhead door closers with a check action can be provided for face or secret
fixing, the latter requiring doors of some thickness to acoid cutting away too
much of the top rail and thus weakening it at the joint between the top rail
and stile. Overhead door closers must be obtained with the correct frame fixing
depending on its position within or without the soffit of the frame.

Bolts are often unsightly and difficult in practice to operate. Flush bolts are
especially difficult to use unless they are provided with a projecting knob on
the slide. Small morticed espagnolette bolts are available operated by an oval
knob which are more satisfactory.

Sash fasteners are of various patterns and are best supplied with a double keep
to allow a small degree of ventilation in bad weather. Casement stays should be
provided with two pins to ensure secure locking when fastened.

Lever door furniture can be obtained with long plates incorporating a keyhole or set on a round plate called a rose. If locks are provided with the latter pattern a separate key escutcheon must be provided. Knob furniture usually has a rose fitting. Case must be taken to select a long cased lock or latch for knob furniture to avoid catching the knuckles on the door lining.

Locks and latches are usually morticed into the edge of the door, made of steel with a face plate and keep to suit ironmongery finishes. Nylon latches are also available.

Cylinder locks for use on external doors are either rim or mortice pattern depending on whether they are face fixed or morticed.

Dead locks for security purposes are always morticed and the keep and bolts are designed to resist forcing which is fairly simple with the usual rim cylinder lock.

Fix the whole of the ironmongery in accordance with the following schedule, ease and adjust and lightly oil all locks on completion

All ironmongery should be fixed with matching screws of correct size and length. This is often ignored and it is common to find only half the number of screws inserted in butt hinges. The screws should be driven home without burring the edges of the slot.

Sinkings for hinges should be neatly formed to receive the appropriate item and this should be set in flush with the edge of the timber. Packing due to faulty workmanship must never be accepted. Similar standards of workmanship are required for fitting locks and keeps. Back plates should be upright and parallel with the frame of the door and items which should be central shall be exact and not approximate.

All joinery moves slightly and as the building dries out so will the doors and windows. To avoid rattles and banging ironmongery must take the butting surfaces up tight and before completion any looseness should be corrected.

All locks and moving parts should be lightly oiled with a good quality light machine oil before the contract is completed.

10 External Plumbing

BS 569: 1967	Asbestos cement
BS 460: 1964	Cast Iron
BS 1091: 1963	Pressed steel
BS 2997: 1958	Aluminium
BS 4576: Pt. 1: 1970	uPVC (half round gutters & round drain pipes only)
BRS Digest 107	Roof drainage

Precise calculations for the design of roof drainage are given in BRS Digest 107 (Second series). Practically the capacity of the gutter depends on several factors, the design of the outflow, the fall provided, frictional resistance and cross-sectional area. Sharp bends near a downpipe restrict the flow, sharp cornered outlets reduce the flow into the downpipe. Gutters should be set to falls to increase the flow but these should never be such as to exceed 51 mm below the roof drip, although falls are discounted in Digest no. 107. A fall of 12 mm in 1 m is a reasonable fall which will clear the gutter of any standing water. Unless fixing holes are provided in the body of the gutter, brackets should be provided at least every 2 m run (or as recommended by the maker) with extra on either side to support outlets. Care must be taken to ensure that the roof sarking felt projects sufficiently to be dressed into eaves gutters. Water penetrating under the tiles may otherwise be trapped behind the fascia, causing it to rot, or discharge between the fascia and the gutter.
Downpipes can be discharged over gullies or connected direct to stormwater drains. Discharge from the gutter outlet can be either direct to the pipe or through a swan neck offset pipe. Discharge at the foot to gullies is generally through a rainwater shoe. Fixings are peculiar to the constituent material but in general pipes should be provided with fixings every 2 m in length with one at the head to support the swan neck, one at each socketted joint and one at the foot to support either the shoe or the connection to the drain.
All gutters should be provided with special stop ends to close the free end and the sections jointed in accordance with the peculiar requirements of the material of which the gutter is composed. Jointing shall be similar for downpipes except that open joints are often left in pipes connected direct to stormwater drains to relieve air pressure in heavy downpours. Downpipes when connected direct to the drain are best jointed in a cementitious cold caulking compound. Stormwater discharged from a downpipe onto an adjacent flat roof can cause

damage to the surface. If this is covered with chippings, these will be disturbed. A quarry tile bedded in mastic or bitumen under the outlet will prevent this occuring.

To avoid leaves and other wind blown debris being washed into downpipes, with the danger of blockage, a guard should be provided to the outlet in the gutter. The galvanised wire balloon guard is probably the best answer to this problem.

The storage of gutters and downpipes should be in racks to prevent damage to the sockets and spigots when stood on end. For small quantities, horizontal storage clear of the ground is satisfactory.

*Provide to eaves ...... mm .... gutters of ....
(all in accordance with BS ....) complete with all necessary outlets,
stop ends, brackets, internal and external angles. Joint and fix the gutters
in accordance with the manufacturer's instructions.
(5)22:1
(5)22:1f6.30+

Asbestos cement gutters to BS 569: 1967, are provided in 2 m lengths with holed spigots and sockets for galvanised countersunk screws for fixings, half round and ogee sections.

Normal gutter sizes H/R – 76, 102, 114, 127, 152 and 203 mm
                    Ogee – 102, 114, 127, 152 and 203 mm

Joints shall be made in the direction of flow and screwed tight with either a cementitious cold caulking compound or a jointing compound supplied by the gutter manufacturer. Fixing is by means of m.s. galvanised brackets screwed to feet of rafters or fascia. Ogee gutters can only be fixed to fascias.

(5)22:1hl.304

Cast iron gutters to BS 460: 1964 are provided in 2m lengths with holed spigots and sockets for galvanised jointing screws for fixings, half round and ogee section.

Normal gutter sizes H/R – 76, 102, 114, 127 and 152 mm
                    Ogee – 102, 114 and 127 mm

Joints should be made in the direction of the flow and screwed tight with a bedding of either red lead and mastic or a cementitious cold caulking mastic. Half round gutters are fixed with mild steel galvanised brackets screwed to feet of rafters or fascia. Ogee gutters are fixed every 610 mm through holes cast in the back of the gutter with galvanised mushroom headed gutter screws.

(5)22:1h2.40+

Pressed steel gutters to BS 1091: 1963, are either light or heavy gauge with holed spigots and sockets, light gauge being in general use for domestic work. They are produced in lengths up to 2 m in half round and ogee sections.

Nominal gutter sizes H/R − 76, 89, 102, 114, 127 and 152 mm
                    Ogee − ditto
Joints should be made in the direction of the flow and screwed tight in bedding
as for cast iron. Fixing to the fascia is with galvanised No. 16. wood screws
with slotted mushroom heads.
(5)22:1h4.50+
Aluminium gutters to BS 2997: 1958, may be cast, extruded or wrought. They
should not be used with copper roofing due to possible electrolytic action.
Gutters are produced holed with spigots and sockets in lengths of 2 m and
more in half round, rectangular and ogee section.
Nominal gutter sizes H/R & Rect. − 102, 114, 127 and 152 mm
                    Ogee − 102, 114 and 127 mm
Joints should be made in the direction of the flow with aluminium or sheradised
fixing bolts and any bituminous mastic. Fixing to rafters or fascia is by either
aluminium or galvanised m.s. brackets.
(5)22:1m6.30
Plastic gutters generally utilise rigid or unplasticised p.v.c. BS 4576: Pt. 1: 1970
refers only to half round gutter and circular down pipes. Manufacturers' sizes
are varied but generally gutters are produced in 2 m and 4 m lengths and in
102 and 114 mm sizes. Integral colours are black, white and grey. Jointing is
generally by integral soft plastic jointing strips which seal the socket and spigot
joints. Fixing is by plastic or plastic coated m.s. brackets and jointing brackets
clipped to the gutter and screwed to the fascia, usually at 1 m centres.
*Provide and fix in position shown on the drawings .... mm ....
downpipes (all in accordance with BS ....) complete with all necessary
swan necks, offsets, r.w. shoes and fixings. Joint and fix the downpipes in
accordance with the manufacturer's instructions.
(5)22:1
(5)22:1f6.10
Asbestos cement down pipes to BS 569: 1970, are produced in lengths of 2 m,
2.5 m and 3 m in nominal pipe sizes of 50, 63, 76, 102 and 152 mm. Socketted
joints may be filled if required with cement and sand 2:1. When sealed jointed
pipes are required for internal use, pipes which conform to BS 486: 1973,
should be used and the joints caulked with a cementitious jointing compound.
As the pipes are not made with ears, fixing is by means of galvanised mild steel
clips fitted below the socket to provide a projection of 38 mm.
(5)22:1h1.12.
Cast iron down pipes to BS 460: 1964, are made in lengths of 2 m and in
nominal pipe sizes of 50, 63, 76, 102, 127 and 152 mm. Unless specifically
ordered pipes are supplied with ears, fittings being generally without. Socketted
jointing may be with red and white lead putty but pipes are often unjointed.

When ears are provided fixing is by means of galvanised pipe nails driven
through holes in the ears to hardwood plugs in the wall. Otherwise stout
galvanised holderbats are fixed below the socket.

(5)22:1h2.10

Pressed steel down pipes to BS 1091: 1963, are of 24 BG black mild steel
galvanised after manufacture in lengths of 1 m, 1.5 and 2 m nominal pipe
sizes of 50, 63, 76 and 102 mm. Socketted joints are left loose socketted and
the pipes are fixed with galvanised pipe nails driven through holes in the ears
welded to the pipe sockets into hardwood plugs in the walls.

(5)22:1h4.35. 1h4.40

Aluminium down pipes to BS 2997: 1958, are either extruded as seamless
tubing or manufactured from sheet or strip in lengths of 2 m upwards and
in nominal pipe sizes as follows:
Round – 50, 63, 75 and 102 mm
Rectangular – 50 x 50, 63 x 63, 76 x 76 and 102 x 102 mm
Socketted joints may be loose or caulked with bituminous mastic. Pipe lengths
and most fittings are fixed with galvanised pipe nails driven through holes in
the ears into hardwood plugs in the walls.

(5)22:1n6.10

Plastic down pipes to BS 4576: Pt. 1: 1970 are generally 63 mm diameter and
in lengths of 2, 2.5, 3 and 6 m depending on the manufacturer. Joints are semi-
tight fit socketted and the pipes are fixed with plastic coated or galvanised
mild steel screws to holderbats.

External plumbing: aluminium:
BSCP 143 Pt. 7: 1965   *Sheet roof and wall coverings – Aluminium*
BS 1470: 1972   *Wrot aluminium and aluminium alloys.........*
                        plate, sheet and strip
BS 747 Pt. 2: 1968   *Roofing felts – Metric units*

The substructure for aluminium roofing must be stable and free from movement
under temporary load. Timber decking is generally used and should be well
seasoned material, tongued and grooved and not less than 25 mm nominal
thickness. Wood preservatives using copper salts should be avoided. On flat
roofs the boarding should be laid in the direction of the fall although on
pitched roofs the boarding may be laid diagonally. Joints should be staggered,
nail heads well punched home and screws countersunk.
Concrete decks should be provided with falls, preferably by a cement/sand 1:4
screed and with a steel float finish. Composition or nailable plugs must be
provided for fixing slips and rolls and timber, if used, must be properly impregnated against rot.

All decks should be provided with a minimum fall of 17 mm in 1 m and any pitch from the minimum to vertical. Aluminium sheets should be stored dry under cover on a clean flat surface clear of the ground. Coils of aluminium strip should be stood on end and preformed profiles should be stored flat, nesting and protected from damage. Felt and wood rolls should also be stored dry and under cover.

All pieces to complete the work must be fabricated from material of the same gauge.

Tools used for working copper or brass must not be used on aluminium as the transfer of any quantity of these metals can cause the aluminium to be attacked by electrolytic action.

Aluminium for roofing will be No. .... gauge of British manufacture in accordance with BS 1470: 1972. The sheet will be clean, flat, cut square, free from all cracks, blisters or scale.

M11 et seq

Aluminium for building purposes is normal commercial grade 99% pure (IC). Where additional ductility is required, for example in complicated flashings, super purity grade 99.99% pure (1) can be used. Sheets can be obtained in any length up to 3.66 m and widths up to 1.22 m. Coiled strip for fully supported roofing is supplied in widths of 457 mm and 610 mm. Aluminium is produced in three thicknesses, 0.91, 0.71 and 0.56 mm but for most work 0.91 mm is used for sheet and either 0.91 or 0.71 for long-strip system roofing.

Aluminium is a basic non-ferrous metal, bright silver in colour which gradually dulls to a light grey colour. The material is ductile and has good cold working properties. In industrially polluted atmospheres the surface may turn into a matt dark grey finish but the effect of weathering is only surface and does not harm the body of the metal. While aluminium has no effect on other materials, the reverse effect is true. Cement/lime, lime, hydraulic-lime mortars and concrete causes interaction and corrosion and the surface of any aluminium in contact with these materials should be provided with a protective coat of bituminous paint. Contact with copper or copper alloys must be avoided and care must be taken to avoid water from copper sources such as roofing, lightning conductors and copper water system overflow pipes discharging onto aluminium roofs.

Aluminium roofing should be laid by competent and skilled craftsmen strictly in accordance with BSCP 143 Pt. 7.: 1965.

M11:1

M11:2

M11:3

M11:4

Aluminium roofing laid over boarded decking should be provided with an insulating felt underlay as BS 747: 1968, type 4A(ii) Brown No. 1 inoderous, weighing 23 kg/10m^2 . The underlay should be butt jointed and secured to the decking with aluminium nails or zinc coated steel nails. Bituminous felt underlays are not satisfactory as they tend to stick to the deck and the sheeting. The felt underlay will help to reduce drumming caused by the impact of rain on the roof, condensation on the underside of the metal and prevent contact between the aluminium and any timber containing acids which will cause chemical interaction. Concrete and screeded surfaces should be provided with a 500 gauge clear polythene sheet underlay laid with joints lapped 150 mm. Whatever the surface or the underlay used, all decking surfaces must be perfectly dry before the aluminium roofing is put on. A coat of paint on timber surfaces can be applied, e.g. an aluminium primer, if there is any question of the dryness of the timber.

The composition of nails and screws is important to prevent electrolytic action. Aluminium nails to BS 1202 Pt. 3 or zinc-coated steel clout nails to BS 1202 Pt. 1 should be used. Screws should be sheradised steel countersunk wood screws to BS 1210 – Wood Screws.

All constructional work should be completed before the aluminium roofing is commenced. Damage will certainly be caused to the roof by workmen having access to it. Before laying the deck must be swept free from all debris and kept clean throughout the work.

Three systems are in general use for aluminium roofing, their choice depending on pitch and practical considerations. Where foot traffic is likely on occasions the 'batten roll' system should be used, otherwise the 'standing seam' system is satisfactory. Batten roll is preferable on low pitches as its greater depth provides greater resistance to weather penetration. Both systems use sheet or strip material. The recently introduced 'long strip' system utilised the benefits of material lengths up to 11 m and can be used for all pitches as heading drips are few in number or even non-existant. Fewer cross welts allow a harder tempered material to be used.

Splay side batten rolls of impregnated deal size 38 x 38 mm at 546 mm centres should be fixed to the deck with wood screws at 620 mm; centres with clips passed under the rolls at 305 mm centres. The roofing sheets are dressed up the sides of the rolls, welted and secured to the clips, the whole being finished with a separate capping strip. Heading joints are made with double lock welts which are staggered in adjoining sheets for appearance. The topmost cross welt should be provided near the ridge so that the rigidity of the joint holds the sheet securely to the roof at this point. Double lock welted joints on pitches below 20° should be sealed by painting the edges with a full coat of boiled linseed oil before welting.

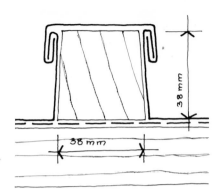

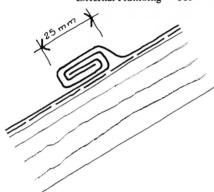

Detail of splay sided batten roll   *Double lock welt for pitches from 4-40°*

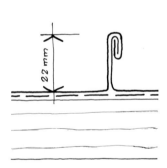

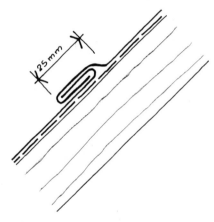

Detail of standing seam   *Single lock welt for pitches above 40°*

Standing seams incorporate an aluminium clip at least 51 mm wide fixed to the deck at 305 mm centres. This system, used for pitched roofs employs the single welted heading joint for longitudinal jointing.

Drips should be provided at 3.0 – 4.5 mm centres in roofs of pitch less than 5° to accelerate the flow of water from the roof. Batten system roofing should have drips 64 mm and standing seam 51 mm deep. When a roof of less than 60° slope discharges into a box gutter a drip should be provided.

Flashings and aprons should be welted to folded roofing sheet upstands and dressed into the brickwork with aluminium wedges, the ends being painted with bituminous paint. All vertical joints should also be welted.

Soldering and brazing should never be used, but aluminium welded fabrication is recommended in some cases using special welding strip.

Inspection of the work on completion should ensure the following have been correctly carried out:

1. All welted seams properly formed without any cracking of the folded parts of the metal
2. The covering is laid with the run of the substructure
3. Apron flashings are properly wedged, pointed, painted and welted to the roof covering and to adjacent lengths
4. The upper surface of the roof is clear of all debris, including nails and metal objects which might damage the surface
5. There is no discharge of water onto the roof surface from any copper piping or copper piped system
6. No water discharges onto the roof from copper roofs, guttering or downpipes or copper lightning conductors

External plumbing: copper:

BS 2870: 1968   *Rolled copper and copper alloys: sheet strip and foil*
BS 747 Pt. 2: 1968   *Roofing felts – metric units*
BSCP 143: Pt. 12: 1970 *Sheet roofing and wall coverings; copper*
Copper Development Association: Traditional Copper Roofing
Technical Note No. 17 Long strip copper roofing

The substructure for copper roofing must be stable, free from movement under temporary load and wind tight. Timber decking is generally used and should be well seasoned material, tongued and grooved and not less than 25 mm nominal thickness. On flat roof slopes of less than 20° the boards should be laid in the direction of the fall or diagonally. Joints should be staggered, nail heads well punched home and screws countersunk.

Concrete decks should be provided with falls, preferably by a cement/sand 1:4 screed and with a steel float finish. Screeds with a sulphate content should have a sealing coat of bitumen primer. Composition or nailable plugs must be provided for fixing copper clips and cleats. When wood dovetail battens are used they should be treated with a preservative against rot.

Other decking materials may be used providing they meet the requirements provided by timber decking and concrete. Apart from structural and dimensional stability they must be smooth, capable of receiving fixings and have a smooth surface to receive the copper sheet.

All decks should have a minimum fall of 40 mm in 2.4 m. Roofs less than 5° should have 65 mm deep drip at not more than 3 mm centres depending on the gauge of copper used.

The storage of copper on site is important. Sheets should be stored dry and nesting under cover on a clean flat surface clear of the ground. Coils of copper should be stood on end and all preformed profiles stored flat, nesting and protected from damage. Felt and wood rolls should also be stored dry and under cover.

All pieces to complete the work should be fabricated from material of the same gauge.

Copper for roofing will be dead soft (quarter hard) temper No. .... gauge of British manufacture, in accordance with BS 2870: 1968. The material will be clean, flat, cut square and free from all cracks and other physical defects.

M12 et seq

Copper for building purposes may be either hot or cold rolled strip or sheet and is generally supplied anealed unless specified to the contrary. Sheets are produced in stock sizes of 1.22 x 0.61 m, 1.83 x 0.91 m and 2.44 x 1.22 m. With domestic work the normal thickness used is 0.457 mm and sheets of this material should not exceed 1.11 m^2. For other work 0.71 and 0.61 mm thicknesses are used and the maximum sheet size may be increased to 1.30m^2. Copper strip is produced in many thicknesses from 0.15 to 3 mm of any width and not cut to length. It is usually supplied in coils of about 51 kg in weight.

Copper is a basic non-ferrous metal which on exposure to the air forms a thin stable insoluble film of copper salts. Once this patina forms it protects the underlying metal from further atmospheric attack. The colour varies from green to black when masked by sooty deposits and takes from 5 to 20 years to form, depending on the degree of atmospheric pollution.

The use of zinc protected ferrous fixings must not be allowed due to probability of electrolytic action. Any bolts or similar fixings which are structurally necessary should be protected by painting with bitumen or covering with a felt ring or washer.

Silver brazing can be employed for the formation of small weathering details. For joints where no stresses occur, e.g. to soil pipes flashings, low melting point copper welding can be used.

Copper roofing shall be laid by competent and skilled copper smiths, strictly in accordance with BSCP 143, Pt. 12: 1970.

M12:1 M12:2 M12:3 M12:4 M12:5

Copper roofing should be provided with a felt underlay, not only to prevent the material from the possibility of galvanic attack from ferrous deck fixings but also to prevent condensation on the underside of the metal and reduce drumming due to the impact of rain on the roof. A felt which will also not adhere to the metal or decking under temperature changes is BS 747: 1968, type 4A(ii) Brown no. 1 inoderous weighing 23 kg/10m^2. The felt should be laid with butt joints and secured to timber decking with copper nails. Felt should be fixed to concrete with cold bonding mastic. Once laid the felt should be immediately covered with copper.

The composition of nails and screws is important to prevent electrolytic action. Nails should be of copper not less than 25 mm long with barbed shanks and minimum 6 mm heads. Screws should be brass countersunk wood screws.

All constructional work should be completed before the copper roofing is commenced. Damage will be caused to the roof surface by traffic and must be discouraged at all costs. Before laying the deck must be swept free from all debris and kept clean throughout the work.

Two systems are in general use for copper roofing, their choice depending on pitch and practical considerations. Over a pitch of 6° long strip welted employing standing seams is used; for pitches of 5° and below traditional wooden roll roofing is used as the upstand of the roll gives greater protection against water penetration. On low pitches foot traffic may cause standing seams to be trodden flat allowing water to penetrate through capillary attraction.

Splay sided batten rolls of impregnated deal size 44 x 40 mm are secured by bolts or long screws into the rafter or decking framing. When the decking is formed from low density insulation boards (strawboard, woodwool slabs or fibreboard) brass bolts with large washers under the locking nut or countersunk long brass screws through the board into 100 x 100 x 25 mm timber blocks should provide sufficient fixing. Rolls should be fixed at 500 m centres for 23 and 26 g copper sheet and 650 mm centres for 22g material.

Cross joints may be double or single lock welts or drips on pitches below 5° Cross welts are usually staggered with standing seams but can be continuous with batten roll joints. Below 20° pitch all cross welts should be painted with boiled linseed oil or a non hardening mastic sealant before being folded together. This procedure should always be followed with diagonal falls and will prevent joints being primed with water and set up a syphonic action leading to water penetration of the roof.

Clips should be of the same gauge of material as the roofing sheet, each fastened to the deck with two brass screws, copper nails or as described for rolls. The sizes of clips and their fixing centres are as follows:

Rolls	38 mm wide at 460 mm centres
Standing seams	38 mm wide at 380 mm centres
Ridge and hips	50 mm wide at 2 clips per bay
Cross welts (double)	50 mm wide at 1 clip per bay
(single)	50 mm wide at 2 clips per bay
Drips and eaves	50 mm wide at 2 clips per bay
Verge	50 mm wide at 300 mm centres
Upstands	38 mm wide at 460 mm centres

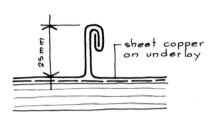

Standing seam detail

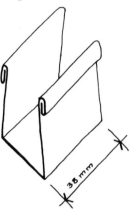

Detail of clip incorporated into standing seam

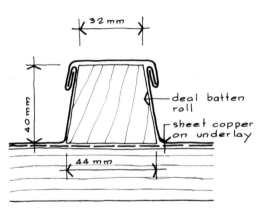

Detail of splay sided batten roll

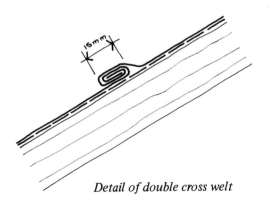

Detail of clip set under deal batten roll

Detail of double cross welt

Falls and drips in gutters The minimum fall in a gutter should be 30 mm in
2.4 m and drips should be at least 50 mm deep. Gutters should discharge into
a cesspool not less than 75 mm deep, the wholé shaped from one piece of
copper with either dog eared or silver brazed corners. The sides of the cesspit
should be taken up and welted to the adjacent copperwork. Gutters can be
discharged direct into a rainwater head without a cesspool if there is no change
in direction of flow.

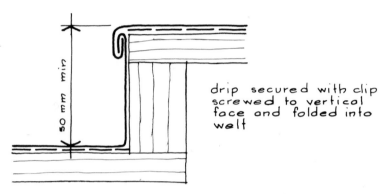

Detail of drip in gutter sole or cross joint for pitch below 5°

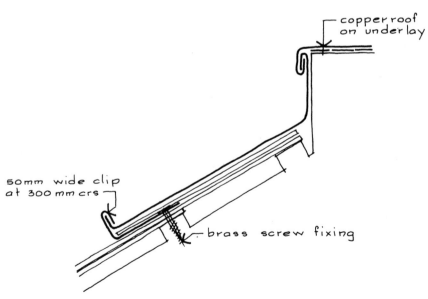

Detail of copper roof discharging onto slates or plain tiles

Drips have the upper and lower bays welted together with a single welt with the turned up edges between the upstand of the drip and standing seam or roll dog eared together. Timber angle fillets are fixed against vertical abutments. Edge details at junctions with tiled or slated roofs have the apron flashing welted to the copper flat over the front edge of the tilting fillet. Where copper is dressed down over tiling or slating a drip should be formed by welting the copper roof to the vertical upstand, dressing the apron over the sloping roof and securing the bottom edge with 50 mm wide clips at 300 mm centres with brass screws to sub-structure rafters.

Valleys have a separate valley gutter welted to the roof sheeting. Jointing is carried out over a timber angle fillet with single welt to front edge. Transverse jointing is by double cross welts.

Ridge & hips are formed either by standing seams or rolls at least 38 mm higher than intersecting rolls.

Vertical abutments are formed either by flattening the standing seam to enable the sheet to be folded up the vertical face or a small triangular fillet is fixed to the top of the roll and the copper flattened as before.

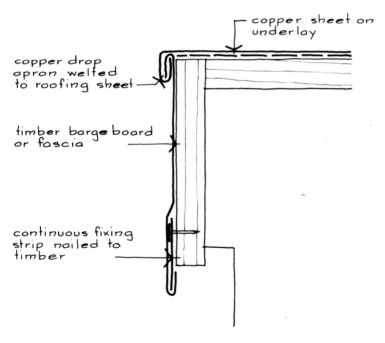

Detail of copper faced fascia or barge board

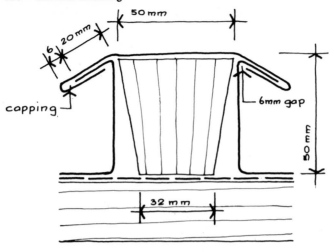

Section through expansion joint

Aprons and flashings should not exceed 1.8 m in length and should be welted to the roof sheet to provide 100 mm minimum cover to the vertical upstand. The upper edge should be folded 25 mm into the wall, wedged with copper or lead and pointed up. A bead on the free bottom edge gives greater rigidity. Eaves and verges should have the main sheet welted to an independant drop apron fully secured with a continuous fixing strip. Where a batten is provided this must be impregnated and preferably screwed, not nailed.

Expansion joints to accommodate thermal expansion in gutters at high points should be provided and the copper used for these gutters should be formed from quarter hard temper copper.

Where flue terminals are adjacent to copper roofs, they should project sufficiently to ensure that flue gases do not come into contact with the copper. Any natural catchment areas adjacent to the flue such as back gutters should be protected by two coats of bituminous paint. Copper roofs discharging onto old litchen covered tiled roofs will kill off the growth, possibly an undesirable occurrence.

External plumbing: lead:

BS 1178: 1969	Milled sheet and strip for building purposes
BS 747 Pt. 2: 1968	Roofing felts – Metric units
BS 1521: 1972	Waterproof building papers
BSCP 143 Pt. 11: 1970	Lead – Metric units

Lead Development Association: Plumber's Handbook

The substructure for lead roofing is always invariably constructed of timber. Due to the very considerable expansion and contraction of lead, the surface of the deck must be as smooth as possible to reduce impedence to the minimum. Well seasoned tongued and grooved rift sawn deal boarding is the best material to use although sawn square edge boards covered with plywood is an alternative. Boards should either be laid diagonally or in the direction of the fall with staggered heading joints. Fixing nails must be well punched home and any screws countersunk. Free edges over which the lead will be dressed should be rounded off with a plane. All timbers should be impregnated against infestation and rot.

All flat roofs should be provided with falls not less than 12 mm in 1 m. Lead roofing can be laid at any pitch from the minimum fall to vertical. A pitch greater than 15° is termed a pitched roof and changes in the design of joints and fixings are necessary.

Lead is a valuable material and easily damaged. It is also very heavy and the rolls should be stored under cover, laid flat on a sheet of building board to protect the soft exposed surface from abrasive damage. Prefabricated lead components should be stored as the rolled lead, or on racks. Felt and wood rolls should be stored dry and under cover.

Lead will be milled sheet of British manufacture in accordance with BS 1178: 1969, and of the thickness specified. The material will be clean, uniform in thickness and texture and free from all cracks, laminations and inclusions. M14

Lead for general building purposes is milled sheet produced in commercial sizes 2.40 m wide and in lengths up to 12 m. It is available cut to any width in rolls up to 12 m long for specific purposes. Lead strip is available in flanged reels, which protect the material from superficial damage, and in such a form is convenient for many flashing and weathering applications. Lead is produced in a range of six thicknesses which cover all practical requirements. The code number applied to each individual thickness relates to the original Imperial weight in pounds per square foot. The ends of the lead rolls are marked with a colour code indicating the respective code and this enables the weight of material used to be checked against the specification, and lead sheet and strip is marked with its code number, British Standard and manufacturer's mark impressed into the metal in letters not less than 12 mm high as follows: Code No. 3 BS 1178.

BS Code No.	Thickness (mm)	Colour marking
3	1.25	Green
4	1.80	Blue
5	2.24	Red
6	2.50	Black
7	3.15	White
8	3.55	Orange

The thickness of lead suitable for various applications depends on a variety of factors. The thinnest lead available will, so far as corrosion goes, outlive almost any building, but mechanical damage and working requirements usually require additional thickness. The following table is a guide to recommended thickness for particular applications:

Flat roofing (depending on traffic)	No. 5 or 6
Pitched roofing	Ditto
Dormer cheeks and roofs	Ditto
Vertical cladding	Ditto
Parapet gutters	Ditto
Chimney flashing complete	No. 4 or 5
Soakers	No. 3 or 4
Cloaks or trays in cavity walls	Ditto
Lead slates	No. 4 or 5
Valley gutters	No. 5 or 6
Hip and ridge saddles	Ditto
Flashings to roof lights and glazing	No. 4 or 5
Damp proof courses	No. 3, 4 or 5
Lining to flower boxes	No. 6

Small qualities of cast sheet lead are produced by specialist firms for the repair of old roofs. Molten lead is run over prepared sand on a casting bed, producing sheets up to 5.5 x 1.8 m in size and 24.5 to 49 Kg/m^2 ($5-10lb/ft^2$). Scrap cast lead is usually used for this purpose and the resultant texture is rough from contact with the sand.

Lead is the softest of the common metals and has a high degree of ductility, malleability and resistance to corrosion. The material is easily cut and shaped and does not appreciably work-harden. Lead is very resistant to town, country and marine exposure, the bright metal being tarnished by atmospheric action to produce a fine grey film on the surface with protects the underlying metal. This tarnish will not stain or harm masonry and it not generally affected by mortars. When lead is buried in concrete or partial cement mortar it should be provided with a good coat of bitumastic paint as slight corrosion is caused by moist materials containing Portland cement. Corrosion of lead can occur when it is in direct contact with some timbers, especially oak and teak. Well seasoned softwoods and elm give little trouble but the use of a felt or waterproof building paper as a separating layer is sufficient to obviate any trouble.

Lead roofing shall be laid by competent and skilled plumbers, strictly in accordance with BSCP 143, Pt. 11: 1970.

M14:1 M14:2 M14:3 M14:4 M14:5

Lead sheet roofing should always be provided with a felt or building paper underlay to reduce irregularities in the surface, reduce frictional resistance to the surface under thermal movement and, in the case of felt, provide additional accoustic insulation caused by rain beating on the surface of the lead. A suitable felt is BS 747: 1968 type 4A(ii) Brown no. 1, inoderous weighing 23 Kg/$10m^2$ and waterproof building paper should comply with BS 1521: 1972 Class A.1. The felt and building paper should be laid butt joint and secured to the timber deck with copper nails.

Nails and screws used in leadwork are always non-ferrous. Nails should be of copper not less than 25 mm long with barbed shanks and minimum 10 mm heads. Nails should be covered as they have a tendancy to work out in use. Screws should be brass countersunk wood screws.

Copper nailing can be specified 'close' or 'open'. Close copper nailing is spaced from 25 – 50 mm centres and is used when the nails have to support any stress or weight. Open copper nailing is from 75 – 150 mm centres and merely holds the lead in position. Vertical surfaces of lead are often fixed by means of a lead dot. A brass screw and washer secure the lead through a countersinking in the surface to the structure and the whole secured by wiping on a soldered dot. A lead plug is used to receive the screw when fixing is being made to concrete or masonry.

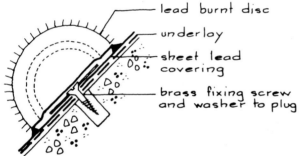

Lead burnt dot, usually for fixing to horizontal surfaces

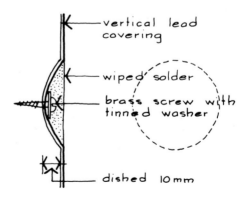

Wiped soldered dot for vetrical surfaces

All constructional work should be completed before lead roofing is commenced. It will be necessary, however, to supply certain flashings and trays for building in and care should be taken to see that these are properly lapped and project sufficiently to provide enough weathering. Any lead surfaces which are likely to receive any traffic whatsoever after fixing must be completely covered and protected from damage. Before laying, deck must be swept free from all debris and kept clean throughout the work.

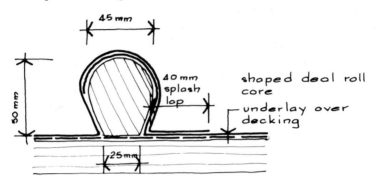

A wood cored lead roll for use on flat roofs

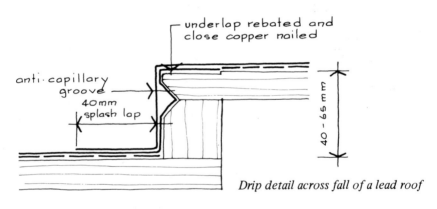

Drip detail across fall of a lead roof

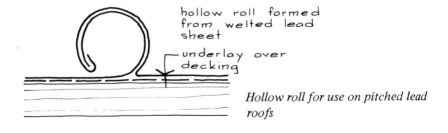

Hollow roll for use on pitched lead roofs

Flat Roofs (below 15° pitch) usually have longitudinal joints formed over tapering deal rolls size 50 x 45 mm wide, tapering to 25 mm at the base and with the top surface rounded. The rolls are placed at centres to limit the size of each piece of lead so that expansion is not excessive and ensure there are no undue restrictions on movement. The centres of rolls and the appropriate centres of cross joints are given below:

BS Code No.	Centres of joints with fall (mm)	Centres of joints across fall (mm)
7 and 8	675	2750
6	675	2500
5	600	2250
4	500	2000

Generally joints at 600 and drips at 2250 mm centres will be satisfactory. Drips – joints across the fall of the roof should be at least 40 mm and preferably 60 mm deep. The lower depth should be provided with an anti-capillary groove in the timber upstand, with the end of the undercloak well dressed into it before being let flush with the roof boarding and copper nailed.

Pitched roofs (from 15° to 70°) usually incorporate hollow rolls for joints with the falls although on very steep pitches double welts are satisfactory. With hollow rolls the undercloak is turned up 100 mm with copper tacks at 600 mm centres, the overlap is turned up 125 mm and the edge welted over the undercloak. The tall welt is then turned over to form a roll. The centres of rolls or welts and the appropriate centres of cross joints are given below:

BS Code No.	Centres of joints with fall (mm)	Centres of joints across fall (mm)
7 and 8	675	2500
6	600	2500
5	550	2250
4	500	2000

Adequate support must be given to the lead in slopes to retain the lead in position without restricting its natural movement.

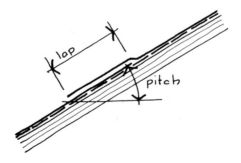

Lap joint across the fall of a lead roof

For joints across the fall, laps are used, the undercloak open nailed with copper nails in two rows 25 mm apart. The lap length is dependent on pitch, as follows:

Pitch	Lap Length (mm)
15°	300
20°	225
25°	175
30° and over	150

In bays of maximum width a copper clip may be provided to secure the centre of the bottom edge.

Roll end details depend on the method of roll construction. At eaves solid rolls are usually bossed with the bay in position and the undercloak clipped to the overcloak and a copper tack provided in the centre of the bay. Lead burning can also be employed to seal the joint. In any event the end of the wood roll should be cut to an angle of not less than 60° with the lower edge in line with the edge of the roof. Hollow rolls can be either double welted to form an open ended hollow roll, turned down with the apron or provided with a lead burnt end. At vertical abutments for both types of roll a gusset is prepared and the whole burnt in to seal the joint.

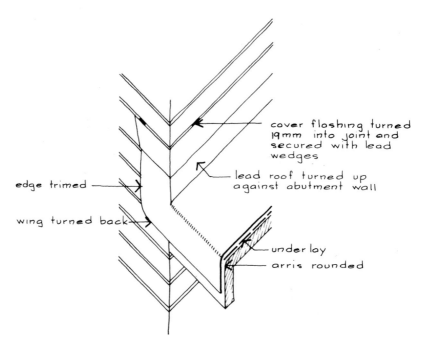

Flashing – abutment of eaves and wall

Where rolls abut drips the undercloak is dressed up the face and onto the higher deck to butt against the felt and copper nailed, the overlap from the upper bay being bossed over the roll and dressed into position.

At abutments the roof covering is dressed up the wall a minimum of 100 mm to receive a cover flashing. Where eaves meet abutments the wing of the upstand is turned back along the wall face, the corner trimmed to radius and the cover flashing dressed round the corner over the top of the wing.

At the ridge the roll is usually finished under a ridge roll capping or the roll carried right over the ridge itself.

Vertical cladding to dormer cheeks and similar situations should not be more than 1.7m^2 or 2.4 m in length, supported at between 500 mm centres for code No. 4 and 600 mm centres for code Nos. 5 and 6 lead by a wiped soldered dot. When the width of the panel exceeds 600 mm the free edge of the lead should be secured by copper clips. Vertical joints are usually double welts, header joints being formed by simple laps of not less than 50 mm, the undercloak being close copper nailed.

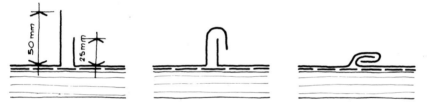

Three stages in the formation of a double welt joint for use on vertical cladding

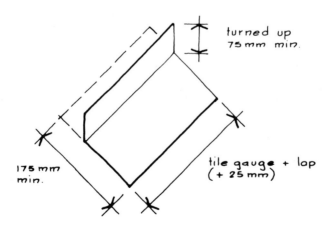

Lead soakers

*Soakers will be Code No. 3 (4) lead one to each tile (slate), properly fixed
with adequate weathering to tile and against the abutment.*
    N22:2551
The length of a soaker is governed by the length of the tile or slate used. The
length is equal to the guage plus the lap. With a plain tile of 265 x 165 mm
laid to 95 mm gauge the length of the soaker will be 95 + 75 = 170 mm plus
25 mm extra to enable the top to be turned down and nailed to the batten with
a copper nail to prevent the soaker slipping. The soaker should be wide enough
to lie 100 mm under the tile or slate and be dressed 75 mm up the wall. Soakers
provided by the Plumber are fixed by the Slater or Tiler.
*Flashings will be Code No. 4 (5) lead either stepped or straight, 150 mm in
height, the top edge to be dressed to a right angle and inserted 25 mm into
the joint in the brickwork to marry with the d.p.c. (cavity tray) and the
remainder to be neatly dressed over the turned up portion of the roof (or
soakers) or 150 mm over the surface of the roof.*
    M14:5
Stepped flashings are used for raking flashings in brick or regularly coursed
masonry. Horizontal flashings and raking flashings in uncoursed masonry require
a groove parallel to the pitch of the roof into which the lead is turned. Cover
flashings should be dressed at least 50 mm (75 mm) over the upstand of the
soakers. Where soakers are not employed the flashing should be dressed 150 mm
minimum over the surface of the roof or 175 mm when interlocking tiles are
employed. Flashings should not exceed 2.1 mm in length, laps should be at
least 100 mm and each 'step' should be wedged into the brick joint with a lead
wedge and the whole joint pointed up on completion in cement/sand 1:3.

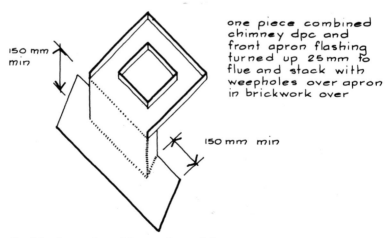

150 mm min

one piece combined
chimney dpc and
front apron flashing
turned up 25mm to
flue and stack with
weepholes over apron
in brickwork over

150 mm min

Combined one piece chimney dpc and front apron

Provide and insert to chimney stack at a point above its intersection with the rake of the roof a Code No. 4 (5) lead d.p.c., perforated for the flue and complete with and including front apron flashing dressed down the face of the brickwork and over the tiling a minimum of 150 mm.
F11:Mh8.10

The d.p.c. to the stack must be formed in one piece including the front apron and it is set in the stack at the normal position occupied by the front apron, i.e. not less than 150 mm above the top of the roof tiling. The outer edges of the d.p.c. and the perimeter of the perforations for the flue should be dressed up 25 mm to collect any water penetrating through the top of the stack allowing it to flow out over the front apron through weep holes left in the brick joints for this purpose. The whole of the bedded surfaces of the lead should be painted with a bituminous paint to prevent corrosion.

The front apron flashing should be the width of the stack plus 150 mm on either side for dressing behind the cover flashing.

The d.p.c. and apron are supplied and fixed by the plumber on a prepared level bed of mortar by the bricklayer.

Provide and fix to back of chimney stack Code No. 4 (5) lead back gutter of minimum width 150 mm dressed over tilting fillet under slates and dressed 150 mm up face of stack, 225 mm around returns of chimney and covered with Code No. 4 (5) flashings as previously described.

The lead should be the width of the stack plus 225 mm on either side for working down under the cover flashing. The sole of the gutter must be wide enough for a man to stand in it, 150 mm being the minimum width acceptable. The lead should be dressed up over a timber tilter fillet to a vertical height not less than 150 mm under the tiling and the upstand to the stack protected by a cover flashing as described before. The back gutter is placed in position before the roof covering is fixed and is supported on a lier board of 25 mm sawn fir brackets provided by the carpenter.

Provide and fix to junction of ridge and chimney stack Code No. 5 (4) lead saddle, neatly dressed to stack and tiling.

This saddle protects the joint between tiling and stack at the ridge. The lead is dressed 150 mm along the ridge and 100 mm or so down the roof on either side and the ridge tile is bedded down on top of the lead. The saddle is fixed by the plumber when the cover flashings are fitted and prior to the bedding of the ridge tiles by the tiler.

Provide and fix to cills of windows Code No. 4 lead flashings dressed down over tile hanging.

Windows in tile hanging, and also preferably in similar claddings, should be provided with an overhanging cill and lead cover flashing close copper nailed in the groove provided for the window board and dressed under the cill and

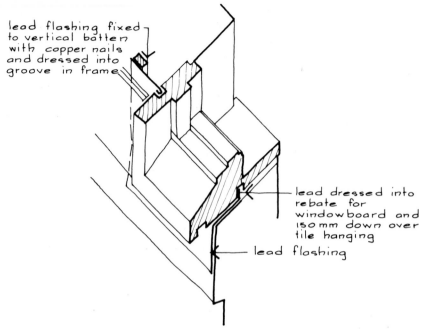

lead flashing fixed
to vertical batten
with copper nails
and dressed into
groove in frame

lead dressed into
rebate for
windowboard and
150 mm down over
tile hanging

lead flashing

Lead flashing to cill and jambs of window in tile hanging

down the face of the tiles by at least 100 m. The free edge can be cut straight or with a decorative finish.

At the head of the window similar lead should be fixed above the tilter and dressed down over the same.

Tile hanging abutting a brick return should be provided with a stepped lead flashing dressed 75 mm behind the tiling and finished with a single welt.

Fixing blocks in tile hanging should be covered in code No. 4 lead to provide fixing for r.w.p.'s and vent shafts.

Provide and fix to head of c.i. vent shaft where it penetrates the tiled roof code No. 4 lead slate with upstand, neatly dressed to roof and vent shaft.

The size of the base varies slightly with the size and type of roofing unit and with contoured tiles allowances must be made for dressing into the contours. For standard plain tiles, the base should be 375 mm wide and 450 mm deep, the circular upstand projecting 100 mm minimum at the back.

The slate is placed in position before the roof covering with the back dressed down and the front turned up so that the tiler can work up to it. Afterwards the lead is neatly dressed down to a close fit with the roofing and the upstand dressed tightly to the pipe.

External Plumbing: zinc:
BS 849: 1939   *Plain sheet zinc roofing*
BS 747: Pt. 2 1968   *Roofing felts – Metric units*
BSCP 143 Pt. 5: 1964   *Sheet roof and wall coverings - zinc*
Z.D.A. Information sheets 1 – 12 Zinc in Building

The substructure for zinc roofing must be stable and free from movement
under temporary load. Timber decking should be of well seasoned material,
preferably tongued and grooved, not less than 25 mm nominal thickness and
laid in the direction of the fall or diagonally across it. Joints shall be staggered,
nail heads well punched home and screws countersunk. Impregnation of timber
should be carried out using only non-corrosive preservatives and fire retardants
should be based on sodium silicate or sodium phosphate.
Concrete decks should be provided with falls, preferably by a cement/sand 1:4
screed with a steel float finish. Composition or nailable plugs must be provided
for fixing clips and rolls and timber, if used, must be properly pressure impregnated against rot.
All decks should be provided with a minimum fall of 50 mm in 3 m. Zinc
roofing can be laid from any pitch from minimum to vertical.
The storage of zinc on site is important. Sheets should be stored dry under
cover on a clean flat surface clear of the ground. Coils of zinc should be stored
on end and preformed profiles should be stored flat, nesting and protected from
damage. Felt and wood rolls should also be stored dry and under cover.
All pieces to complete the work must be fabricated from material of the same
gauge. Holding down clips should be made with the grain of the metal running
with the length of the clip.
Zinc should never be marked with a steel scribe or any similar sharp tool as
this may well cause mechanical failure.
*Zinc for roofing will be No. 14 gauge of British manufacture in accordance
  with BS 849: 1939. The sheet will be clean, flat, cut square, free from all
  cracks, blisters and scale.*
  M13
Zinc sheet for building purposes is produced by hot rolling the material until
the right thickness (gauge) is produced. The sheet is then cropped to provide
stock sizes of 910 x 2440 and 910 x 2130 mm. Although zinc is produced in
three gauges No. 14 gauge is generally used for building purposes and weighs
5.82 Kg/m^2. Its thickness is 0.813 mm.
Zinc is a basic non-ferrous metal light grey in colour, available in sheet or strip.
The material is ductile, has good cold working properties and weathers to a
matt grey colour. Its life under average conditions when properly laid to
adequate falls is not less than 40 years in urban conditions. Heavily polluted

atmospheres should have the pitch increased to allow corrosive deposits to be quickly washed away. Zinc is seriously affected by acids and strong alkalis and by electrolytic action from water draining off copper or copper rich materials. Care must be taken to isolate copper lightning conductors from zinc roofing. Iron, aluminium and lead have no effect on zinc. Although not affected by cement mortar or concrete, the metal should be coated with bituminous paint if these is any likelihood of sulphate or chloride attack. Condensation is an enemy of zinc and consequently the roof structure should be properly ventilated.

Zinc roofing shall be laid by competent and skilled zinc workers strictly in accordance with BSCP 143 Pt. 5. 1964.

   M13:1 M13:2 M13:3 M13:4 M13:5

Zinc roofing must be provided with a felt underlay not only to prevent the material from possible chemical attack from the materials forming the decking but also to reduce drumming caused by the impact of rain on the roof. Felt should be open textured impregnated felt as BS 747 Type 4A (roofing felts – bitumen and fluxed pitch) laid with butt joints and secured to the decking by rolls or clips provided to secure the zinc sheeting. Temporary fixing can be provided by galvanised clout nails.

The composition of nails and screws is important to prevent electrolytic action. Nails should always be galvanised steel clout nails to BS 1202 – Wire and Cut Nails, and never less than 25 mm long. Screws should be sherardised steel countersunk wood screws to BS 1210 – Wood Screws.

Roll capping which is supplied machine made in lengths not exceeding 1200 mm should be of the same gauge as the roof covering.

All constructional work must be completed before roofing operations are started. The roof deck must be dry and swept free from all loose debris and kept clean throughout the work. Laying commences from the lowest edge and from an abutment or verge at one side and in the following sequence:

Cesspools to box gutters

Box gutter linings and outlets

Drop aprons

Main roof and capping

Cover flashings

Rolls of impregnated wrot deal size 38 x 44 mm should be spaced 840 mm apart to allow for 38 mm turn up at each side of the sheet. End bays against abutments should not be more than 788 mm to allow for turn up against the wall. Drips should be spaced 150 mm less than the length of the sheet with 100 mm allowed at the top abutment if required or 75 mm at ridges.

Rolls are fixed through the felt at 525 mm centres either by skew nailing to timber decking or by screws to concrete or similar substructures. Fixing clips are inserted under the rolls as the latter are screwed to the deck, not more than 75 mm from the ends of the rolls and spaced not more than 1100 mm centres, secured either with the roll fixings or by two clout nails or screws.

Eaves aprons should have fixing clips every 300 mm secured either by folding round top and bottom edge, or by sheradised round head screws and dished zinc washers. Horizontal joints should be lapped 50 mm.

Roofing sheets should have either a beaded or welted drip to the sheet below secured with fixing clips folded over the upstand.

Capping should be secured over the rolls by holding down clips not exceeding 1100 mm centres each clip secured with clout nails or screws to the roll.

Verges are formed either with a roll or a drop apron as provided for the eaves.

Flashings can be either straight or stepped and lap over the edges of roof sheets at least 50 mm, turned into the wall, wedged every 600 mm centres and pointed up. The free edge should be stiffened by a half bead or a roll.

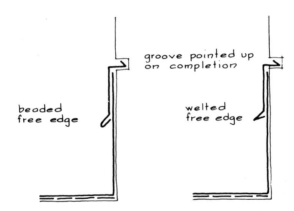

Alternative details to free edge of flashings

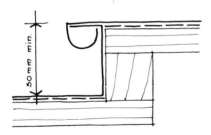

Detail of beaded finish to drip

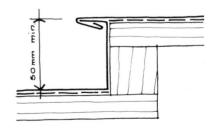

Detail of welted finish to drip

<u>Hips and ridges</u> are formed with rolls 38 mm higher than normal sheet jointing rolls and the joints between hips and ridge are soldered as necessary. The solder should be 50/50 or 60/40 tin/lead composition.

<u>Valleys</u> are formed either by box gutter or, where the pitch is less than 15°, by a 450 mm girth sheet with welted joints to adjacent sheets and joints in its length secured with hanging clips.

<u>Cross joints</u> between ends of sheets by means of a single lock welted joint are suitable for roofs of 15° pitch and above. Below 15° drips not less than 50 mm deep are required.

<u>Free edges</u> of all zinc sheets should be stiffened with a bead.

Inspection of the work should be carried out to ensure the above requirements are followed, no damage to the surface of the zinc has occurred and no nails or similar ferrous material is left on the surface of the roof. Any traffic over the roof after laying should be prohibited unless the roof is properly sheeted and protected from damage and swept clean on completion.

11 Internal Plumbing

Pipes and fittings: Cast iron
BS 416: 1967   *Cast iron spigot and socketted soil, waste and*
                             ventilating pipes and fittings
Copper:
BS 659: 1967   *Light gauge copper tube (light drawn)*
BS 2871 Pt. 1: 1971   *Copper and copper alloy tubes*
BS 3831: 1965   *Hard drawn thin wall copper tubes*
Steel:
BS 1387: 1967   *Steel tubes .... for screwing to BS 21 pipe threads*
Lead:
BS 602, 1085: 1970   *Lead and alloy pipes*
Pitch fibre:
BS 2760: 1966/7   *Pitch impregnated fibre pipes and fittings for*
                             drainage below and above ground

Polythene:
BS 1972: 1967   *Polythene pipe (type 32) for cold water services*
BS 3284: 1967   *Polythene pipe (type 50) for cold water services*
UPVC:
BS 3505: 1968   *Unplasticised pvc for cold water services*
BS 4514: 1969   *Unplasticised pvc soil and vent pipe fittings and*
                             accessories
BS 3943: 1965   *Plastic waste traps*
Stop valves:
BS 1010: 1959   *Draw off taps and stop valves for water services*
                             (screw down pattern)

Cisterns:
BS 417: 1964   *Galvanised mild steel cisterns and covers, tanks and*
                             cylinders
BS 2777: 1963   *Asbestos cement cisterns*
BS 4213: 1967   *Polyolefin or olefin copolymer moulded cold water*
                             cisterns
Ball valves:
BS 1212 Pt. 1: 1953   *Piston types*
       Pt. 2: 1970   *Diaphragm types*
BS 1968: 1953   *Floats for ball valves (copper)*

BS 2456: 1954	Floats for ball valves (plastic)
Cylinders:	
BS 699: 1972	Copper cylinders for domestic purposes
BS 1566 Pt. 1: 1972	Copper indirect cylinders for domestic purposes: Double feed indirect cylinders
BS 1566 Pt. 2: 1972	Copper indirect cylinders for domestic purposes: Single feed indirect cylinders
BS 417: 1964	Galvanised mild steel cisterns and covers, tanks and cylinders
Codes of Practice:	
BSCP 99: 1972	Frost precautions for water services
BSCP 304: 1968	Sanitary pipework above ground
BSCP 310: 1965	Water supply

BRS Digests:
15   Pipes and fittings for domestic water supply
69   Durability and application of plastics
98   Durability of metals in natural waters

The design and installation of internal plumbing services, in the main, are carried out to conform to BSCP 304 and 310. Both these Codes give detailed guidance on specific matters for water supplies and sanitary pipework in such buildings as houses, flats, schools, offices and industrial premises.

In addition, local water boards are empowered to issue Byelaws for the control of plumbing services and water supplies in their areas and due regard must be paid to these requirements. The Public Health Acts lay down certain minimum requirements and these are taken into account in approvals which are required under the Building Regulations for building proposals.

*Give notice to the .... Waterworks Company for a ..... mm supply to the premises and pay all fees.
   A22:1101

The local water authority has a statutory duty (subject to certain conditions and reservations) to afford a supply of water to premises on demand. This is usually effected by completing an application form or notice of requirement and forwarding this to the authority.

Connection to the water main will be made by the water authorities staff who will usually insert a ferrule in the pipe and run a communication pipe of the correct bore to a position immediately outside the boundary of the site or premises, terminating in a stop tap or valve with a key head, in a box with a c.i. cover over. From this point the provision of the supply pipe is the responsibility of the building owner.

The cost of making the connection and providing the communication pipe, stop valve, pit and cover is charged to the contract either by means of a fixed charge or at the net cost of the work at the supply authority's discretion.

Excavate trench not less than 1 m deep, make connection to Water Company's stop valve with copper to iron coupling and run .... mm diameter copper supply to BS 2871. Pt. 1 Table X. into the building to the point shown on the drawings terminating in a brass screw down pattern combined stop and drain cock set 225 mm above the floor.

(5)31:1151 1152 1153

(5)31:Xh6.20 Xh6.26

The minimum depth of main supply below ground is designated in the Model Water Bylaws. This is to prevent water in the pipe freezing in cold weather. The total depth of cover should not be less than 750 mm but in the light of local experience a greater depth should be specified. Care must be taken to see that the minimum depth is maintained throughout the length of the pipe and where this rises in the building, the pipe should not be less than 750 mm from the inner face of any external wall. Care must be taken to see that site works do not reduce the cover provided, otherwise the pipe should be properly lagged as described elsewhere.

Copper supply pipes can be used as well as plastic. Metal pipes are best protected with a proprietory wrapping to stop mechanical damage during backfilling of the trench and, in some soils, chemical attack. Details of copper and plastic pipes are described elsewhere.

Immediately on entering the building the supply pipe should terminate in a screw down stop valve conforming to BS 1010. These can be obtained combined with a drain cock which, when the stop valve is screwed down shut, allow the whole of the mains water distribution system to be drained down. Alternatvely a separate drain cock can be fitted immediately above the stopcock to serve a similar purpose. Make sure that both are placed in a position where they can be easily operated.

Provide and install in the roof space a .... litre (actual capacity) .... storage cistern complete with cover, conforming strictly to BS ....

(5)31:Xf6.10. Xh2.10. Xn6.10

Storage cisterns for water storage are made in a variety of sizes in three main materials. The size required depends on the number of sanitary fittings installed, the number of occupations, the number of persons occupying the building and the estimated volume of water likely to be used over a period of 24 hours. The three materials commonly used in the construction of water storage cisterns are: galvanised mild steel; asbestos cement or various plastics.

It is important to know the overall sizes of cisterns constructed of different materials for various actual water çapacities. As the level of the water below the cistern top is a further check on the actual capacity of a cistern of specified capacity, this dimension is also important. The overall sizes and capacities of cisterns of different capacities and materials is as follows:

Galvanised mild steel to BS 417 (Grade A or B)

BS Ref.	Dimensions (mm)			Capacity to water line		Distance of water
	L	W	D	(litres)	(gall.)	line from top (mm)
SC 20	610	410	380	55	12	111
SC 40	690	510	510	114	25	114
SC 70	910	610	580	227	50	114
SC 80	910	660	610	264	58	114
SC 100/1	1220	610	610	327	72	114
SC 150	1090	860	740	491	108	146
SC 350	1520	1140	910	1250	270	146
SC 600	1830	1220	1220	2137	470	191
SC 1000	2440	1520	1220	3364	740	254

Asbestos cement to BS 2777

AC 20	533	406	495	61.37	13.5	111.12
AC 30	635	482	571	113.65	25.0	114.30
AC 60	787	609	648	227.30	50.0	114.30
AC 80	940	686	648	300.03	66.0	114.30
AC 130	1016	863	736	472.77	104.0	146.05
AC 180	1232	1029	736	700.07	154.0	146.05

Polyolefin or Olefin Copolymer to BS 4213

PC 15			430	68	15	114
PC 25			560	114	25	114
PC 50			660	227	50	114
PC 60			660	273	60	114
PC 70			660	318	70	114
PC 100			760	455	100	114

In addition to dimensional checks for capacity cisterns are marked as follows: Galvanised mild steel to BS 417: BS 417/reference/grade and thickness/ Manufacturer's name or identification mark/Capacity to water line.

Asbestos cement to BS 2777: Manufacturer's name or identification mark/ BS 2777/BS type reference/Capacity.

Polyolefin Copolymer to BS 4213: Manufacturer's name or trade mark/ Type reference no./BS 4213.

Galvanised mild steel cisterns in some water areas of the U.K. require additional internal protection to reduce the risk of chemical attack from deleterious chemicals in the water supply. This protection should be provided by two coats of a black bituminous coating solution to BS 3416 applied by brush or spray to whole of the interior of the cistern after it has been installed. After the coating has hardened the cistern should be filled with water, allowed to stand for four hours and then drained down.

Cisterns should always be fully supported over the whole area of the base to prevent deflection when full of water. This may be provided by means of a boarded platform securely supported by timber joists carried on the main structure. A good alternative is provided by wood wool slabs in place of the boarding with a layer of bitumen roofing felt between the slab and the cistern bottom.

Care must be taken in cutting holes in all types of cistern. With galvanised steel, all swarf must be removed and the holes carefully reamed smooth. Plastic and asbestos cement cisterns should have holes with clean edges, free from notches and with plastic cisterns scratching or scoring should not be permitted for setting out the holes. With the nature of the material in mind, plastic tanks must not be positioned close to sources of heat and pipes must be supported so as not to distort the cistern and backnuts not over-tightened.

All cisterns must be carefully stored to prevent damage to the cistern or its coating, and must be kept clean.

Provide and fit to cistern. . . . . . mm ball valve to BS 1212 complete with plastic float to BS 2456 (copper float to BS 1968) and secure with back-nut. (5) 31: Xh6.30. Xh6.40. Xh5.20. Xn5.10. Xn6.30. 35 seq.

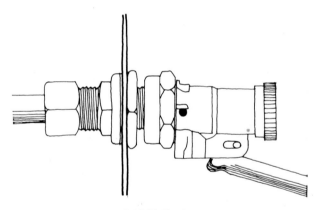

Piston ball valve to BS 1212 Pt. 1

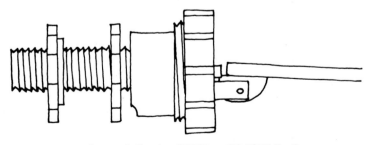

Garston or diaphragm ball valve (BRS) to BS 1212 Pt. 2

Types of ball valve in common use are as follows:

Piston Ball Valve to BS 1212 Pt. 1 has a horizontal cylinder with the float arm operating on a seating under the body of the valve. BS 1212 makes recommendations for varying sizes depending on the nominal bore of the seating and the water pressure. Generally all metal parts are made of brass or gunmetal with nylon seatings and brass levers.

Diaphragm Ball Valves (known as Garston or BRS) to BS 1212, Pt. 2 devised by the Building Research Station, consist of a simple diaphragm operated by the float lever arm on a tapered seating in the body of the valve.

As ball valves are made to suit varying pressure, the correct valve for the pressure should be fitted. All ball valves complying with British Standard Specifications are marked as follows: BS 1212/manufacturer's name or mark. The floats for ball valves may be of copper or plastic. Ball valves to BS1212 are fitted with floats, complying with the following and marked as described:

BS 1968: Floats for ball valves (copper)

Identification marking/BS 1968/manufacturer's identity.

BS 2456: Floats for ball valves (plastic)

Identification marking/BS2456/manufacturer's identity.

*Provide and fix ...... mm diameter copper (lead or plastic) overflows to all
   cisterns with w.w.p.'s.*

All cisterns must be provided with efficient overflow pipes to safeguard the building against defective ball valves. These overflows must discharge in a conspicuous position and be of sufficient bore to carry away water faster than it can be delivered. The usual procedure is to provde an overflow pipe one size larger than the delivery pipe. The pipe should be fixed to the cistern and turned down at the discharge point as recommended elsewhere.

Copper, lead or plastic pipes are best for this work, galvanised steel tubes not being satisfactory due to corrosion problems.

*The whole of the internal hot and cold water distribution pipes will be carried
   out in copper tube conforming in all respects to BS 2871 Pt. 1: 1971,
   jointed with approved compression fittings (capillary fittings, silver brazing
   or bronze welding).
   (5)31:1h5.10 1h6.15*

Copper tubes are virtually inert to potable water and they are strong enough to withstand any permanent deformation due to the stresses caused by expansion and contraction. The tubes are easy to manipulate and fabricate, light to handle and sufficiently rigid and flexible to meet variations in dimensional requirements so often required in buildings.

Copper tube for building purposes is covered by BS 2871 Pt. 1 1971. These tubes are in metric dimensions and are suitable for connection by a number of different methods as follows:

(a) Using compression fittings of two main types
   (i) non-manipulative type A
   (ii) manipulative type B
(b) Capillary soldered joints
(c) Silver brazing
(d) Bronze welding

All fittings must be of copper or corrosion resistant copper alloy.
<u>Compression joints</u> In the manipulative type the square cut end of the tube is
flared, cupped or belled by means of special forming tools and compressed by
a coupling nut against the shaped end of a corresponding section on the fitting
or a loose thimble insert. In another type a swaging tool is used to roll a bead
on the tube about 12 mm from the end. This bead is compressed against the
mouth of the fitting making a fluid tight joint.

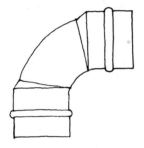

Capillary joint incorporating
solder ring

Compression joint

The manipulative joint only requires the end of the tube to be cut square.
The joint is made by a loose copper ring gripping the outside wall of the tube
when the coupling nut is tightened.
<u>Capillary joints</u> are cold wrot from copper tube. Capillary fittings operate
by the action of the solder contained in the fitting which, when melted
by the heat from a blow lamp, is drawn into and seals the narrow space between
the two closely fitting metal surfaces of the tube end and the interior of the
fitting. These joints are very resistant to temperature stresses and vibration.
To ensure a good joint the tube end and fitting must be thoroughly cleaned
and the flux used must be that recommended by the manufacturer of the fittings
and in moderate quantities. Two types of capillary fittings are:
(a) those containing an integral soldering, and
(b) those where the solder is applied in the form of thin wire to the mouth of
    the fitting (end feed capillary joints).

Silver brazed or bronze welded joints These jointing techniques require a higher temperature than that required for soft soldered capillary joints and in general are used for large bore pipes.

Copper pipes are easily bent but unless a proper bending machine or spring is used, deformation of the tube will result. This is because the inside or throat of the bend is compressed and the outside or back is stretched. Unless precautions are taken the tube will collapse in the bend. Support is provided by the insertion of a spring or use of a bending machine. This latter can be operated by hand or through a ratchet gear employing formers and back guides to ensure that the tube when pulled to the required angle maintains its true diameter and shape throughout the bend.

Copper tubes can be easily and neatly installed without much trouble. Parallel runs of pipe should be parellel, plumb and equidistant apart. Where pipes change direction through 90° it is better to use bends rather than fittings. Pipes should be set far enough apart for fixings to be inserted. Provision for expansion in long runs of pipe must be made, either:

(a) by a loop, or

(b) by the insertion of bellows, or

(c) by the insertion of glands

The first is a loop of copper jointed in fittings, welded or brazed. The loop must be horizontal to avoid air locks.

Bellows fittings are obtained in sizes of 22 mm and upwards. The gland is of cast bronze or gun metal, compact in size, but access must be provided for maintenance.

Noise transmission in pipelines from high water pressure, faulty ball valves or pumps can be eliminated by using flexible connectors (vibration eliminators) at terminal ends and pump inlets and outlets. Noise can occur from inadequate use of fixings as described elsewhere.

Copper of small diameter must be jointed to cast iron or steel by copper alloy fittings to prevent corrosion or electrolytic action. With galvanised cisterns the painting of the interior of the cistern with two coats of a bituminous solution as described elsewhere should also be considered.

Cold water distribution pipes throughout the building will be copper (galvanised – iron – polyethylene – p.v.c.)

(5)31:1h5.10. 1h2.13. 1n6.20. 1n6.25. 1n6.10

Copper pipes supplied for this work should conform to BS 2871. Two conditions of copper tube are supplied suitable for building purposes, those to Table X which are drawn from half hard material which is suitable for bending to appropriate radii and those to Table Z which are drawn from hard material not suitable for bending.

Both grades of copper are suitable for jointing by means of compression or capillary fittings but *only* tube to Table X is suitable for silver brazing or welding.

The tubes should be round, clean, smooth, free from harmful defects and from deleterious film in the bore. The tubes should be solid drawn and the ends cut clean and square with the axis of the tube.

All tubes from 15 mm diameter up are marked with the following identification: BS 2871/Table designation/Manufacturer's identification mark.

Tubes from 15 – 42 mm diameter are so marked at intervals not exceeding 500 mm. Above 42 mm, the identification marking is at one end of the tube only.

Galvanised iron tube is required to conform to BS 1387. This tube is suitable for screwing to BS 21 pipe threads and is jointed by means of malleable galvanised fittings such as elbows, tees etc. The tube is supplied in three thicknesses, light, medium and heavy, the two latter being used for building purposes.

The tubes should be cleanly finished, free from harmful defects and reasonably free from scale. The screw threads are to be clean and well cut, the ends of the tube cut cleanly and square with the axis of the tube. Galvanised tubes should have reasonably smooth surfaces.

Distinguishing colour bands about 50 mm wide are provided to each tube as follows:

Light tubes: brown. Medium: blue. Heavy: red

Lengths *below* 4 m have one band at the end, lengths *above* 4 m have a coloured distinguishing band at each end.

Galvanised tube is often provided with short lengths of lead pipe when making connection to fittings as this method is more convenient than g.i. connections. For details see 'Hot Water Distribution pipes'.

Polyethylene pipes for cold water services are subject to two BSS, LD polyethylene in sizes up to 100 mm nominal bore being covered by BS 1972: 1967, and HD polyethylene in sizes up to 153 mm nominal bore being covered by BS 3284: 1967. Jointing methods are by means of plastic or metal compression fittings and the pipe is available in coils of 150 m and above. Three pressure classes are available as follows with colour marking imprinted longitudinally incorporating the following information: Manufacturer's identification/ BS 1972. 3284

Nominal size and class.

Class	Max.working pressure	Colour code
B	6 bar (60 m head)	Red
C	9 bar (90 m head)	Blue
D	12 bar (120 m head)	Green

The internal and external surfaces of the pipe shall be smooth, clean, reasonably free from grooves and other defects and the ends of the pipes shall be plugged or covered on delivery.

Polyvinylchloride pipes for cold water services conform to BS 3505 in sizes from 9 to 600 mm. The pipe, being fairly rigid, is supplied in lengths of 6 and 9 m and changes of direction are usually formed by the use of moulded fittings although hot bending techniques are available. Jointing may either be by a mechanical joint or by the use of a solvent cement with plain socket fittings, the former method being demountable.

All pipes must be indelibly marked at intervals not exceeding 3 m with the following: Manufacturer's identification/BS 3505/Nominal size and class. Marking will be in colour, imprinted longitudinally, classifying the pipe in accordance with the sustained working pressure as follows:

Class	Max.working pressure	Colour code
B	6.0 (60 m head of water)	Red
C	9.0 (90 m | ditto	Blue
D	12.0 (120 m ditto	Green
E	15.0 (150 m ditto	Brown

The pipes shall be reasonably round, external and internal surfaces smooth, clean and reasonably free from grooving and other defects which would impair performance in service. The ends should be cleanly cut and square with the axis of the pipe.

Storage: with the exception of polyethylene coils all lengths of pipe should be supported throughout their length in prepared racks in a clean dry store.

Provide and fix where shown on the drawings (or where specified) brass stop valves conforming strictly to BS 1010.

(5)31:Xh6.26

The provision of stop valves and their location is covered in some detail in BSCP 310. The recommendations of the Code are briefly as follows:

(a) A stop valve should be provided on the service pipe as near the point of entry into the building as practicable. A drain cock should be provided just above this valve

(b) Each separate occupation in multi-occupational buildings (e.g. flats) should have a separate stop valve to isolate the individual supply from a common service pipe. Where this is under the control of the occupiers a separate lock shield pattern should be provided outside the flat for emergency use

(c) Distribution services from a common cold water storage cistern should be individually controlled in a similar way

(d) External supplies to isolated draw off points should be provided with a stop valve inside the main structure

(e) In large buildings stop valves should be provided on branch pipes to control ball valves and draw off taps to minimise interruption of supplies during repairs and fixed in accessible positions

Stop valves to BS 1010 may be brass, gunmetal or, if not pressings, of brass or manganese bronze. Castings must be sound, free from laps, blowholes and pitting, smooth and free from sand. Castings must not be patched, burned, plugged or stopped. Pressings must be truly machined so that the assembled parts are axial, parallel and cylindrical with the surfaces smoothly finished. Check that the word 'INLET' or a direction arrow stamped in the body of the stop valve points in the direction of the flow.

All stop valves must be legibly marked with the following information: Manufacturer's name or mark/Nominal size/BS 1010.

Provide and install in the cylinder cupboard a .... gallon hot water cylinder conforming strictly to BS ....

Storage cylinders for hot water are made in a variety of sizes in either copper or galvanised steel sheet. In addition, cylinders may be obtained in two patterns, either direct or indirect patterns depending on the method of water circulation from the primary heater. All are made in grades, manufactured in accordance with the requirements of maximum working head pressure. Connections are provided for standard requirements and in addition connections for specific requirements can be provided if so specified at the time of ordering. The sizes of cylinders in common use are as follows:

BRS Type Ref.	Dia. (approx) (mm)	Ht. over capacity Dome (mm)	Litres	Gall.
Y28	465	790	114	25
Y33	465	910	136	30
Y39	465	1070	159	35
Y78	615	1220	332	73
Y100	615	1600	441	97

Copper (direct) cylinders to BS 699

BRS Type Ref.	Dia. (approx) (mm)	Ht. over capacity Dome (mm)	Litres
3	400	1050	116
8	450	1050	144
9	450	1200	166
13	600	1500	370
14	600	1800	450

Copper (indirect) cylinders to BS 1566 Pt. 1 (double feed cylinders)

BRS Type Ref.	Dia. (approx) (mm)	Ht. over capacity Dome (mm)	Litres
3	400	1050	114
8	450	1050	140
9	450	1200	162
13	600	1500	360
14	600	1800	440

Copper (indirect) cylinders to BS 1566 Pt. 2

BRS Type Ref.	Dia. (approx) (mm)	Ht. over capacity Dome (mm)	Litres
3	400	1050	104
7	450	900	108
8	450	1050	130
9	450	1200	152

In addition to dimensional checks for capacity cisterns are marked as follows:
Galvanised mild steel to BS 417 – BS 417, grade and thickness/Manufacturer's
name or identification mark/Capacity (in gall.)/Maximum permissible working
head (in feet)
Copper (direct to BS 699 – BS 699, reference and grade/Manufacturer's name/
Max.permissible working head (in metres)/Storage capacity (litres)/Thickness
of copper body and ends
Copper (indirect) to BS 1566 Pt.1. – BS 1566 Pt. 1 reference and grade/
Manufacturer's name/Max. permissible working head (metres)/Storage capacity
(litres)/Thickness of copper body, ends and primary heater/Max.length of
immersion heater to be fitted/Location for immersion heater if connection not
fitted during manufacture/Primary heater surface area
Copper (single feed indirect to BS 1566, Pt. 2 – BS 1566 Pt. 2, type reference.
grade & heater class/Manufacturer's name/'Cylinder to be fixed in vertical
position only'/Maximum permissible working head (metres)/Maximum permissible quantity of primary water/Water content of primary heater/Thickness
of copper body, ends and primary heater/Max. length of immersion heater to
be fitted to cylinder/Location for immersion heater if connection not fitted
during manufacture/Primary heater surface area
All cylinders should be installed clear of the floor so that air can circulate
under the domed bottom to prevent condensation. Two lengths of 50 x 100 mm
prepared softwood are ideal.
The same care must be taken in cutting holes in cylinders as for cisterns. This
is especially so with galvanised steel products as swarf falling into the body of
the cylinder will set up rusting in the interior.
Cylinders should be carefully stored in a dry store prior to fixing. Any with
dents or abrasions to the sides should be rejected.

Hot water distribution pipes throughout the building will be copper (galvanised iron with lead tail connections to fittings).

(5)31:1h8.12

Materials for hot water distribution pipes are usually copper or galvanised iron tube. The requirements for these materials are as for cold water distribution services.

Connections between fittings and g.i. tubes are usually made with short lengths of lead pipe which should conform to BS 602, 1085. This BS specifies two grades of pipe for distribution services in buildings, Table 3 dealing with cold water distribution pipes. Both these applications require lead complying with BS 602 Chemical Composition No. 1 and a certificate of compliance can be requested from the manufacturer.

The sizing of pipes is by Code number and lead pipe sizes in common use are as follows:

Code No.	Nominal bore (mm)	Nom. wall thickness (mm)
1	10	5.00
3	12	3.60
9	20	3.20
14	25	3.30
15	25	8.00
18	32	3.60
21	40	4.00

All pipes are legibly embossed at intervals not exceeding 500 mm with the following: BS 1085/Code no. of pipe/Manufacturer's identification mark. The embossing is formed on a raised rib so as not to lessen the true wall thickness of the pipe.

Lead pipes shall be sound in all respects, free from all laminations, flaws, pronounced extrusion marks and, as far as possible, cylindrical and smooth. The material is supplied in coils which must be carefully stored to prevent damage.

All pipework shall be properly fixed and supported throughout its length to prevent deformation or distortion.

(5)31: 3051 3052 3101

Fixing clips and holderbats for tubes are made in a wide variety of types and patterns, both built in and screwed to wall. Where several tubes are run in parallel sufficient space should be allowed between them to provide clearance for fixings.

Noise transmission may occur as a result of inadequate use of fixings or spacing clips. Suggested spacing of fixings for different materials are as follows:

Material	Bore (mm)	Horizontal Spacing (mm)	Vertical Spacing (mm)
Copper	12	1200	1500
	18	1200	1500
	28	2000	2500
Mild steel	12	1850	2450
	18	2450	3050
	28	2450	3050
Lead and	All sizes	600	760
plastic	All sizes	12 x OD pipe	24 x OD pipe

All pipework or fittings concealed in the floor or positioned in roof spaces are to be protected from frost throughout their length with approved lagging. (5)31:H et. seq. 1401 1402

The best precaution against pipes and fittings freezing in a building is to keep the inside continuously warm. When this is not possible or convenient and to protect pipes and fittings located where heating is wasteful or impracticable these should be protected with thermal insulating material. In addition, where pipes are concealed in voids within the structure, insulation should be provided to reduce heat loss in hot pipes and prevent condensation occuring on the outer surfaces of cold pipes.

Good advice on the protection of water services against frost damage is provided in BSCP 99. Recommendations are given on those areas of a building which are most prone to freezing and these include the following:

(a) Unheated roof spaces

(b) Unheated outhouses, garages or cellars

(c) Positions near windows, larder vents and external doors

(d) Inside faces of external walls including ducts and chases

Precautions should be taken to protect pipes and fittings in these locations and should include the following:

Roof spaces Pipes other than overflow pipes should be kept at least 750 mm away from the roof covering and external walls. Pipes should be fixed, where possible to take advantage of any heat rising through the ceiling by placing them under the ceiling insulation.

Cisterns should preferably be insulated in conjunction with the ceiling but insulation should be omitted below so that the cistern has the advantage of heat rising through the ceiling. This is helped by placing the cistern over the cylinder cupboard and where the ceiling is insulated with foil backed plaster lath a fibrous plaster vent should be provided through the ceiling under the cistern. An alternative position for the cistern is adjoining the chimney stack passing through the roof space. Care must be taken to provide access to the ball valve when required.

In exposed positions overflow pipes should be turned down 50 mm below the water level in the cistern and outside the building the end of the pipe should be turned down. This will prevent an inward flow of cold air into the cistern.
Pipes and fittings above ground within buildings Service pipes entering a building should be insulated if they are located with 750 mm of an external wall. Pipes rising out of the ground should be insulated for a depth of 750 mm if they are also located within 750 mm of an external wall. Any pipe in an air space under a suspended ground floor must be insulated throughout its length and similar precautions should be taken in unheated cellars, garages and outhouses. The lagging used should be waterproof. Pipes on the internal faces of external walls in heated parts of a building need not be surrounded with insulation so long as they are fixed to a wood pipe board or fixed 20 mm clear of the wall on brackets. Metal brackets should be insulated from the wall or the pipe.
Insulation Minimum thickness of insulation will depend on the declared thermal conductivity of the thermal insulating material. Insulation will not protect against freezing, only delay the process. Three types of material suitable for insulation are as follows:

Material	Thermal conductivity
Glass wool, mineral wool, slag wood as loose fill, felt or mat	0.03 to 0.045
Preformed sections of above	0.045 to 0.06
Exfoliated vermiculite (loose fill)	0.06 to 0.07

The minimum thickness of thermal insulating materials for pipe sizes from 15 to 40 mm are as follows:

Thermal Conductivity $(W/m^{\circ}C)$	Minimum thickness of insulation (mm)	
	Internal	External
0.03	22	27
0.04	33	40
0.05	46	54
0.06	61	72
0.07	82	99

Thermal insulation materials must be fixed in accordance with the manufacturer's instructions. All must be kept dry before, during and after fixing and gaps should not be left at the ends of sections. While lagging should be continuous over fittings, care must be taken to ensure that these can be operated satisfactorily.

The one pipe soil and vent shaft will be .... mm diameter cast iron (asbestos cement, copper, pitch impregnated fibre, unplasticised pvc) installed, jointed and fixed strictly in accordance with BSCP 304, 1968, or the manufacturer's recommendations

(5)21:1h1.21. 1h1.10 et. seq. 1h5.10. 1n2.10. et. seq. 1n6.10. 5151 et. seq.
(5)21.1
(5)21.3

The choice of materials and the design of one pipe systems for dwellings and small projects is fully described in BSCP 304, 1968. The following should be guarded against as they will effect the efficiency of the installation:

Location	Possible Defect	Design Recommendation
Bend at foot of stack	Back pressure at lowest branch, detergent foaming	Bend to be 150 mm min. root radius, vertical distance between branch fitting and drain invert minimum 460 mm (760 mm over two storeys)
W.C. branch connection to stack	Induced syphonage lower in stack when W.C. discharged	Connections should be swept in direction of flow with radius of 50 mm Max. branch length of 1.5 m
Basin waste 32 mm trap and waste pipe	Self-syphonage	'P' traps to be used, max. waste lengths of 2.3 m to fall of min. 1 in 48. Also recommended that wastes up to 50 mm diameter should be provided with 76 mm seal traps.
Bath waste 38 mm trap and waste	Self-syphonage	'P' or 'S' traps may be used, max. length 2.3 m at fall of 1/48 to 1/12. Point of entry to waste stack must be above centre line of W.C. branch or below a level 200 mm below this. See also note under basins re deep seal traps.
Sink waste 38 mm trap and waste	Self-syphonage	'P' traps to be used. For lengths between 0.70 m and 2.3 m a fall of 1/24 up to 0.70 m. 1/12 is sufficient. See also note under basins re deep seal traps
Waste disposal units	Foaming and blockage	The waste should connect directly to the main stack without any intermediate connection with a fall of not less than 15°. Tubular traps should always be used.

The sizes of suitable one pipe stacks for various purposes are as follows:

Purpose	Diameter of stack (mm)
Two storey dwellings with max. branch dia. of 76 mm	76
Two storey housing	89
Flats up to 5 storeys	100
Maisonettes up to 4 storeys	100
Buildings up to 12 storeys with one set of appliances on each floor	125
Buildings up to 10 storeys with two sets of appliances on each floor	125

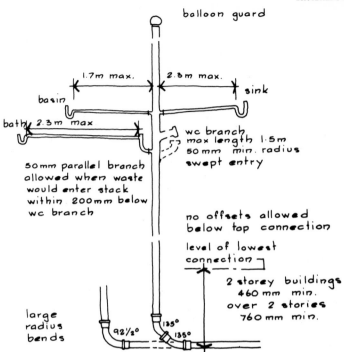

balloon guard

1.7m max.   2.3m max.   sink

basin

bath 2.3m max

wc branch
max length 1.5m
50mm min. radius
swept entry

50mm parallel branch
allowed when waste
would enter stack
within 200mm below
wc branch

no offsets allowed
below top connection

level of lowest
connection

2 storey buildings
460mm min.
over 2 stories
760mm min.

large
radius
bends

92½°   135°   135°

One pipe soil stacks

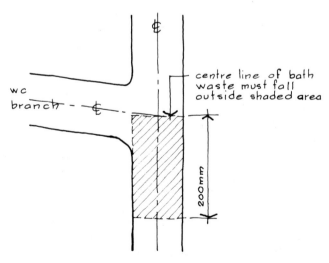

centre line of bath
waste must fall
outside shaded area

wc
branch

200mm

Prevention of cross flow in one pipe stacks

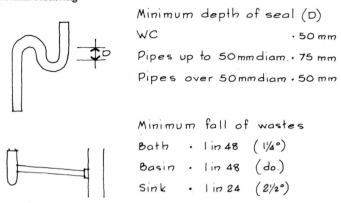

Minimum depth of seal (D)

WC   · 50 mm

Pipes up to 50mm diam. · 75 mm

Pipes over 50mm diam · 50 mm

Minimum fall of wastes

Bath   · 1 in 48   (1/4°)

Basin   · 1 in 48   (do.)

Sink   · 1 in 24   (2½°)

Minimum depth of trap seals and inclination of waste pipes

Materials and jointing The following materials, properly coated and installed, are suitable for normal discharges from sanitary fittings. Electrolytic action may occur between dissimilar metals and this problem must be prevented. Cast iron pipes depend for their durability on their black protective coating and must be examined to see that this is intact and undamaged. Spigot and socket should be packed with firmly caulked tarred yarn and with a minimum of 38 mm deep run molten lead or fibrous lead yarn. Alternative jointing materials are asbestos fibres incorporating a cementitious material, caulked dry into the previously wetted socket (BS 416: 1967).

Asbestos cement pipes need care in handling as well as jointing to prevent damage. Pipes may be dipped in a bituminous composition but this is not obligatory. When used externally, the usual methods of jointing are 1:2 cement/sand mortar or a fibrous cementitious jointing compound. If synthetic rubber rings are used the space above the rings should be packed with a mastic compound.

Copper pipes are obtainable in long lengths but as expansion of copper can be a problem, expansion joints may be necessary. Jointing is usually by welding or brazing and flanges may be provided with gaskets to join long lengths (BS 2871 Pt. 1.)

Pitch impregnated fibre are subject to greater thermal movement than copper. The pipes need no protection by painting but need to be installed in fire resistant ducts internally of the same grade as the compartmenting structure. For building up to three storeys in height the taper joint to couplings or fittings is satisfactory but above this height telescopic joints may be required. Branches up to 50 mm diameter are connected to stacks with metal or plastic fittings designed for the purpose (BS 2760 Pt. 1 and Pt. 2.)

Unplasticised P.V.C. is the most common material used for large diameter

discharge and ventilating pipes but should not be used when the temperature
of the discharge water exceeds 60°C. Jointing is either by solvent cementing
(when expansion joints must be incorporated in the system) or by synthetic
rubber 0 ring joints. As fittings for different systems are rarely interchangeable
care must be taken to see that all used are compatible. The pipes need no
painting but must be installed in fire resistant ducts of the same grade
as the compartmenting structure (BS 4514).

With all materials joints must be made air and water tight and remain so in
use. No jointing material should project into the pipe and obstruct the bore.
Joints between pipes of different materials are common and should be
carried out as follows:

Glazed stoneware drainpipes/cast iron or asbestos cement pipes: Joints made
with yarn and cement/sand joints of 1:2 or 1:3

Cast iron/lead pipes: Joint made by caulking a copper alloy sleeve with yarn
and lead into the cast iron socket with a wiped or lead burned joint between
the sleeve and the lead pipe

Glazed stoneware/lead and copper pipes: Joint made by caulking a copper
alloy sleeve with yarn and 1:2 cement/sand mortar into the stoneware socket
with a wiped or lead burned joint between the sleeve and the lead pipe

Copper/lead pipe: Joint made by a wiped or lead burned joint to a short
copper-alloy connector attached to a normal copper joint

G.I. tube/lead pipe: Joint made by a wiped joint to the spigot end of a copper-
alloy connector screwed to the g.i. tube

Copper/G.I. Tube: Joints made either by a compression, capillary or brazed
joint to a copper-alloy caulking bush to the cast iron socket (caulked as
described for c.i. stacks) or by a threaded copper-alloy connector preferably
of a pattern which can be readily disconnected

Glazed stone/pitch impregnated fibre: Joints should be spigot and socketted
and made either by purpose made adaptors supplied by the manufacturers
or with yarn and 1:2 cement/sand mortar

Glazed stone/uPVC: Joints should be made with purpose made sleeves caulked
with yarn and 1:3 cement/sand mortar

Cast iron pipes/uPVC: Joints made by purpose made cast iron sleeves jointed
as for cast iron pipes.

All stacks must be firmly fixed in position and where painting is specified at
least 32 mm clear of the wall. The fixing centres of vertical stacks are as follows:

Material	Bore	Vertical fixing centres (mm)
Cast iron	All sizes	3.0
Asbestos cement	ditto	3.0
Copper	63–100	3.7
Pitch fibre	76–100	3.0
uPVC	76–100	1.8

Horizontal fixing centres for waste pipes in various materials are given elsewhere.
Fixings depend on the pipe material and can be summarised as follows:

Cast iron   ears on pipe sockets
                       holderbats for building in, nailing or screwing to the
                       structure
                       purpose made straps
Asbestos cement   Galvanised m.s. holderbats as above
Copper   Copper alloy holderbats as above
                       Strap clips of copper or copper alloy
Pitch impregnated fibre Galvanised m.s. holderbats as above
uPVC   Holderbats of metal or plastic coated metal. When
                       fixed to the pipe sockets these control thermal
                       movement, intermediate holderbats fitted to the
                       pipe barrel are stays only and allow thermal movement.

All stacks must be inspected during erection and tested before being cased in
ducts. Details of testing are generally described in Chapter 18. Water testing
should only be carried out up to the level of the lowest fitting and thereafter
the air test should be used. This must be equal to 38 mm water gauge and
remain constant for not less than three minutes.

To test for the effect of self syphonage the fitting should be filled up with
water and discharged in a normal manner. The seal should be measured and
conform to requirements. This test applies to baths, basins and sinks only.

*Waste pipes will be copper to BS 659 (unplasticised pvc to BS 3506: 1968)
and fitted with 75 mm c.p. deep seal traps to BS 1184: 1961 (unplasticised
pvc traps to BS 3943: 1965).*

Light gauge drawn copper tube to BS 659 is an ideal material for wastes from
sanitary fittings. The tubes should be solid drawn, round, clean, smooth, free
from harmful defects and deleterious film in the bore. The ends shall be cut
clean and square with the axis of the bore.

All tubes shall be marked as follows:

Bore (mm)	Marking
13, 19 and 25:	marked at intervals of not more than 0.61 m with BS 659 and manufacturer's identification mark
Over 25 to 51:	either as above or a 25.4 mm band of waterproof adhesive tape with BS 659 and manufacturer's identification mark

Unplasticised pvc to BS 3506 is being increasingly used for wastes where hot
water is not carried. For all practical purposes Class O is generally satisfactory
where pressure is unlikely, otherwise Class B is specified (up to 60 mm head
of water). The pipe should be reasonably round with internal and external
surfaces smooth, clean and reasonably free from grooving and other defects

which would impair its performance in service. The ends should be cut clean and square with the axis of the pipe. The pipes should be indelibly marked at intervals not greater than 3 m as follows: Manufacturer's identification mark/ BS 3506/Nominal size (inches)/Class 0 — white/Class B — red.

Copper and p.v.c. tubes should be supported throughout their length in racks in a clean store.

Copper traps to BS 1184 may be formed in three ways as follows: tubular (solid drawn), or cast, or hot formed.

Traps are provided in a number of sizes, for particular situations and with or without clearing eyes. The standards of workmanship generally are as follows:

Tubular (a) Walls free from cracks and splits and should be watertight

(b) The bore should be reasonably uniform throughout the trap

(c)The exterior of the trap should be either

(i) Self finish, free from grease or tool marks

(ii) Polished

(iii) Plated to BS 1224

12 Metalworking

Items manufactured for use in small building contracts under the trade heading
of Metalworker are relatively few in number. The number of separate and
individual metals used has dwindled in recent years due to the introduction
of plastics. Some items are still required and specified, usually by means of a
prime cost sum, and the nomination of a specified supplier. While the composition of the metal and methods of fabrication are usually controlled by BSS
and BSCP's, fixing and protective treatment are usually matters either of
preference, tradition or chemistry. Treatment is dealt with primarily in
Decorative Finishes except for immediate protection necessary either prior
to fixing or while the item is exposed to the elements. Fixing and the
preparation for fixing is dealt with under specific items.

Structural steelwork:
BS 4. Pt. 1: 1972   *Hot rolled sections*
BS 4. Pt. 2: 1969   *Hot rolled hollow sections*
*BS 449. Pt. 2: 1969   The Use of Structural Steel in Buildings (deemed to
satisfy clause in Building Regulations. All structural steelwork in G.L.C. area
must comply with this specification)*
BS 4360: 1972   Weldable Structural Steels
BSCP 3 Chap. 5: Loading Pt. 1: 1967 Dead and imposed loads
Pt. 2: 1972   Wind loads
BSCP 117   Composite construction in structural steel and concrete:
Pt. 1: 1965   Simply supported beams in building

*Include the P.C. Sum of £   for the shop fabrication, delivery to site,
offloading and erection complete of all structural steelwork by a specialist
sub-contractor to be nominated (by the Architect). Add for profit and
attendance.*
The design of structural steelwork is generally entrusted to an independent
consultant engineer who, working from the design drawings and in consultation
with the designer, prepares the steel design drawings on which the steelwork
sub-contractor can base his tender. In many small works contracts, however,
the design is carried out by the fabricator who may be paid a separate fee for
his work or incorporate the cost in his tender for the steelwork. On commencement of the sub-contract the steelwork sub-contractor will make a visit to the

site to agree with the contractor and/or the design consultants the levels and positions of all steel beams in relation to floors and column centres and the column centres in relation to the structure. Any variations in column length will also be agreed. From this information and that given on the steelwork design drawings, the sub-contractor will prepare his shop details for approval prior to putting the fabrication in hand. It is not just sufficient for the engineer to approve the shop drawings. Both the designer and the contractor must have an opportunity of going through the details as only they have the whole project under their control and can anticipate practical problems in other trades which may arise from the particular method of connection or fabrication employed. Care to anticipate problems at the detail stage can prevent delays and difficulties at a later stage of construction. For example, by setting beams down slightly floor trunking may be installed without having to notch the bottom to pass over every top flange of each beam, a costly business.

One administrative danger which must be avoided is the informal communication by word of mouth or telephone concerning matters affecting the steel proposals. All communications should be in writing and copies sent to all parties as a matter of course.

The inspection of structural steelwork to ensure that it follows the requirements of the design drawings and specifications will be the responsibility of the consultant structural engineer. If no consultant is appointed the steelwork should be checked as described later in this trade.

Delivery to site is usually on large vehicles and proper lifting tackle has to be provided to off-load the steelwork. Mobile cranes are usually employed and these require hard standing on which to operate. The provision of hard covered areas or sleeper roads is generally necessary and provided by the contractor under attendance. If the steel sections are of such sizes as to require cranage of any sizes, the contractor's attention should have been drawn to the additional provision at tender stage. Unless the floor slab has been specially designed and reinforced to carry heavy loads such as are imposed by mobile cranes and their jacking points, traffic over the slab by the crane should be prohibited or, in consultation with the structural engineer, a sleeper access be provided over the slab to distribute the load. In general, the steelwork sub-contractor will try to deliver and offload his steel direct to the position where it is required and in most cases the erectors will commence erection as soon as they have off-loaded and sorted the sections. It is the contractor's responsibility to ensure that not only does he arrange for the steel to be delivered in the right sequence, but also that when delivered the sub-structure is ready for erection to commence. It is also his responsibility to ensure that the steelwork is completed in a manner which will enable him to carry out his contractural works in cladding and encasement in a proper and workmanlike manner, and the checks and precautions he must take are as described later in this trade.

Provide structural steelwork shown on the drawings from steel of British manufacture complying in all respects with BS 4. Pt. 1 1972. Hot-rolled sections (BS 4 Pt. 2: 1969, Hot rolled hollow sections) and BS 4360: 1972 Weldable structural steels Pt. 2: 1969 Metric units, fabricated in accordance with BS 449, Pt. 2: 1969 Metric units
H11:Hh2.10

Steel of British manufacture is marked in the web during rolling with the name or trade mark of the manufacturer. This identification can be accepted as implying compliance with BS 4 and that the steel is of the strength designated as mild steel, the usual material for small steel structures. Should a steel of higher quality be specified or there is any reason to suspect that the requirements of the specification are not being met, a certificate of proof should be requested from the fabricator for the steel supplied.

Design and fabrication should be in accordance with BS 449. This is a 'deemed to satisfy' provision of the Building Regulations. In addition all steelwork in the area covered by the London Building Acts must comply with this BS. It will generally be found that all design and detail drawings prepared for structural steelwork will give this undertaking.

Certain matters should always be checked during general inspection of the works. The ends of steel members should always be smoothed off sufficient to allow proper priming of the surface. Where structural splices occur, as in stanchions or the butt joints of other compression members such as stanchion caps and bases, the ends of steel members must be machined or accurately prepared to spread the load evenly over the whole surface of the steel. The only exceptions are when the bolts are of sufficient strength in sheer to carry the load imposed on the connection, a condition often found in small works. All steel members must be straight and free from twisting. Steel occasionally becomes distorted during delivery and must be straightened on site prior to erection. Erection clearances should generally not be greater than 2 mm except for beam ends without web cleats where 3 mm is permissible. Holes for black bolts up to 24 mm diameter should not exceed 2 mm over the nominal diameter of the bolt and the respective holes should register accurately one with another and no drifting should be permitted.

Prepare, prime, hoist and fix structural steel sections shown on the drawings. Erection to be in accordance with BS 449. Pt. 2. 1969.
H11:2051 H11:2 H11:3 H11:4 H11:5 H11:6

Steelwork is usually specified painted with a preservative primer such as red oxide, applied before delivery to site. Prior to application the surface of the steel is wire brushed to remove mill scale and loose rust. This treatment is quite satisfactory for steel which is being encased in concrete but where it is exposed, any rust which has been left on the original surface will break through the paint film. The problem of divided responsibility will then occur, the contractor, quite rightly, disclaiming responsibility for the defect. Exposed steel is best delivered to the site clean, free from all mill scale, loose rust and unprimed. The painting specification should direct the contractor to clean off any remaining rust and apply an inhibitor immediately prior to applying the priming coat. A primer compatible with the painting system can then be employed and the responsibility for preparation is placed squarely on the contractor's shoulders. When friction grip bolts are employed for the connections the bearing surfaces must be left unpainted to ensure close contact between the steel surfaces. This is not important when black bolts are used. Then the bearing surfaces can be prepared, primed and the surfaces brought together while the paint is still wet. The rest of the steelwork can be prepared and primed after erection. It is, however, necessary to advise the steel fabricator or those responsible for erection at the time the tender is being invited that this procedure will be followed, so that any delay can be financially covered and allowed for in the preparation of the tender. Otherwise a claim will ensue for any delay caused to the erection gang.

Successful rust exclusion from steelwork depends on a speedy follow up from one stage of preparation to the next. As soon as any loose rust has been removed with a wire brush, the surface of the steel should be treated with an inhibitor. These are usually acidic in character. As soon as this is dry or when the manufacturers advise, the priming coat should be applied. It is obvious that this work must be carried out in dry, frost and condensation free conditions. The protection process must be carried out without a pause as successful treatment depends on preparation and priming being carried out without giving rust a chance to reform on any part of the surface, which will happen if an inhibited area is allowed to remain unprimed overnight. When this occurs due to special circumstances, a further coat of inhibitor should be applied before the priming coat. A second coat of primer is an advantage to ensure the complete sealing of the surface. Before any further application of paint is applied any damaged primer should be treated as before to prevent pockets of rust breaking out under the final paintwork. All steelwork in columns and bases cased in concrete below ground floor level should, in addition, have a good coat of black bitumastic paint before grouting and encasing to give the steel still further protection from deterioration.

The erection of structural steelwork is generally carried out by specialist fixing gangs employed for the purpose by the fabricator. These men are highly skilled and fully competant in the use of erection plant. On occasions their desire for speed can cause problems especially if the steelwork is not as true and straight

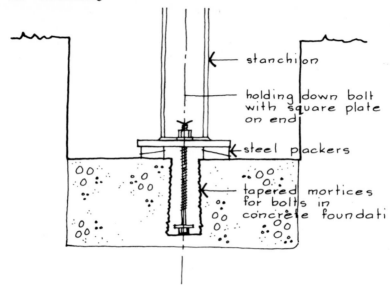

Detail of holding down bolts to stanchion bases prepared for grouting

as it should be. Never accept a framework which is in any way distorted or twisted or allow the use of steel hawsers to restrain the frame during casing in concrete. Such work should be taken down, straightened or replaced before re-erection.

All holding down bolts must be so placed that they pass freely and upright into holes provided in the baseplates. This should be squarely at right angles to the column and secured with m.s. angle cleats. The baseplate should be packed off the concrete by steel packers and the 50 mm gap filled by ramming in a dry cement/sand 1:1 mix after the steel frame has been plumbed and accepted as straight, true and upright. Holding down bolts should be of adequate length and include allowance for variation in foundation level. A full turn of thread should project above the nut, otherwise the baseplate is set too high, the bolt is too short or the top of the concrete too low. Have the bolt broken out of the concrete, reset or replaced. Do not accept site welding of the nut onto the bolt.

Plumbing and checking the level and positioning of all steel work prior to packing the baseplates is essential as any discrepancies will have a cumulative effect on the main structure. The checking will usually be carried out by the general foreman and foreman erector as the acceptance of the work is the responsibility of the contractor. It is advisable to ask for and obtain a certificate from the contractor to the effect that the steelwork is level and plumb, the columns set on the correct grid lines and all beams at the specified levels. All holes should be provided with bolts sufficiently long for the purpose complete with washers, taper pattern being used where necessary to ensure the satisfactory bearing of boltheads and nuts to tapered flanges. All bolts must also be properly tightened before the erectors leave the site.

Metal windows and doors:

BS 990: Pt. 2: 1972   *Steel windows generally for domestic and similar building (for Module 4 windows)*
BS 1285: 1963   *Wood surrounds for steel windows and doors*
BS 1422: 1956   *Steel sub-frames, sills and window boards for metal windows*
BS 1787: 1951   *Steel windows for industrial buildings*
BS 4330: 1968   *Recommendations for co-ordination of dimensions in building – controlling dimensions*
BS 4873: 1972   *Aluminium alloy windows*
PD 6444 Pt. 2   *Co-ordinating sizes for fixtures ..... etc.*
DD 4: 1971   *Recommendations for the grading of windows*
Steel Window Association, Specification SWA 201: 1972
BS 729: 1971   *Hot dip galvanising*
BS 1706: 1960   *Electroplated coatings .... on steel (Classification ZN3 – zinc plating)*
BS 4315: 1968   *Methods of test for resistance to air and water penetration:*
Pt. 1   *Windows and gasket glazing systems*

*Include the P.C. Sum of £   *for the supply, delivery to site and fixing complete of .... windows by a sub-contractor to be nominated. Add for profit and attendance.*
(3)11:X

Aluminium and steel are the principal materials used in the manufacture of metal windows. The use of bronze is very rare due to the extremely high cost of the basic material. Both aluminium and steel need to be protected from the effect of atmospheric pollution. Aluminium is usually anodised either with a clear natural finish or coloured. Steel has various levels of protection. The most expensive is the use of an alloy of 18/10/3 chromium nickel molybdenum (type 316) stainless steel which is available in the wide range of finishes in thin gauge strip used in the manufacture of stainless steel windows. Rolled steel bars and sections which are used for the bulk of steel windows manufactured in U.K. are galvanised to BS 729 by the hot dip method which produces a cheap article with reasonable freedom from maintenance problems.

Aluminium windows are usually extruded, which process enables complicated sections with a high strength/weight ratio to be provided to meet the requirements of wind pressure, air infiltration and water penetration grading. Jointing of sections can be either by the use of corner cleats or direct screw fixing, allowing the final finish to be applied prior to assembly. The fixings and fastenings should be of aluminium or non-magnetic stainless steel where visible or passivated zinc plated or hot dip galvanised where hidden. All aluminium windows should be constructed to BS 4873 and if the manufacturers subscribe to the Kitemark scheme there will be certified performance ratings. Steel windows are usually manufactured from rolled steel sections mitred and welded at the corners in accordance with BS 990: 1972, and SWA: 201. Fully purpose made steel windows are usually fabricated from the metric W20 range of sections. After manufacture the windows are protected by hot dip galvanising. Used correctly steel windows perform adequately. Performance standards are laid down in SWA publication 'Specifier Guide to Window Performance' which deals with the degree of water tightness of steel windows generally and includes tabulated information which reduces the amount of calculation required to determine Design Wind Pressures. Generally W.20 weather stripped windows are satisfactory for the following exposures:

Type of Casement	Performance for air and water when tested flush	Expected recessed site performance
SH o/out) TH o/out)	Severe	Severe
HP, VP	Sheltered	Sheltered to moderate

(from SWA: 201: 1972)

(See also Window Performance – a Specifier's Guide - SWA).

*Include the P.C. Sum of £   for the supply and delivery to site of steel windows manufactured by Messrs .... The windows will be hot dip galvanised and manufactured in accordance with BS 990: 1972 (or SWA: 201). Add for profit.
(3)11:Xh2.20. Xh2.23*

Two publications deal with the manufacture of steel windows and to some extent they are complimentary. Whereas, however, BS 990 deals with a range of windows which are known as Module 100 (including the earlier N and Z ranges still available for replacement and renovation works) SWA: 201, 1972, refers to the W20 range of steel window sections used both within the preferred range of sizes and for purpose made windows to specified sizes.

Methods of protecting the surface of the steel are dealt with in both documents. These comprise hot dip galvanising to BS 729 for the window itself and

zinc plating to BS 1706 for fixing and small compounds. The method
which is thus generally accepted as being best suited to the U.K. climate
is hot dip galvanising. SWA members use the approved quality mark
'Galvaguard'.

Windows are tested to BS 4315 Pt. 1 to meet requirements of DD4: 1971.
Weather stripped windows constructed of W20 sections to SWA: 201: 1972,
can be provided to meet the requirements for weather tightness by consultation with the manufacturers.

Windows manufactured to SWA: 201, are always provided with internal glazing,
using either putty or beads as specified. Beads are screwless snap on pattern
with corner pieces fabricated from pre-galvanised steel sheet or aluminium alloy.
Fixing studs should not be more than 70 mm from the ends and not exceed
300 mm centres spaced to suit the glass or panel thickness specified.

*Take delivery, store on site, sort, move to position and fix metal windows all
  in accordance with the manufacturer's recommendations (and the following
  schedule).

  (3)11:2 (3)11:3*

Damage occuring to metal windows is generally due to careless site handling
and storage. Great care must be taken in the loading and stacking of individual
units. Windows should always be kept upright during handling to prohibit
sagging and stacked on level battens on hard standing clear of mud and site

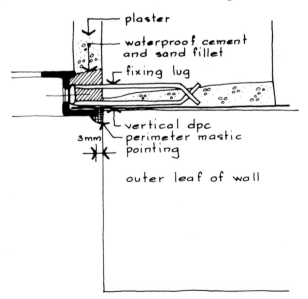

Detail – fixing metal window to brickwork detail at jamb

traffic, never on ashes whose sulphur content would attack the metal. Windows can be stored in the open but never either on top of other materials, when they may be roughly handled to get to the materials below, or under materials whose weight may cause deformation.

All opening lights are checked for clearance before leaving the factory and should be left fixed until glazed. Access should never be allowed through fixed windows or scaffold poles, boards or similar placed in such a manner as to bear directly onto the frame.

It is essential that prepared openings are plumb, square and to the correct size allowing 6 mm over and above the work size of the window in height and width. Oversized openings can present difficulties in fixing and weathering and windows must never be forced into undersized openings.

When windows are built direct into brickwork care must be taken to ensure the window is held plumb and square and any composite units should line across the couplings. With cavity brickwork the back of the long leg of the frame section should line up with the inner face of the outer leaf and the vertical d.p.c. inserted into the frame section against the long leg to prevent ingress of water. The brickwork forming the outer leaf must be at least 3 mm clear of the metal frame allowing proper pointing up in mastic and the space at the back of the frame filled in with a waterproofed cement and sand fillet. The fixing lugs supplied with the frames should be fixed to the frames in the holes provided, located in the brick courses and solidly bedded in mortar. When it is necessary to proceed with brickwork, due to windows not being on site, sand courses should be left to allow building in of the fixing lugs to be carried out later and the vertical d.p.c. set to project 15 mm into the prepared opening. It is always best, however, to build the windows in, and this course should always be preferred.

Fixing at the head will vary with the construction. With single full width concrete or cast stone lintol, plugs or fixing blocks are cast in at appropriate

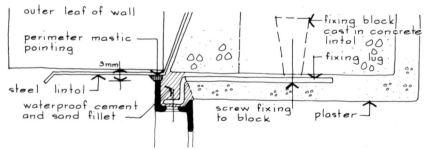

Detail – fixing metal window to concrete lintol supporting inner leaf of cavity wall

positions to receive No. 10 rustproof countersunk wood screws provided by the fixer. With double lintols e.g. brick external lintol and concrete supporting the inner leaf of a cavity wall, fixing lugs similar to the reveals may be used. Some new proprietory lintols may require special lugs to be supplied by the window manufacturer and need site drilling of the steel soffit to take self-tapping screws securing the end of the lug. The gap between window section, structure and back of section should be filled in as required for the reveals.

Cills of whatever material must be located to provide a weather check behind the long leg upstand of the window section to prevent ingress of water at this very vulnerable point. The gap must be well filled and pointed up so that the whole of the metal section sits down on a solid bed of mastic. Fixing is generally by means of plugs and screws as described for lintols but a special lug allowing fixing to be provided to the upper face of the inner leaf can be provided when pressed metal cills or brick on edge or tile creased cills are used.

The fixing of timber surrounds follows that of timber windows. The steel light may be fixed before or afterwards. Any raw edges of timber frame caused by cutting back projecting horns must be well primed before fixing to stop any water penetration into unprotected wood, and cills are best bedded on a d.p.c. for extra protection. Metal frames should be set on bedding compound spread continuously along both rebates in the timber frame and fixed with No. 10 rustproof countersunk wood screws. The gap between metal and wood externally should be neatly pointed up in mastic. It is advisable to prime the metal window before fixing, with the appropriate metal primer for galvanised surfaces. If this is not possible the rebates must be primed before glazing is carried out.

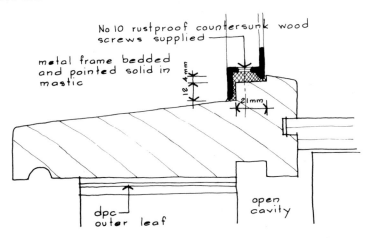

Detail – fixing metal windows to timber frames: detail at cill

Metal Balustrades

The height and, by implication, the extent, construction and material used in the construction of screens, balustrades and railings is specifically determined by the Building Regulations (Sections H5 and H6). This requires that private and common stairways shall have protection to a height of 840 mm above the pitch line and on landings such height will be increased to 900 mm for a private and 1.1 m for a common stair. Externally the height of protection to balconies, roofs etc. to which persons have regular access will also be 1.1 m in height. Care must be taken to ensure that these requirements are complied with by the metalworker, who may, in fact, be working from small scale drawings where the detail may leave much to be desired.

Include the P.C. Sum of £   for the supply and delivery to site of wrot iron (mild steel) balustrades and rails by a specialist sub-contractor to be nominated (by the Architect). Add for profit and attendance.

Balustrades and rails are a specialised craft and care must be taken to ensure that the firm entrusted with the work is capable of giving satisfaction. The advice of the contractor might well be sought if there is any doubt on this score.

Balustrades must be rigid in construction and be so balanced as to allow the hand to flow easily from one flight to another. Ideally the handrail should sweep naturally from one to another, but where this is not possible care should be taken to allow the hand to retain its grip with the least effort. Handrails are used for assistance and in emergency and nothing in their design or construction should make this difficult or impossible.

The fixing of balusters to handrail should ideally be by means of countersunk self tapping screws or the balusters tapped to take bolts passing through the handrail. The connection should be tight and the splay cuts neatly and correctly formed. Any welding should ideally be carried out on the underside where it is less visible and ground off smooth on completion. If the handrail is to be of hardwood the metal core rail should be at least 9.5 mm thick and 50 mm wide, let flush into a groove on the underside of the handrail and fixed with countersunk steel screws. If a plastic handrail is to be provided, care must be taken to provide a core rail of suitable size to receive the plastic, which is generally either clipped over the metal or slid on from the end. The manufacturer of the plastic should be consulted before agreeing the size of the core rail. While plastic can be mitred and welded at right angles, sharp radius bends often provide difficulties.

Set the balustrade in position in mortices provided in concrete treads and landings and grout in position

It is usual to deliver the balustrade in lengths of one flight and to assemble these in position, usually by bolting the handrails or their cores at each floor

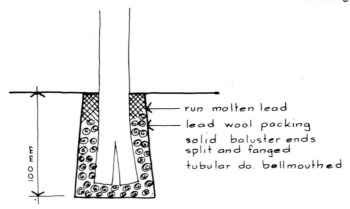

run molten lead
lead wool packing
solid baluster ends
split and fanged
tubular do. bellmouthed

Detail of fixings to concrete for balusters etc

and landing level. The balustrade is then wedged up to the correct height, not forgetting to make due allowance for the screed and floor finishes which follow later, with the balusters or supports set into mortices formed in the concrete staircase treads. These mortices must be accurately positioned and at least 100 mm deep to allow 75 mm of metal to be incorporated. To ensure proper fixing the sides of the mortice should be undercut and the ends of the metal either bell mouthed or split and fanged.

Two methods of fixing are in general use. Neat cement grout is cheap but tends to shrink on hardening and can break up under the constant movement of the baluster. Lead is perhaps the best material to use, lead wool being packed in the bottom of the mortice around the baluster and the mortice filled in with molten lead flush with the top surface of the concrete.

The preparation and priming of iron and steel balustrades should follow that suggested for structural steelwork.

Matwell frames

Provide .... No. matwell frames size .... constructed of ....
   ...... with corners square and complete with 4 No. sherardised fixing
   clamps, and fix in position where shown on the drawings and as directed

Matwell frames are often manufactured to suit coir or similar mats provided. If this is so, the size should be about 13 mm larger than the overall size of the mat and about 6 mm shallower. These tolerances allow the mat to tread down to suit the matwell.

Various materials are used for the frames, the most common being wrot iron or mild steel. These should have welded angles and the fixing cramps welded to the botton edge and so designed as not to interfere with the thickness of the floor finish. After manufacture, including welding on the lugs, ferrous frames should be sherardised, zinc sprayed or hot dip galvanised prior to delivery to site. The lugs can be set in the screed when this is laid making sure that the rim of the frame protrudes the full depth of the final flooring material and finishes level with it.

Bronze, brass and aluminium frames are usually manufactured from angle sections, mitred at the corners and welded. Sometimes the frames are supplied loose and screwed down through the floor finish into a hardwood frame provided to form the perimeter of the matwell. This timber should be treated and backed with bitumastic paint. Care must be taken to protect these relatively soft metals from scratching and damage prior to completion.

13 Electricity

BS 1454: 1969   *Consumer's electricity control units*
BS 6004: 1969   *P. V.C. insulated cables for electric power and lighting*
Institution of Electrical Engineers: Regulations for the Electrical Equipment of Buildings

*Include the P.C. Sum of £ .... for the electrical installation, the work to be carried out by a nominated sub-contractor. Add for profit and attendance on the following electrical points
The electrical installation should be carried out by a competent specialist. While much of the work must, of necessity, be left to the competance of tradesmen working within controlling regulations, certain matters which will affect other trades or have a bearing on the life of the installation need to be supervised in the interests of the contract. These matters are dealt with later.
The main contractor should be advised at the time of tendering of the number of electrical points included in the installation so that he can assess the monetary value of attendance which he will have to provide. Some electrical contractors carry out their own cutting away and chasing and if this is so the contractor must be advised. Otherwise the work may be paid for twice, once to the electrician and once to the contractor.
*Include the Provisonal Sum of £   *for the electric supply cable from the supply authority main to the intake position*
A price for the installation of the service cable from the main supply to the intake position will be obtained from the supply authority. As discounts are not given by statutory authorities this will usually be dealt with by the inclusion of a Provisional Sum in the contract.
Overhead supplies often require a pole and the position of this should be negotiated to avoid any unfortunate siting. The cable will usually be connected to an insulated bracket fixed to the structure and the cables brought to the intake. Unsightly layouts can be avoided by negotiation and careful planning and the provision of a conduit of suitable diameter through the wall will avoid cutting away the facework.
Underground supply routes should be agreed to avoid either disturbance of finished areas or possible interference from future extensions. Some supply authorities excavate their own trenches, others require the trench to be prepared for them. This matter should be cleared up at the drawing stage and any work

by the contractor included in his specification. Underground cables are about 30 mm in diameter and, being armoured, are difficult to bend. A 100 mm stoneware or pitch fibre easy bend should be inserted through the foundations, terminating against the wall at floor level under the meter position, through which the cable can be drawn. The bends should be extended under any adjacent paving to clear site and the cable sealed around with an asbestos collar before the floors are screeded.

Provide and install in the position indicated on the drawings a consumer's supply control unit as Messrs .... surface pattern conforming to BS 1454: 1969, mounted on an approved 12 mm blockboard backboard Provide tails in P.V.C. insulated and sheathed cables from consumer unit for connection to meters

The electrical installation on the consumers side of the meters is controlled by a unit which incorporates a main switch isolating the whole of the circuits provided. Inside the unit, the individual circuits are controlled by one of three methods against excess current as follows:

Re-wireable fuses

Cartridge fuses

Circuit breakers

The two latter methods are more satisfactory and should be employed as standard. There are several sizes and patterns of consumer unit to satisfy the requirements of various installations. Generally for domestic installations separate circuits will be required as follows:

Ground floor lighting	5 amp
First floor lighting (etc.)	5 amp
Ring power circuit ground floor	30 amp
Ring power circuit first floor	30 amp
Cooker circuit	30 amp
Immersion heater	30 amp
Spare (or boiler circuit)	15 amp
Bell installation	5 amp

With some of the very large electric cookers now provided a separate 60 amp fused switch may be necessary or a 50 amp circuit breaker unit if these are incorporated in the main consumer unit.

The consumer unit is mounted on a backboard which should be kept 25 mm off the wall to allow the cables to be concealed in the void. The backboard should be large enough to accommodate the supply authority's meter and sealing chamber into which the main supply cable is drawn. The bell installation, being low voltage, will require a separate small transformer complete with isolating switch and this should be placed close to the consumer unit on the backboard. Cupboard units are available which incorporate the whole of the control gear

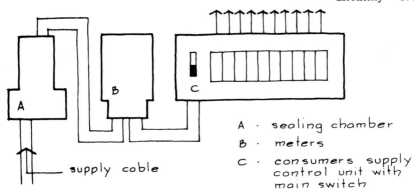

A · sealing chamber
B · meters
C · consumers supply control unit with main switch

Layout of typical domestic fuseboard

and meters, are accessible from outside and are provided in some cases with viewing panels allowing meter reading from outside the property without disturbing the occupants.

The earthing of the whole installation is completed by bonding a green insulated earth conductor to the metal case of the consumer unit and connecting this either to the sheath of the main supply cable or to a separate earth electrode driven into the soil outside the building. This latter method is necessary for overhead supplies. An alternative to both methods is to provide an earth leakage circuit breaker which automatically isolates the main current in the event of an accident.

The connection between the sealing chamber and the meter is carried out by staff of the supply authority. The electrical contractor is required to leave short lengths of cable (called 'tails') from the consumer unit of sufficient length to allow the supply authority to connect these to the meter.

The whole of the installation will be carried out strictly in accordance with the 14th Edition of the I.E.E. Regulations and the requirements of the supply authority

The installation of electrical equipment in buildings by qualified electrical contractors is carried out to the minimum standards of the Regulations for the Electrical Equipment of Buildings issued by the Institution of Electrical Engineers and revised by them from time to time. These are the minimum standards to prevent the risk of fire or shock. Unfortunately, they have no statutory force but a supply authority must connect to an installation which complies with the regulations, as required by the Electricity Acts. Some authorities insist on strict compliance with the regulations, others show little interest.

*The internal wiring will be carried out using p.v.c. sheathed cable, twin
with earth or three core with earth conforming to BS 6004 and of
British manufacture*

Plastic insulation for the metallic conductor is now almost universally
employed, the principal material used being p.v.c. Plastic insulation is less
affected by damp than rubber and can be used with confidence on the surface
where condensation may be a problem. The incorporation of an earth wire is
to protect against faults in the installation. As the resistance of these wires
is low a heavy current flowing along them will be sufficient to blow the fuse
and make the whole system safe. This procedure has been followed for many
years in connection with power but the incorporation of metallic lighting
fittings in many lighting schemes has rendered the inclusion of an earth wire
in lighting circuitry an essential.

*Wiring will be carried out on the 'looping in' principle, all joints being made
at main switches, sealing boxes, socket and lighting outlets and switch
boxes only*

The 'loop in' method of wiring requires ceiling roses with three terminals, two
of which are used to maintain a completed circuit of all fittings. The wiring to
switch and lamp utilises the third terminal as a common connection, a second
being connected to the circuit line terminal which connected to the isolating
switch forms the lamp connection. The neutral cable is taken from the lamp

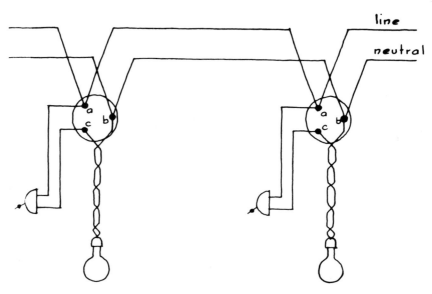

Diagram of loop-in method of wiring to lighting points

to the neutral terminal of the ceiling rose thus completing the circuit.
As it is necessary to strip a portion of the sheathing to the cable to make a
connection, the exposed cores must be enclosed in an incombustible unit. At
ceiling roses these may be provided by a plastic backplate to the rose. Switch
points must be provided with switch boxes to both carry the switch plate and
seal in the connection.
In positions where there is a possibility of contact with water, such as bathrooms, ceiling rose pull switches should be used operated by a cord. A similar
switch can be provided over bedhead positions to provide switching facilities
for the main ceiling light.
*Socket outlets will be flush pattern ivory plastic switched (unswitched)
13 amp complete with fused ivory plug heads. Outlets will be set .... mm
above the floor level. The system of wiring will comprise the 'ring main'
circuit controlled by a 30 amp fuseway (m.c.b.) Fixed appliances will be
controlled from flush pattern irovy fused spur boxes*

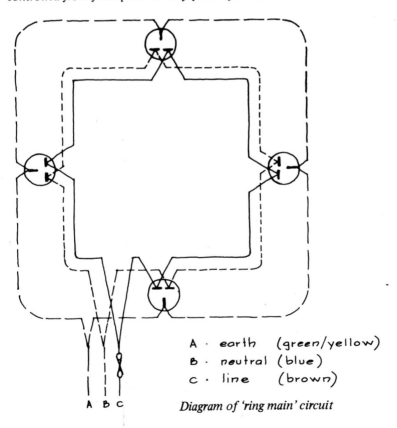

A · earth   (green/yellow)
B · neutral (blue)
c · line   (brown)

A B c   *Diagram of 'ring main' circuit*

Socket outlets should be mounted on metal or plastic boxes. Wiring is carried out by the 'ring main' circuit which provides for a twin cable plus earth to be taken from a 30 amp fuseway or the consumer unit to the socket outlets in turn returning in due course to the fuseway. A new circuit is required for every 100 m^2 of floor area and, so long as the outlets are reasonably well distributed along the run of the circuit, the number of outlets which can be provided is unlimited. Socket outlets may be connected to a spur, subject to a limitation of two outlets to each spur, but in practice this method is usually reserved for extensions to the original installation or the provision of power to fixed appliances. The outlet then incorporates its own fuse and the cable connection is made direct to the outlet terminals, dispensing with a fused plug head.

Cables will be run as far as possible in roof and floor voids, properly secured and supported to avoid strain or distortion. Cables buried in walls or on the surface shall be protected by means of approved plastic (black or galvanised steel) conduit

To operate with maximum efficiency and enjoy long effective life cables must be protected from damage. For ease of installation it is usual to install cables in roof and floor voids. To avoid reducing the strength of timbers, cables which pass through joists should do so at the neutral axis but in any event not closer than 50 mm from the top of the joist to avoid penetration from nails used in fixing the flooring. Holes should be drilled through the joist, notching should never be permitted. Cables in floor and roof voids should be supported against the sides of the timber by rust proofed buckle clips at maximum 1 m centres and where they cross voids the cables should be supported on battens. On no account should cables be supported on the tops of ceiling joists in roof spaces as they are liable to damage by abrasion from possible foot traffic. Cables should be dressed flat and not twisted or buckled and where they change direction there should be sufficient slack to prevent any tension due to movement in the timbers.

Cables on the surface or in plastered walls should be protected throughout their length with mild steel or plastic conduit. Steel conduit will generally be painted with black enamel but on surface, in areas of high humidity and externally, conduit should be galvanised. In plastered walls the conduit should be chased in so that at least 6 mm of plaster cover is provided. Horizontal chases in walls should never be permitted as these seriously weaken the structure. The conduit must be securely fixed with rust proofed fixings and free ends either smoothed for plastic or, in the case of metal conduit provided with rubber protective bushes.

Care must be taken to keep all cable runs at least 230 mm from any hot water pipes as the heat will cause deterioration of the protective sheathing.

Nothing is more untidy than electrical outlets which are not plumb or level. This is very apparent with switch plates close to architraves. All plates should be levelled up satisfactorily on completion.

14 Glazing

BS 544: 1969   Linseed oil putty for timber frames
BS 952: 1964   Classification of glass for glazing etc.
BRS Digest 106   Painting woodwork (putty and glazing compounds)

Glass may be delivered to site either in a special container or brought to site by the glaziers when glazing commences. If by container, this should be stored upright as indicated and carefully protected from damage. If allowed to get wet, glass is difficult to separate and the risk of damage is greater. Storage under cover is therefore recommended.

Roof-light domes are always delivered in a case which should be stored as directed on the case. Care must be taken to fix roof-lights in such a way that they are secure from external attack. Fixings should be secured inside the building and any exposed portions should be strong enough to resist break-in. Unventilated glass domes are prone to condensation troubles which can be reduced by leaving small gaps in the perimeter seal allowing external air to pass over the underside of the glass.

Glass for glazing will be of British manufacture complying with BS 952: 1964, and free from bubbles, scratches, wavy surfaces, spikes and other imperfections.
R21:R

All glass for glazing should be accompanied by the makers name, guarantee of compliance with BS 952, type of glass and nominal weight. This should be made available to the supervising officer on request.

Glass for glazing small works is either float glass, sheet glass (also known as flat drawn) and translucent or patterned glass.

Float glass obtained in various nominal thicknesses and sizes is flat, parallel and fine polished giving clear undisturbed vision. It has largely replaced plate glass for most applications and is available as follows:

Nom. thickness (mm)	Nom. max. size (mm)
3	1270 x 1270
	1520 x 1010
5	2540 x 2280
6	4560 x 3170
10	7110 x 3300

Float glass can be obtained in two qualities for building purposes:

GG – glazing glass – for general purposes

SG – selected glazing quality – for better class work such as shop windows

Sheet glass obtained in various thicknesses and sizes is never perfectly flat always providing a degree of distortion and reflection. Because of its relative cheapness it is generally used for most building purposes especially for housing.

Nom. thickness (mm)	Nom. max. size (mm)
3.0	2030 x 1220
4.0	2030 x 1220
5.0	4.65 m^2 (max. dimension not exceeding 2640 mm)
5.5	9.3 m^2 ditto
6.0	Ditto

The thicker glasses may well be replaced with the more expensive float glasses which provide better vision, especially in large areas. Sheet glass can be obtained in three qualities:

OQ – ordinary glazing quality – for general building work

SQ – selected glazing quality – for better class work

SSQ – special selected quality for cabinet work

Translucent glasses usually referred to as 'obscured' or 'patterned' are rolled glasses with one flat surface and one textured or patterned. The pattern or texture obscures the vision in varying degrees which can be classified from low (a) to high (e). Reeded and ribbed glass are not classified in this way.

In addition, these glasses are segregated to three groups, depending on price, the cheapest being group one. To avoid extras being claimed care must be taken to select glass from the group specified. Patterns are available as follows:

	Pattern	Degree of obscuration	Thickness (mm)	Colour
Group 1	Arctic large	b	3	White & some tints
	Arctic small	c	3	White & some tints
	Atlantic	c	3, 5	White only
	Flemish large	a	3	White only
	Flemish small	a	3	White & some tints
	Hammered No. 2.	a	3	White & some tints
	Pacific	c	3, 5	White only
	Sparkle	d	3	White & some tints
	Stippolyte	c	3, 5	White only
Group 2	Borealis	e	3	White only
	Broad reeded	a	3, 5	White only
	Deep Flemish	b	5	White only
	Gross Reeded	b	3	White only
	Festival	c	3	White only
	Narrow reeded	a	3, 5	White only
	Broad Reedlyte	b	3, 5	White only
	Narrow Reedlyte	b	3, 5	White only
	Cotswold	c	3, 5	White only

Frostlyte	b	3, 5	White only
Ralton	a	3, 5	White only
Reedrop	a	3, 5	White only
Spotlyte	c	3, 5	White & some tints
Group 3 Autumn	b	3, 5	White only
Discus	b	3, 5	White only
Siesta	b	3, 5	White only
Plain cathedral	a	3*	White & some tints

Patterned glasses are available in the following stock sizes:

Thickness (mm)	Size (mm)
3	1270 x 1520
	1270 x 1830
	1270 x 2130
4	1320 x 1830
	1320 x 2130

Standard tints normally available in a maximum size of 1830 x 1220 mm are:
Blue tint   Nos 302, 402
Pink tint   Nos 904, 951
Green tint   Nos 21, 23, 24
Amber tint Nos 503, 804, 806

*All glazed panels in doors will be provided with .... wired
.... glass of British manufacture complying with BS 952, 1964.
Ro4.10.*

For safety reasons, some areas of glazing need special glass to protect the public
and occupants of the building from the dangers of breaking glass. Special glasses
are available which, while preserving a varying degree of opacity, are strong
enough to resist shock or heat.

Georgian polished wired glass is transparent with a polished plate finish reinforced with a 13 mm square wire mesh. The glass is obtainable in the following
sizes:

6 mm x 3300 x 1830

A better quality glass with similar properties is diamond polished wired
distinguishable by the diamonds having sides of approximately 20 mm thickness
and overall sizes as for Georgian polished wired.

This glass is used for windows and doors of public areas, where clear view and
fire retarding properties are required.

Georgian wired cast glass is a translucent rough cast glass reinforced in a
similar manner to polished wired and obtainable with the same alternative reinforcement. The size obtainable varies and is as follows:

6 mm x 3710 x 1830

The glass is used for glazing in areas where damage from falling glass is important
and where maximum protection from spread of fire is required. Roof lights and
patent roof and sliding glazing are good examples.

The panels to the main entrance will be glazed in Armourplate glass supplied by an approved manufacturer

Ro8.01

Where great mechanical strength is required to glazed areas subject to impact or sudden changes in temperature, armourplate glass is to be reommended. It is made by subjecting ordinary float or clear plate glass to heating and sudden cooling. Any working required such as edge polishing, drilling or recutting cannot be carried out after the process has been completed and the glass can only be supplied within specific sizes:

Thickness (mm)	Maximum size (mm)
5	1524 x 914
6	2540 x 1524
10	3950 x 1524
12	3175 x 2540

When one dimension exceeds 1524 mm the other must not exceed 3175 mm Armourglass doors can be supplied as standard prepared from 12 mm glass complete with all hinges and fittings.

Glaze all timber framed windows in linseed oil putty conforming to BS 544: 1969

R21: Yt4.10

R21: 2051 2101

R21: 4051 4151 4201

R21: 6153

Putty glazing is only satisfactory for face glazing and as putties harden quickly they must be painted regularly to retain a degree of flexibility. The maximum size of pane for face putty glazing should not exceed the following:

Sheltered conditions — 4800 mm (perimeter measurement)

Exposed conditions — 3600 mm (perimeter measurement)

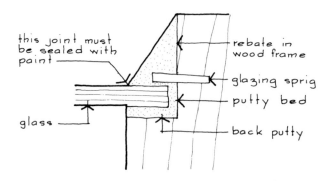

this joint must be sealed with paint

rebate in wood frame

glazing sprig

putty bed

glass

back putty

Detail – glazing to timber with putty

Before glazing all rebates must be properly primed with a good quality wood primer to seal the surface and prevent oil in the putty being leached out into the timber. Putty is generally supplied in drums and the label should be checked to ensure that the material complies with BS 544.

Before glass is placed in the rebate, this must be back puttied to ensure that the glass is bedded solidly against the timber to provide a weatherproof seal. The glass should fit easily into the rebate with a small clearance all round and secured with small metal sprigs driven into the timber to give mechanical support to the glass. To complete the work the front should be splay puttied the full depth of the rebate and the full height of the sight line. If this is not done there will be insufficient weather seal around the glass, there will be insufficient strength to hold the glass in position and the appearance will be unsatisfactory. The angles should be neatly formed as here water can penetrate more easily than in the main run of puttying.

Glaze all steel windows in metal glazing compound of approved manufacture.
   R21: Yt4
   R21: 4101

The general remarks concerning putty glazing to timber windows apply equally to steel. The material used, however, differs and is coloured green to distinguish it from pale biscuit coloured linseed oil putty. In addition, small pegs or clips are used to secure the glass in place instead of metal sprigs. Rebates should be primed with an approved zinc plumbate or red oxide primer before glazing is commenced.

All glazing to timber doors and screens will be carried out by bedding the glass in wash leather with beads (supplied) and brass sockets and screws
   R21: 2201
   R21: 5401 5421

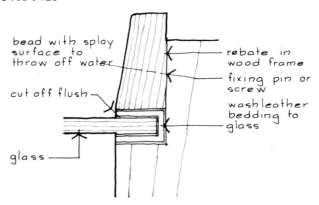

Detail – glazing to timber with beads

Where glazing is subject to vibration glass must be set in a resilient bedding and washleather has been found, over the years, to be most suitable for this purpose. Beads to hold the glass in position can be either hardwood or softwood. Rebates must be sealed with wood primer as well as the bedding faces of the beads, which should be bedded in the primer while it is still wet. Fixing can be either by screws and sockets or screws and cups, the former being neater but more expensive. Alternatively, in cheap work, the beads may be secured with panel pins. Care must be taken to see that the washleather is of sufficient girth to completely surround the glass in the rebate and cut flush with the shoulder and the bead on either side.

Hack out any cracked or broken panes and replace on completion, clean and polish all glass both sides.

R21: 6251

Breakage of glass on all contracts is considerable and where double glazing is provided by sealed units these should not be fixed until immediately before decoration, temporary enclosure being effected to keep out the weather.

It is almost impossible to paint window frames without spotting the glass. Care must be taken in removing these not to scratch the surface and any panes so damaged should be replaced. Immediately before handover the glass should be cleaned and polished both sides. The work is sometimes carried out as the scaffold is struck. Consequently the glass is dirty by completion. This will not do.

During decoration make sure that the putties both inside and outside the building have the full number of paint coats specified for the frame and that the joint between the glass and the putty is sealed with paint.

15 Plastering and Wall Tiling

Plastering:

BS 12: 1958	*Portland cement*
Pt. 2 1971	*Metric units*
BS 890: 1972	*Building limes*
BS 1191 Pt. 1: 1967	*Gypsum building plasters*
Pt. 2: 1967	*Premixed light-weight plasters*
BS 1198 and 1199: 1955	*Building sand from natural sources*
BS 1230: 1970	*Gypsum plasterboard*
BS 1369: 1947	*Metal lathing (steel) for plastering*
BSCP 211: 1966	*Internal plastering*
BSCP 221: 1960	*External rendered finishes*
BRS Digests 49	*Chosing specifications for plaster*
104	*Floor screeds*

Gypsum Plasterboard Development Association, Dry lining 1961
British Gypsum Ltd., British Gypsum White Book 1972/3

External Renderings should be porous and provided with an open textured finish to be successful. Weak mixes based on lime with a wood floated or steel scraper finished surface, while tending to absorb more moisture during wet periods, help to dry out the rendering in dry conditions, eliminate the possibility of water being trapped behind the rendering. By distributing the water evenly over the face, these renderings weather more evenly than smooth finishes. In addition the pronounced tendency to crack which is such a feature of hard, dense cement sand mixes is wholly absent when lime is incorporated in the mix.

Adhesion is an important consideration. Hard dense impervious backgrounds such as concrete, dense concrete blocks and bricks need a spatter-dash coat of cement and sand cast onto the surface to assist in providing adhesion. The greater suction provided by most other bricks and blocks renders this precaution unnecessary.

Where bricks are known to have a high soluble sulphate content care must be taken to use sulphate resisting cement in the mix.

Prepare, render the external walls where shown on the drawings in two coat work, 1:1:6 Cement/lime/sand in accordance with BSCP 221: 1960, and finish from a wood float (steel scraper).

P.11:1 P11:2 P11:3

As indicated before, preparation is an important constituent of a successful rendering. Dense impervious backgrounds should have the surface splattered with a wet mix of portland cement/sand 1:1½–2 by volume and left to harden without further working. New brickwork with reasonable suction with the joints deeply raked to 19 mm during construction needs little further preparation but old brickwork will require the joints to be deeply raked or cut out. All mould growth or efflorescence wire brushed away and the surface hacked if smooth and likely to cause absorbtion problems. Areas of differing suction should always be splattered to even up the background absorbtion.

Materials for external rendering should conform to the appropriate BSS laid down for general plastering. Materials are normally proportioned in gauge boxes by volume. Mixing may be by mechancial mixers or on a boarded platform. Either method requires cleanliness which is discussed in detail in Concretor. A mix of 1:1:6 (cement/lime/sand) is a good reliable finishing mix which is suitable for all surfaces and degress of exposure when textured. An undercoating of a similar mix is first applied to the surface about 13 mm thick with a trowel and the surface well scratched before setting to provide a good key for the finishing coat. Free bottom edges of rendering should be bellied out 25 mm for a height of 100 mm and undercut to throw any surface water clear of the wall below. A similar detail may be carried out above openings. The undercoat should be set to the appropriate thickness and true face by the use of wrot timber rules set at all openings and returns and allowed to thoroughly dry before the finishing coat is applied. To prevent too rapid drying the surface should be cured by spraying with water through a fine rose at frequent intervals. The second coat should be about 10 mm thick. If a fairly smooth finish is required, the surface should be smoothed with a wood float, the use of a felt float will tend to pick up the surface more. The use of steel scraper will remove surface laitence and open up by the surface and if carefully carried out a very pleasing natural open texture will result. More accentuated textures can be obtained by the use of expanded metal wrapped round a wood float or a nail studded board.

Prepare and render the external walls where shown on the drawings with 1:1:6 cement/lime/sand in accordance with BSCP 221: 1960, and finish with a white Tyrolean rendering coat in accordance with the manufacturer's recommendations

The preparation of the background and the provision of the rendering coat follow similar lines to two coat external rendered work. The application of Tyrolean finish direct to brick or blockwork is not wholly successful as the joints and irregularities of the surface tend to grin through the finished material. Protection and masking from polythene or paper is necessary for adjoining fair brickwork, painted surfaces to doors and windows and this should be adequate to remove any possibility of damage from the application. The finishing material will usually be thrown onto the rendered coat by means of a hand powered machine, the finish being built up to a textured coat of a granular consistency. In rural areas this finish is eminently suitable but in urban areas dirt tends to accumulate and the external finish becomes sordid.

Provide and lay to oversite concrete cement/sand 1:3 floor screeds, well tamped, consolidated and levelled to a finished thickness of ...... mm. Cover up, protect and properly cure all screeds and hack up and relay any hollow or defective areas.

P13:2 P13:3 P13:4

The preparation of the base and its stability is an important factor in the success of a dense floor screed. Most screeds are laid on the 'separate construction' basis where the oversite concrete has been allowed to harden. If the surface has been well roughened during laying, a coat of cement grout applied to the surface immediately prior to laying the screed will usually suffice to provide adequate adhesion. If the surface is smooth it will be necessary to hack the surface well before grouting. In any event the surface of the concrete must be clean and free from dust and dirt immediately. before grouting is commenced.

Dense screeds should be laid in bays, the size of which relates to its thickness and the state of the concrete base. With a screed thickness of 40 mm, which is generally accepted as being the minimum acceptable to average conditions, the bay size should not exceed 15 m^2 and the ratio of sides should be near to 1:1½. Expansion joints in the concrete floor should be repeated in the screeded finish.

The standard of screed is directly relevant to the skill of the operative. The surface finish should be suitable for the final floor finish, a smooth finish from a steel float for thin sheet or tile floorings, the textured surface produced by a screeding board for blocks and clay tiles. The material is prepared and laid as dry as possible and it should not be possible to squeeze any water out of a handful of mix. Too dry a mix will make compaction difficult producing a weak mix with poor adhesion which may cause corner and edge curling. Specified thicknesses are maintained with rules and the surface compacted and finished with a screeding board and finally with a steel trowel or float. Permissible variations in surface tolerances depend on the area involved, large open areas can carry a variation of ± 10 mm whilst variations in small areas should be restricted to ∓ 3 mm under a 3m straight edge.

Curing and drying is important to ensure that the screed gains initial strength before the onset of drying shrinkage which induces the risk of cracking and curling. The screed should be covered with polythene or tarpaulins for at least 7 days after laying. Thereafter surplus water must be removed by natural evaporation and good ventilation before water sensitive flooring can be laid. Initially, the screed will be dark in colour or green and will lighten to pale grey as it dries out. Natural drying will take approximately four weeks for each 25 m thickness of screed laid. Acceptance of the screed by the flooring sub-contractor should be on the basis of acceptable water content as well as surface finish.

Hollow areas can be detected by tapping the surface of the screed with a stick when the difference in impact sound with securely adhering surfaces will be readily apparent. Such areas should be hacked up and relaid. Other defects can be caused by water from failure of temporary internal rainwater pipes, impact damage from heavy equipment, cracking due to movement of the substructure. Minor iregularities can be accommodated by the application of a latex screed over the affected portions to level up the surface.

Provide and lay to .... flat roofs 40 mm minimum thickness cement/ sand 1:4 screed, well tamped, consolidated and laid to a minimum fall of .... Cover up, protect and properly cure and hack up and relay any hollow or defective screeds

The preparation of concrete flat roofs for screeding follows that previously specified for oversite concrete. The mix used is slightly weaker and the sand used should be coarser than that for floor screeds as the surface smoothness is not so important when covered with built up or asphalt roofing. The screed should be laid in alternate bays not exceeding 15 m^2 and the mix shall be as dry as possible. The minimum falls provided should suit the roofing material to be accommodated:

Built up bitumen roofing – 1 in 60
Asphalt   – 1 in 80

Woodwool slabs are usually themselves set to appropriate falls. Screeding is therefore required only to provide a smooth finish to receive the roofing and of nominal thickness of 13 mm.

Mixing, laying and ruling is generally carried out in a similar manner to floor screeds and similar care must be taken in curing and drying out. Water trapped in screeds (especially light weight specifications) can cause bubbles in the felt. The problems of clearing stormwater from screeded roofs can be dealt with by drainage holes in low areas with provision for catchment below the roof. Lightweight and aerated concrete screeds are usually carried out by specialist sub-contractors. The problems of trapping moisture in the structure are greater than with dense screeds and in addition to the use of drainage holes, provision may be necessary for the installation of edge and intermediate vents to release any moisture trapped in the structure by the waterproof roof finish. Lightweight screeds always require a protecting layer of 1:4 cement/sand 13 mm thick to provide a wearing surface for the underlying screed which is very weak in compression and likely to break up under light foot traffic.

The backgrounds for plastering are very varied and all present their own particular problems of adhesion, suction and movement. A very wide range of plastering techniques are available to meet specific contingencies and new materials are available to meet problems created by increases in the speed of building and mechanisation.

Three main groups of plastering materials are available for use and these used singly or in combination cater for most building requirements. The basic materials, lime, portland cement and gypsum plasters, are produced to comply with relevant BS and the general principles and plastering techniques are set out in BSCP 211: 1966, Internal Plastering. Plastering materials are easily damaged by moisture and great care must be exercised in their storage and handling.

All plasters delivered to site must be kept in clean dry covered stores and free from contact with the ground. Sand for plastering should also be kept clean and dry to ensure that no contaminating matter — cement, ballast or mud — can be incorporated in the plaster mix and cause blemishes in the finished work. Water must be kept clean, drawn from the main supply and when stored in a tank, should be separate from any concreting supply and not used for washing tools. Any cement incorporated in gypsum plaster mixes will cause an expansion reaction under damp conditions. Plasterboard should be carried on edge and carefully stacked without scuffing the surface on a large flat, clean and dry platform, to a height not exceeding 900 mm. Cement and gypsum plasters are supplied in multi-wall paper bags in 50 Kg, and lime in 25 kg weights. Gypsum lath and wallboard is supplied in two thicknesses, 9.5 and 12.7 mm, the thickness used depending on the centres of fixing and of the following sizes:

Gypsum lath — 406 x 1200 mm

Gypsum wall board — Widths 600, 900 and 1200 mm

Lengths 1800, 2350, 2400, 2700 and 3000 mm

As absorbtion of moisture by any gypsum plaster products shortens the setting time and may reduce the strength of the plaster, the period between delivery and use should be kept as short as possible. Plastering or the fixing of boards or lath is normally carried out immediately after first fixings have been completed, floors boarded or screeded, the carcassing of the electrical installation and the first stages of plumbing completed. All linings, frames and grounds should be plumb and set to allow for the full thickness of plaster – 12 mm – with extra thickness when metal lathing is used – 15 mm. Pipes and conduits to be buried should be chased into the walls their full diameter and the surface of any metal parts protected with galvanising or paint to prevent any rusting from water in the plaster. All cutting away, fixings and holes for services should be completed and sleeved (if specified) before plastering is started to avoid unsightly making good to the finished work.

Accurate proportioning of materials and absolute cleanliness is essential for good plastering. Measuring boxes in conjunction with a clean gauging board or banker must be used, the materials being mixed first dry and again after water is added and the mix made ready. Boxes and board must be well washed between each batch. On no account should additional water be added once the mix starts to set and the whole batch must be discarded. Also an old mix must not be used as the basis for a new one. Mechanical mixers may be used and if it is in continuous use no special washing out is necessary. If the use is intermittent the mixer must be washed out after each batch to ensure that no old material is incorporated in the new.

All solid background should be free from dust, efflorescence and loose or projecting mortar blobs before plastering starts. In two coat work the backing coat should be well scratched to provide a key for the finishing coats. Thick coats tend to lose adhesion and good practice is to apply a thin coat first with firm pressure and build up to the required thickness. The floating coat is brought up to a true and level surface to receive the finish by means of a straight edge. Finishing coats are applied in one thickness and should not be over polished or they become dusty. A matt eggshell finish should be produced.

All plastered surfaces shall be finished straight and smooth and left free from all cracks, blisters, rough areas, dents and other defects. All arrises shall be slightly rounded.
P11: 4
P11: 2151

All plastered surfaces should be properly ruled and capable of standing up to a straight edge placed upon its surface. Good plastering should feel smooth all over under the hand and this method of assessing quality will readily expose high and rough spots, especially around the heads of doors and in

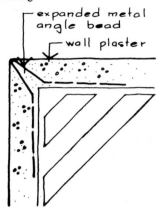

expanded metal
angle bead

wall plaster

Detail – expanded metal angle bead

internal angles. Due to difficulty of application, plaster is often rougher above the skirting and should be carried down sufficiently to be covered if grounds are not used.

Surface cracking is often due to composite wall structures which incorporate materials of differing coefficients of contraction and expansion. To overcome this a heavy building paper should be lapped over the area and covered with expanded metal lath. This will enable the reinforced plaster to bridge over the difficult area, the building paper isolating the plaster from the wall face. This method is particularly useful when concrete piers have infill panels of bricks or lightweight block.

Arrises should be slightly rounded to improve their appearance. As making good to damaged plaster arrises is always unsatisfactory, the provision of expanded metal beads to protect the angles is a worth while measure.

Provide expanded metal lathing all in accordance with BS 1369: 1947, and fix to timber stud partition in accordance with the manufacturer's recommendations.

P11: J

P.11: 4201 4202

Expanded metal lath should be galvanised or black painted although aluminium is now being used more for its non-corrosive qualities. The lath should be fixed with the long way of the mesh running from support to support and with galvanised staples at 100 mm centres. Sheets should be lapped 25 mm on supports, 50 mm otherwise and securely tied with soft galvanised tying wire to keep as taut as possible.

Metal lathing cannot be considered as a rigid background and weak mixes

should be specified for the rendering coats and time allowed for each coat
to dry and shrink before the next is applied. Special hemi-hydrated plasters
containing hair and light weight metal lathing plasters should be used.

*Provide and fix 9.5 mm (12.7 mm) gypsum lath to all ceilings in accordance
with the manufacturer's instructions and set with a retarded hemihydrate
board finish gypsum plaster.*

P11: 2501 2502 2503

Gypsum lath is designed as a base for gypsum plaster, available in standard
and insulating grades, the latter having an aluminium foil bonded to one face.
This enables the material to be used as a vapour barrier when required and
also as a reflective insulant when fixed with the foil facing outwards. Lath
is easy to handle, may be cut using a fine tooth saw or a sharp knife, by
scoring the material, snapping it over a straight edge and cutting through
the paper on the opposite side. Lath should always be fixed across the
supporting joists and laid breaking joint. Sherardised or plated nails should
be used every 150 mm, the cut edges butted and a gap of 3 mm left between
rounded edges.

The thickness of material used depends on the centres of supports, 9.5 mm
is satisfactory up to 400 mm but over this and up to an absolute maximum
of 600 mm, 12.7 mm lath should be used.

Finishing plasters are usually mixed in plastic buckets with clean water in
preference to the mixing boxes or metal containers. This ensures scrupulous
cleanliness and reduces the risk of rust spotting.

The angles between walls and ceiling should be scrimmed with 87 mm wide
jute scrim cloth set in neat plaster to reduce cracking and at the same time
the gaps in the boards should be filled with neat plaster and struck off flush.
Board finish plaster is generally applied neat to a finished thickness of 3 mm
and trowelled to a smooth surface.

Baseboards may be used instead of lath but they should be fixed with a continuous gap all round of 1.5 mm. Even so they have a greater liability to
cracking along the joints and are usually more expensive due to their greater
weight per unit which increases fixing costs. Perimeter scrimming should be
as for lath.

A superior finish can be obtained by two coat work onto the lath. This is best
carried out in lightweight plaster to BS 1191 Pt. 2 1967 (premixed lightweight
plasters) using a bonding grade undercoat. This material is slightly resilient
which reduces cracking caused by structural movement, a feature of rigid
lightweight backgrounds such as plaster lath on timber board and joisted floors.

*Provide and fix 9.5 mm (12.7 mm) gypsum lath to all ceilings with an
approved textured plastic finish all applied in accordance with the
manufacturer's instructions and with approved colour textured finish*

The fixing of the lath is all as described before except the perimeter scrimming is omitted. The finish is mixed on site from self coloured materials and applied direct onto the surface of the lath with a strong texture obtained by a variety of methods. The material being self coloured throughout requires no further decoration and being resilient has good resistance to structural movement. Ceilings should be kept clean as the finish does not take kindly to washing down with warm water.

Render the walls in a lightweight premixed retarded hemi-hydrate undercoat 11 mm thick and finish with 2 mm neat finishing coat conforming to BS 1191 Pt. 2 1967.

Lightweight retarded hemi-hydrate plasters are generally produced from gypsum incorporating aggregates such as vermiculite or perlite. Undercoats are manufactured to suit the appropriate background with a standard finish applicable to all grades. This finish is usually smooth with a matt slightly mealy appearance.

The advantage of pre-mixed plasters is that they require only the addition of clean water and can be mixed indoors to avoid frost damage. If the premises are not warmed, however, frost will disrupt wet backgrounds and plastering on frozen backgrounds can result in lack of adhesion.

As with all plaster, complete drying out must precede decoration. Care must be taken to allow any efflorescence to be eradicated from the surface as this can be damaged if salts are sealed within the plaster by an impermeable paint.

Render the walls in cement/lime/sand (Browning) 11 mm thick and finish with 3 mm neat anhydrous gypsum plaster conforming to BS 1191 Pt. 1 1967 Class C (retarded hemihydrate gypsum plaster conforming to BS 1191 Pt. 1 1967 Class B).
Pll: 5.

For interior work cement/sand backings are rarely used, lime being added to assist in controlling shrinkage cracking. The mixes most commonly used are 1:1:6 and 1:2:9 (cement/lime/sand) by volume. The use of a plasticiser instead of lime can be of advantage in plastering undercoats but are not advised for external renderings. An alternative to cement/lime/sand backings is the use of a slow setting browning undercoat which does not require such a long period to mature as the former mix, which should be allowed to dry thoroughly and mature before the finishing coat is applied. Otherwise cracks will occur in the finished work due to continuing shrinkage of the rendering coat.

The finish applied to cement/lime/sand renderings is usually known as Sirapite. This has an almost indefinite life and develops a high strength immediately on setting. As the plaster deteriorates with keeping, the date of manufacture is stamped on each bag. Plaster over two months old should be discarded. It is usually mixed neat in a plastic bucket with clean water and applied by the trowel/float/trowel technique. As Sirapite has an early initial set the plaster should be applied before this takes place, but the mix may be retempered or knocked back by the addition of fresh water within an hour of first mixing. The surface is usually smooth but an interesting 'antique' finish can be obtained by adding an equal volume of clean sharp sand (coarse or fine to suit the texture desired) to the plaster and finish with a wood float. A deep stippled finish can be obtained while the material is still soft with a hair or rubber brush. An alternative finishing coat to Sirapite and used on browning undercoats is retarded hemihydrate gypsum plaster usually known as Thistle finish. Plaster should be checked for manufacturing date and rejected if over two months old in the same manner as Sirapite. The finish is prepared in a plastic bucket as for Sirapite and care must be taken not to over trowel the finish as described before.

Line the walls of .... with 9.5 mm (12.7 mm) aerated gypsum plasterboard manufactured in accordance with BS 1230: 1970, fixed and jointed by the Thistleboard method dry lining technique (or M/F system or to timber framing) all in accordance with the manufacturer's instructions.

R71:1 R71:2 R71:3

The thickness of lath used depends on the centres of fixing and the width of board employed. Generally 9.5 mm is used except when timber framing is employed as a base when the thicker board may allow considerable saving of timber.

With the thistleboard system, small impregnated fibreboard pads are fixed to the walls with Carlite bonding or Thistle board finish to provide a true flat background. Two pads are fixed at each angle one 230 mm down from the ceiling, and the other 100 up from the floor with intermediate pads at not more than 1070 mm centres, all levelled and plumbed in. Further lines of pads at 1800 mm; centres are provided along the wall, all carefully checked to obviate any high spots. Finally intermediate lines of pads should be levelled and plumbed in at 450 mm centres. The pads should be so arranged that they bridge joints between adjacent boards. After the pads have set, dabs of board finish plaster are applied between the pads, each dab standing proud of the pad, the length of the trowel 50 – 75 mm apart and a similar width. The precut plasterboard 25 mm short of floor to ceiling height should then be placed in position and tapped firmly back with a straight edge tight against the pads and the ceiling. Double headed nails then secure the board through the pad along the edges and removed after about an hour when the board has set. Narrow widths are set with plaster dabs applied to their backs, external angles always having a cut edge mastered by a bound edge. Where cut edges are unavoidable they should be lightly sanded to remove burrs and a 3 mm gap left between the boards.

The Gyproc M/F system of dry lining uses 0.6 mm thick metal channels, in place of alignment pads, which can be bonded to the wall with special adhesive. The method of setting out the vertically set channels is similar to the thistleboard method and the channels are set at 600 mm centres, in dabs of adhesive 200 mm long and 25 mm apart, applied by an applicator, repeated at 460 mm centres from top to bottom of the wall. The metal firring channel is tapped into place and the face cleared of adhesive. Short (150 mm) lengths of channel are placed top and bottom of the wall between the upright channels to take the bottom of the panel. Care must be taken to ensure the channels are plumb and line through one with another, taking into account any high spots in the wall. The panels are secured to the channels with 22 − 32 mm self-tapping screws depending on the thickness of the boards to just below the surface. Cut edges and narrow widths are dealt with as the thistleboard method.

Fixing to timber framing requires the use of well seasoned timber which must be sawn to close dimensional limits. Twisting and warping will exert stresses on the rigid lining causing serious cracking. The face width for fixing the lining should not be less than 38 mm. This allows for 3 mm gap between boards and 13 mm between nails and the edges of the board. Nails should be 2 mm x 30 mm long for 9.5 mm board with a small flat head and smooth shank, fixed at 150 mm centres starting from the middle and working out-wards. All edges of the board should be supported with noggings between uprights where required. The centres of uprights should be at 450 mm centres for 600 mm wide boards and 400 mm centres for 1200 mm boards using 9.5 mm thick material.

Three edge profiles are available for dry lining boards:

Taper edge − by which a flush seamless surface can be obtained by taping and filling the shallow well formed by the edges

Square edge − which may be close butted and finished with a cover strip

Bevelled edge − where the vee joint becomes a feature of the wall.

All boards should be fixed with the foil or grey surface to the framing. Both 9.5 and 12.7 mm thick plasterboard can be obtained with all three profiles as well as a foil backing to act as a vapour barrier. Both thicknesses can be used for the timber frame and Thistle board method but 12.7 mm plaster-board, and 25 mm Gyproc thermal baord are generally used for the Gyproc M/F system.

Care must be taken to ensure that the lining is properly supported at all edges and adequately throughout tis face, that there are no loose or 'live' boards,

that the surface is level and plumb and true and the joints neatly made and,
is filled, are flush with the adjacent surface.

*Provide to perimeter of all rooms 100 mm (127 mm) gypsum plaster cored
cove and fix in accordance with the manufacturer's recommendations
with all butt joints and mitres neatly made and finished.

P11: 6101 6102

This material is used as a cornice at the angle of walls and ceilings to conceal
cracking which often occurs at this point. It is self finished and only requires
decorating with emulsion or similar paint. Lengths obtainable vary from
2 m to 4.2 m depending on the girth selected, and it is delivered in bundles.
The cove is cut with a fine toothed saw and any rough edges are lightly sand
papered. Angles should be properly mitred and the cove is fixed with proprietory adhesive supplied by the makers or through walls to plugs or ceiling
joists with 30 or 40 mm small headed galvanised wallboard nails or brass
countersunk screws. Fixings to walls should be at 305 mm and to ceilings
600 mm centres. Angles and straight joints should be filled with cove adhesive.

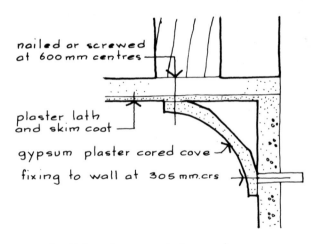

Detail – fixing of gypsum plaster cored cove

*Run vertical quirk in plaster at angles where shown on the drawings to
receive decorative wallpaper*

Decorative finishes such as wallpaper tend to pick up on free edges unless
these are proteced in some way. The easiest method is to run a vee groove
in the plaster finish, into which the edge of the paper can be dressed to
provide protection. Care must be taken to see that the quirk is vertical

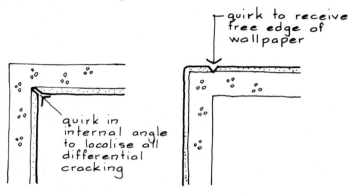

Details of quirks through skim coat plaster

and in complete alignment with any adjacent external angle or feature.
A quirk run in an internal angle joining two materials of differing coefficients of expansion and contraction — brick and lightweight blocks — will
allow movement cracking to take place and be confined to the angle without
spreading across the face and spalling the plaster.
Expanded metal beads can also be used for these purposes and reinforces
the plaster against cracking.

Wall tiling:
BS 1281: 1966 Glazed ceramic tiles and tile fittings for internal walls
BSCP 212: Wall tiling Pt. 1 1963 Internal
Pt. 2 1966 External
The British Ceramic Tile Council, Technical specifications for ceramic
wall tiling
The fixing of ceramic wall tiles to plaster surfaces
The fixing of ceramic wall tiles and mosaics

Ceramic wall tiles can be fixed to a very wide range of backgrounds. Technical
advances in recent years have produced specialised adhesives which allow for
greater adhesion, increased productivity, the elimination of the need to soak
tiles before fixing and the capacity to fix onto almost any surface. The choice
of the correct adhesive is, however, critical and will be governed by the background, the location and duty the tiling is required to achieve.
Despite this, most tile fixing is carried out either on cement/sand renderings
or directly onto plasterwork. The former should always be specified in
preference. Before the cement rendering is applied to the wall, the materials
of which it is composed must be thoroughly dry. Materials with high drying

shrinkage, e.g. lightweight concrete blocks or sand lime bricks, are particularly difficult in this respect. Failure to ensure a properly dry backing will cause the rendering to crack and hollow areas to develop causing consequential tiling failure. If it is necessary to dampen the wall to control water absorbtion before rendering, adequate time must be allowed for the wall and rendering to dry out again before commencing tile fixing. With backgrounds of differing types where differential movement may cause cracking, it may be necessary to control this by incorporating metal lathing in the rendering. Inadequate key is best remedied by hacking the surface in preference to the use of bonding agents.

Plastered backgrounds for ceramic tiles must be strong and fully adhering to the supporting wall. This is especially important where light weight blocks have been used or where light weight plasters provide the background. The water content of the plaster is important and new plaster must have been completed at least four weeks before tiling is commenced. Accelerated heating often only draws moisture from the face leaving the body still damp. A dusty surface, indicating excessive trowelling to produce a finer surface, will need the application of a binding coat of suitable primer brushed over the surface. Since thin-bed adhesives are used for fixing tiles to plaster, it will be appreciated that the surfaces should be plumb, true and level and any loose or hollow areas removed and made good. Gloss paint which is in good condition is quite satisfactory as a background.

Plaster is not satisfactory as a base for tiling in wet areas such as showers. Water resistant tile adhesives are not necessarily water tight. The penetration of water through the joints into the plaster will almost certianly occur. Tiling in these areas should always be carried out on a cement/sand backing.

The ceramic wall tiles for the bathroom and kitchen will be .... mm coloured, all in accordance with BS 1281: 1966, with spacer lugs and cushion edges complete with all necessary rounded edge tiles for free edges. S32: Sg3.10.

Ceramic glazed wall tiles are generally available in two main sizes and associated thicknesses as follows:

152 x 152 x 5 mm (with spacer lugs and cushion edges)
152 x 152 x 6 mm   ditto
108 x 108 x 4 mm   ditto

Tiles are available in other sizes, many of them imported, and most of these are square edge and thicker than those listed above.

Spacer lugs assist in establishing a standard joint width of 3 mm which improves the appearance and provides a crushing point which will fail under compression without shattering the tile. Cushion edges assist in evening out variations in surface planes which are inevitable in ceramic work.

Fittings are produced in a wide variety of angles, coves and cappings, these being mainly used in high quality work. Round edge tiles are the cheapest and probablty by far the most widely used. Glazed earthenware fittings for soap and toilet rolls are available for building in to tiled areas but care must be taken to ensure that colours match as this cannot always be guaranteed due to different manufacturing processes.

Tile the walls of the bathroom (kitchen) to a height of .... mm with ceramic wall tiles as described before, with rounded free edge. Perform all cutting and fitting required and point up on completion with white grout. S32:Y S32:1 S32:2 S32:3 S32:4

As stressed before the backing, whether cement/sand rendered or plastered, must be perfectly dry before tiling is commenced. If any doubt exists special adhesives should be used. Three methods of fixing tiles are in general use, depending on the type of backing, the adhesive selected and the type of installation — interior or exterior.

The thin-bed method for normal dry interior installations uses a thin floated coat of adhesive about 3 mm thick spread in small areas not exceeding $1m^2$ which is carefully ribbed with a notched trowel. The tiles, which are fixed dry, are pressed firmly into position in the adhesive, spacer lugs providing correct spacing for the tiles. If the tile is square edge 1.5 mm joints must be left around each tile as these must never be fixed with tight joints. All adhesive should be removed from the face and joints of the tiles before grouting.

The 'thin-bed' method of fixing with the notched trowel technique is satisfactory for the following dry and dimensionally stable backgrounds with 1:4 cement/sand rendered face:

Common brickwork

Lightweight and aerated concrete products

The technique without the rendered face is suitable for:

Plastered surfaces

Painted surfaces (sound and with good adhesion)

Old glazed tiles and bricks (sound and with good adhesion)

Metal surfaces (rigidly supported and inflexible)

Rendered common brickwork and blockwork

The solid-bed method is used for shower areas where penetration of water is a possibility. After spreading the adhesive to an area of about $1m^2$ the dry tiles are pressed directly into the solid bed tapping each tile firmly and carefully into position to ensure solid bedding and no voids. Jointing and preparation for grouting are as for thin-bed tiling.

The thick-bed method is only used when the background surface is not sufficiently true to permit thin-bed fixing (for example on fiar face brickwork) and where a cement/sand rendering is not acceptable. A setting bed up to 13 mm thick consisting of a proprietory cement or rubber based 'thick-bed' adhesive is applied to the wall surface and the tiles fixed in accordance with the solid-bed method previously described.

Tiles are cut by scoring through the glaze and breaking the tile across, or in a cropping guillotine. Edges should be fair and joints should not vary from the main body of the work. Holes can be but for pipes and similar obstructions and should be neatly formed. The tiles should be neatly fitted into corners and up to obstructions.

Careful attention must be paid to grouting. The work should not be carried out for at least 24 hours after completion of the tiling on normal surfaces or 72 hours on backgrounds of low porosity to allow the adhesive ample time to set. As the grout should be resilient, neat cement should not be used, a proprietory grout or expanding grout should be used to provide a suitable joint. The grouting mixture should be pressed firmly into the joints and around the outside edges of the tiling. An area of $1m^2$ should be completed before the next area commenced. If a higher degree of impermeability is required (e.g. for shower areas) a second application of grout after 24 hours is recommended. With the use of an epoxy grout, double grouting in wet areas is not required as the material sets to provide an impervious joint. The material should be pressed into the joint with a pointed stick with a point equivalent to the thickness of the joint. After grouting, any excess left on the tiles should be scraped off, the surface wiped down with a damp sponge and then polished with a clean cloth.

All wall tiling should be finished with a straight and level joint, free edges level or plumb as applicable, the surface of the tiling even and smooth without irregularities or distortion and the joints fully and evenly grouted and slightly recessed.

Provide movement joints in the tiled wall surfaces where required
   S32: 4152

Movement in the substructure will be reflected in the rigidity of a tiled wall face by cracking, usually in the adjacent joints. By inserting movement joints in the correct places cracking can be reduced to a minimum if not completely obviated. Joints should be located:

(a)   where tiling abuts onto different backing materials
(b)   over existing structural movement joints, and
(c)   at internal vertical corners in large areas of tiling, and at 3 – 5 m centres horizontally and vertically

To be effective, the joints should be at least 6 mm wide, extend throughout the thickness of tiling and bed and be continuous throughout the tiling.

The joints formed should be kept free from adhesive or mortar droppings and filled completely with either:

(a)   Butyl rubber,

(b)   silicone rubber sealant, or

(c)   polysulphide based sealing composition

The two latter materials have good water resistance and are suitable for exterior use and swimming pools. A cheaper substitute to those materials referred to is polyeurethene foam strip sealed off with silicone rubber of polysulphide composition. Care must be taken to clean these materials off the face of the tiling.

Include the P.C. Sum of £   per meter super for the supply and delivery to site of external quality glazed ceramic tiles size ...... pattern to be as selected by the Architect. Add for profit, taking delivery, fixing in accordance with BSCP 212. Pt. 2 1966, to areas indicated on the drawings. S32: Sg3.60. Yt3.12

Exterior quality glazed ceramic tiles need to be fired to a temperature of about 1250° C to withstand variations in temperature and frost. To withstand these high temperatures the body of the tile needs to be thicker than interior quality tiles.

Many of these tiles are imported and the thickness and overall sizes vary enormously. Specialist suppliers will advise on tiles which are suitable for exterior use.

Methods of fixing exterior grade tiles vary with the background, its surface and porosity. With porous common brick or clay block construction a 13 mm rendering coat of cement/sand 1:4 mortar should be applied and allowed to dry for at least 14 days before fixing the tiles. These are bedded using the solid bed method with a suitable adhesive which must be protected from inclement weather for 24 hours until grouting is carried out, and thereafter for a further 14 days. On dense impervious surfaces such as concrete or certain bricks, it may be necessary to hack the surface to form a key together with metal lathing incorporated in the rendering coat. As the adhesive takes longer to dry out on dense backgrounds, grouting will usually be delayed several days and consequently the period of protection will be extended.

Exterior quality tiles may be fixed direct to common brickwork or other dimensionally stable backgrounds by the thick-bed method as described before. Protection from the weather must be provided until the adhesive has set and the grouting completed and for a further period of 14 days.

Movement joints must be provided in the tiled areas using the same methods as previously described. The standards of workmanship and finish are as for interior glazed tiling.

16 Paving

Floor finishes
*Include the P.C. Sum of £ .... for the supply and laying complete of
.... flooring by specialist sub-contractors to be nominated
by the Architect. Add for profit and attendance.*
T31:Aa0.01
Good standards of flooring are difficult to obtain. High standards are a
requirement for that portion of a building which meets with most abuse.
Traditionally also, when costs are rising and economies have to be made, the
finishing trades (including floors) are cut back to effect the necessary savings.
The usual method by which this is controlled is the inclusion of a P.C. sum
to cover the cost of floor coverings and this is reduced or apportioned as
necessary. This system allows for financial and aesthetic reconsideration up
to the immediate period prior to the laying of screeds and while from the
contractor's point of view the indecision is a problem, the other advantages
to both employer and architect are obvious. It will be appreciated that, unless
the work involved in laying the selected floor includes all the necessary
bedding or making up to the required levels from the structural floor to the
finished floor level, decisions must be finalised in time to instruct the contractor to provide screeds of the required thickness to bring the selected
material up to the required level. Unless this is attended to in good time
claims for delay in issuing instructions may well be made by the contractor.
Where possible explicit instructions and specifications should be included
in the contract documents, although the right to select final colours or
textures may be reserved for a later decision, subject to price fluctuations,
which may result in a variation in the cost of the contracted works.
*Cover up and protect all floor finishes and paving and deliver up perfect
on completion.*
T31: 5315
The protection of floor finishes is the contractor's responsibility until completion of the contract. It is, however, often necessary to remind him of his
duties and responsibilities in this respect to avoid future problems. The usual
method is to cover the floor with a good sprinkling of dry sawdust and this
is quite satisfactory on timber and similar dry floors. On quarry tile flooring
and mortar jointed floors this practice should be discouraged as there is the
possibility of sawdust getting into the green joints and causing weakness.

These floors are better protected with a layer of polythene or building paper which permits curing to continue naturally without speeding up the drying process. The best protection is to prohibit traffic altogether but this is not always possible or practical.

Carry out all cutting and fitting required and allow for all waste.
All floor finishes require cutting and fitting to perimeters and obstructions. This should be carried out without damage to the surface of the flooring and without exposing any of the subfloor to view. Tiles and blocks should be as near as possible full units and the edges of the cuts should be straight without spalling of arrises. Where duct or manhole covers intrude, the pattern should be maintained around and, if the covers so permit, across so that minimum breaks in the finish are provided.

The price allowed for the work should include for all normal waste. The percentage will be calculated on the basis of the requirements of the specification. Any variation on the requirements occasioned by omission of information respecting obstructions may result in extra waste as well as additional cutting and this will usually entail an extra.

Asphalt Flooring:
BS 988, 1097, 1076, 1451: 1966 Mastic asphalt for building (limestone
    aggregate)
BS 1162, 1418, 1410: 1966 Mastic asphalt for building (natural rock
    asphalt aggregate)
BS 1450: 1963 Black pitch mastic
BS 3672: 1963 Coloured pitch mastic
BSCP 204 Pt. 2: 1970 In situ flooring

Asphalt flooring is to be manufactured in accordance with BSS ...... and
    laid strictly in accordance with the provisions of the relevant British
    Standard Codes of Practice.
    P.42 et seq.
The aggregate for asphalt for flooring is usually based on limestone and the relevant BS is selected depending on the aesthetic considerations of black or coloured finishes. Asphalt flooring can be laid over any sound sub-floor but where timber is concerned, an isolating membrane of black sheating felt should be provided to avoid any risk of cracking due to differential movement between the sub-floor and the finish. (See Chapter 6.) Similar precautions should be taken when expansion joints and day work joints occur in concrete subfloors, where movement may occur for a variety of reasons and where the thickness of asphalt applied is less than 25 mm in one layer.
The thickness of asphalt varies with the location:

Light duty – domestic/schools/offices – 15 mm in one layer
Medium duty – factories/stores/shops – 19.25 mm in one layer
Heavy duty – breweries/warehouses/loading platforms – up to 50 mm in
one layer
When the application is to 'wet areas', e.g. suspended floors where wet processes are employed, two coats of asphalt should be employed with laps of
at least 100 mm.
Where skirtings are specified, these should be provided with a full cove or a
fillet at the junction with the floor, otherwise as for roof skirtings (see
Chapter 5.)
In cold weather, the building should be warmed before any asphalt flooring
is laid as accelerated cooling may result in cracking or shrinkage. After laying
the floor should be allowed to cool thoroughly before any traffic is allowed
on it.

Brick Paving
*BS 3921 Pt. 2: 1969 (Metric units) Specification for bricks and blocks of
fired brickearth, clay or shale*

**The bricks for paving shall be .... manufactured in accordance
with BS 3921 Pt. 2. 1969, and equal to an approved sample.
F. 21. et seq.*
Bricks for paving are usually of vitreous or semi-vitreous types of normal size.
Some bricks vary from BSS sizes and these are usually thinner and are known
as true paviors. Facing brick slips are also manufactured and although they
are of standard BSS face sizes, their thickness varies from 25 to 50 mm. It is
important, therefore, to select and approve the brick well in advance of the
construction of the subfloor to ensure that the overall thickness does not
cause problems with the finished floor level.
The selection of bricks for paving purposes should be undertaken with care.
Selection on the basis of colour and texture is not enough, durability is of
great importance due to abrasion, and, where used externally, exposure to
saturation and freezing. Engineering bricks such as Blue Staffordshire and
Southwater Reds are eminently suitable but also some rough hard burnt
stocks and wire cuts obtained in good ranges of red, ochre, and blue can be
safely used. It is best to obtain the manufacturer's advice on the suitability
of the products for the situation and exposure contemplated before taking
any decision on the samples offered for the work.
**Paving bricks shall be well wetted to reduce initial suction, laid on edge (or
flat) in straight courses to patterns shown on the drawings bedded in
mortar, neatly pointed up and brushed to remove all dirt and escrescences*

on completion and protected until properly cured.

F21:Y F21:1 F21:2 F21:3

Clay bricks are often wetted by hosing or preferably by immersion in a tank of water for a short period to reduce excessive suction. Only highly porous bricks such as London stocks should be treated in this way as these bricks have a tendency to extract too much moisture from the mortar thereby drawing fine particles of cement to the surface with insufficient moisture to complete hydration and consequently causing poor adhesion between mortar and brick. It is not necessary to wet highly vitrified bricks such as engineering grades, as this would, due to their low suction, create a film of water between brick and mortar imparting a floating action rendering them extremely difficult to lay.

Clay bricks which are bedded onto a concrete base should be provided with a separating membrane over a screeded base. This allows for differential movement without risk of cracking. A layer of polythene or building paper is suitable. The bricks should be bedded in 1:½:4 (cement/lime/sand) by volume well tamped down with a 10 mm. joint and pointed up on completion.

Externally brick paving can be laid on well consolidated hardcore fill graded to a minimum fall of 1 in 60, the bricks being laid on a 50 mm bed of sand or lime; sand (1:4) or ash with the joints filled with lime:sand or run in grout. This grout can be a mix of 1:¼:3 (cement/lime/sand) by volume.

When brick paviors are provided in areas of potentially high temperature, e.g. around boilers, a bituminous bedding may be used. This should consist of 1 part of aqueous bitumen emulsion to 2½ parts of soft dry sand by volume. The dry screeded bedding surface should be primed with a coat of emulsion before laying the paving, and the water content of the composition should be kept to a minimum consistent with workability.

Make provision in the paving for all necessary expansion and movement at the perimeter of the paving and at all construction joints

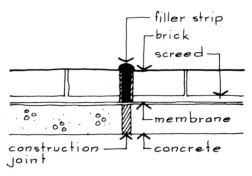

Detail – movement joint in brick paving

Movement joints must always be provided at the junction of paving and a wall. The insertion of a 19 mm sawn batten and the filling of the resultant space on its removal with a prefabricated expansion strip or a non-rigid material such as polyurethane or polyethelene is satisfactory. With the latter materials the joint should be sealed with polysulphide or a similar mastic. Prefabricated expansion strips usually require recommended sealants. Movement joints of a similar construction should also be provided at all construction joints and, when the paviors are jointed with a cement mortar. every 6 m in any direction.

Clay floor quarries:
BS 1286: 1945 Clay tiles for flooring – Type A or B
BSCP 202: 1972 Tile flooring and slab flooring
BRS Digest 79 (2nd series) Clay tile flooring

*Clay quarry tiles will be ...... mm by ...... mm by ...... mm thick heather brown (red or brown) manufactured in accordance with BS 1286 – Type A (or B) by Messrs; .... and laid strictly in accordance with the relevant provisions of BSCP 202: 1972
S31:Sg2.10. S31:1 S31:2 S31:3 S31:4

Clay floor tiles, usually known as quarries, are obtainable in two types depending on the use to which they are to be put and aesthetic considerations. Type A tiles are more uneven with greater permissible dimensional variation. The surface is also rougher and more interesting and sizes up to 225 mm square by 32 mm thick are obtainable. Colour is restricted to reds, blues, browns and buff. Type B tiles have a fine smooth texture, are manufactured to closer tolerances and include vitreous and semi-vitreous tiles in a wide colour range up to 150 mm square by 13 mm thick.

Unless the tile flooring is to be laid in conditions of high temperature (e.g. around boilers) or where there is a risk of chemical attack, the standard method of bedding on a separating layer will avoid the risk of failure by cracking or ridging. This type of failure shows itself by tiles separating cleanly from the bedding due to failure of bonding by shrinkage of the screed and expansion by the laid tiles.

Any method used will, however, require the structural base to be so constituted that it is rigid and stable, any falls required are provided in the structure and not in the bedding and that the bedding is smooth and free from irregularities in the surface. Here a good spade finish can be acceptable but it is generally necessary for the base to be screeded or levelled up for the quarry tile flooring.

The generally accepted method of laying is to spread building paper or polythene over the base concrete or screed, well lapped to avoid any key between bedding and base. The tiles are then laid in as thin a bedding of cement and sand as practicable, 9.5 mm if the smoothness of the base screed allows, 13 mm maximum on spade finish concrete. Where traffic is heavy or impact likely the thickness of the bedding can be increased to 19 mm but never greater than the thickness of the tiles. If a damp proof membrane is provided in the base this can be used as a separating layer so long as it stops any possibility of bonding between base and bedding.

Another method commonly used is the 'thick bed' method where a semi-dry mix of cement and sand (1:4) generally 38 mm thick is packed onto the base, its surface spread with 1:1 cement and sand grout and the floor tiles laid in position dry and tapped into the grout. It is important not to provide greater area of semi-dry mix than can be properly grouted and tiled before its plasticity is lost. A separating layer is not required by this method.

Proprietory cement based adhesives and other types are available and they should conform to BSCP 212 Appendix B Pt. 1. The manufacturer's recommendations should be strictly followed. These adhesives are generally 4.5 mm in thickness and being slightly resilient tolerate some movement between base and tile. The surface level of the screeded base must be of a very high quality as any inaccuracy can be reflected in the surface of the tiled floor. The surface of the quarry tile floors can, with advantage, be dressed with linseed oil on completion, to maintain its colour.

The clay quarry tile flooring in the boiler room will be laid in a bituminous bedding to withstand high temperatures.

  P13:Yr4.20

The method here is to provide a bedding which, although virtually imcompressible, is always of sufficient plasticity to allow the relatively high degree of differential movement which can be expected in such a situation.

The bedding comprises one part of aqueous bitumen emulsion and 2½ parts of dry sand by volume. The base, which should be dry, should be primed by brushing a coat of bitumen emulsion over the surface before the bedding is laid. Care must be taken to reduce the water content to the minimum consistent with workability.

Make provision in the tile flooring for all necessary expansion and movement at the perimeter and at all construction joints.

  S31:4151 4152

Expansion joints should be provided to the perimeter of the floor and to abutments to columns, boiler bases and similar restrictions. These should be formed from suitable water resistant compressible material and either situated between the coved skirting and the floor tiling or against the wall where the joint may be concealed by an applied skirting.

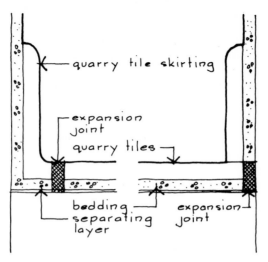

Detail – alternative methods for providing expansion joints in quarry tile floors

Additional movement joints should be provided at all construction joints and at intervals of 6 m in any direction.

Cork tiles:
BSCP 203: Pt. 2: 1972 Sheet and tile flooring

*Cork tiles will be ...... mm by ...... mm by ...... mm thick supplied by Messrs .... or other approved manufacturer. The tiles will be butt jointed (or tongued and grooved) in natural (or specified) colour and equal to samples to be submitted and approved before the work is carried out.

T31: Tj5.30. T31:Ta0.02

Tiles are produced by hydraulically compressing natural cork granules and baking them at high temperatures into blocks. Although the natural resins bond the particles together, synthetic resins are often added to improve the wearing qualities. Two qualities are manufactured, ordinary quality weighing about 488 kg/m^3 and heavy density weighing about 544 kg/m^3. The former quality is in general use. Tiles are manufactured 305 mm square with thicknesses ranging from 4.8 mm upwards, although other sizes can be obtained. The thinner tiles are usually but jointed, the thicker tiles being obtained with a tongued and grooved edge. Colours are in three natural shades of light, medium or dark. Make sure you keep a sample of approved material marked and noted in connection with the appropriate project.

*Lay the cork tiles in a suitable adhesive with straight joints, smooth off with a mechanical sander and, after sweeping clean, apply coats of
.... (seal).*
T31:Yr4.10. Yt3.10. Yi5.10. T31:1 T31:2 T31:3 T31:5
Proprietary adhesives are manufactured for the specific purpose. It is, however, important that the subfloor should be properly prepared and this will depend on the material itself:

(a)   New screeded concrete – all irregularities should be removed and any depressions made good with latex or a non shrinking filler.

(b)   Existing concrete surface – this must have a screeded finish prepared as for new work.

(c)   Wood floors – punch down all nail heads, secure all loose boards, sand to an even surface, sweep and apply a coat of wood primer. Lay a dry felt paper in a suitable adhesive or if the surface is too irregular securely pin hardboard or plywood to the floor to receive cork tiles.

Whatever the adhesive used it is standard practice to secure the tile with nine hardened steel pins per tile. Iregularities in the tile thickness are removed by passing a fine sander over the floor, followed by brushing or vacuum suction to remove the fine dust produced. There are many suitable seals available providing a variety of finishes from matt to high gloss. The number of coats applied will depend on the material selected.

Granolithic paving: topping:
BS 882: 1965 Coarse and fine aggregates from natural sources
BS 1201: 1965 Aggregate for granolithic concrete floor finishes
BSCP 204: Pt. 2: 1970 In situ floor finishes

Materials for granolithic shall be in accordance with BSS 882 and 1202: 1965, and the mix shall be composed of two parts Portland cement to five parts of granite chippings, well graded from 6.4 mm down, with not more than 20% passing a 200 mesh BS sieve.
Y31/C
Granolithic topping is a fine concrete incorporating hard aggregates such as granite or whinstone mixed with portland cement and incorporating just sufficient water to provide sufficient plasticity for laying. The quantity of cement combining with the fine aggregate provides sufficient material to fill the voids but the incorporation of excessive dust produces a material with insufficient wearing qualities. Certification that the aggregate complies with the grading requirements should always be obtained from the suppliers.

*The granolithic paving shall either be laid to the concrete base within 12
hours of the base being laid or the surface must be properly and adequately
prepared to receive the paving without risk of lifting or failure.*

P14:1 P14:2251

It is usually impracticable to apply granolithic paving to freshly laid concrete
slabs. In addition the probability of damage during the progress of works is
increased. It would be much more practical to provide a monolithic granolithic topping in this instance.

When mature concrete has to receive a granolithic finish the problem of
adhesion is of paramount importance. To assist adhesion the surface should
be well cleaned of all cement dabs oil stains and similar deleterious matter,
well hacked and roughened to provide a key and all dust and debris carefully
removed. The surface should be well wetted to reduce suction and immediately
before laying the topping a thick portland cement grout should be brushed
over the whole area.

*Provide and lay to .... granolithic paving as specified
40 mm thick, well trowelled levelled and consolidated and finished
smooth from a steel float.*

P14: 2151 P14:3 P14:4

A finished thickness less than 40 mm always has a tendency to lift. The material
should be well worked with a trowel to close up the surface after excess water
has risen to the surface and evaporated. Trowelling also causes consolidation
of the mass and the removal of voids. Excess laitance must be removed
immediately before final trowelling and the surface is finally polished by
means of a steel float.

It is advisable to divide the finish into bays not exceeding 15 m square by
means of ebonite strips or similar material. This reduces cumulative expansion
problems. The strips are usually set out and supported by dabs of granolithic
material and, providing they are themselves originally set in at the correct
level, provide a useful levelling guide for the whole floor.

To prevent accidental slipping a proprietory abrasive or carborundum may be
sprinkled over the surface and worked into the material on the final trowelling.
This is usually provided on stair treads and thresholds at the rate of 1.25 kg/m^2
Where possible granolithic should be integral with the concrete slab. Laid in
this way it very rarely causes any problems of separation. The materials used
are identical with applied granolithic finish.

*The whole of the concrete floor slabs, unless specified to the contrary, are
to be brought to finished floor level and while still wet, well sprinkled with
a well prepared mixture of two parts granite aggregate as specified and
one part portland cement applied at a rate of 7.5 kg/m^2, well tamped in
with a wood float and well trowelled to a smooth level finish*

In floors of any size, the granolithic finished slabs should be laid in alternate bays to allow drying shrinkage to occur in the concrete before the intermediate slabs are cast. If proper care is taken with the formwork it is possible to use the finished surface as a rule for the intermediates and the presence of the construction joint will be almost unnoticeable. The same precautions in respect of dovetailing and grouting the shallow face of the concrete should be followed as in plain concrete slabs.

The surface of all granolithic paving must be kept damp and properly cured for a period of at least seven days after laying by the application of a thick covering of wet sand, hessian or a polythene membrane, kept moist by frequent sprinkling with water applied through a hose.
    P14:5

The usual method employed today is the use of polythene, the others being liable to cause damage to the surface especially with any accidental traffic. The surface during this period should be a uniform grey green colour, and the area should be fenced off and all traffic over the surface prohibited. The application of a single application of a 10% solution of sodium silicate to the cured surface will assist in reducing the amount of dust which any cement based floor will generate.

Linoleum:
BS 810: 1966 Sheet linoleum, cork carpet and linoleum tiles
BSCP 203: Pt. 2: 1972 Sheet and tile flooring

Plain linoleum will be ...... mm thick supplied by Messrs ....
    or other equal and approved manufacturer to BS 810: 1966. The colours will be as directed and the linoleum will be equal to samples submitted and approved before the work is carried out.
    T31:Tn4.10. T31:Ta0.01

Linoleum is manufactured by applying a mixture of oxydised or polymerised linseed oil, driers, resins, cork and/or wood flour, colouring and fillers under pressure onto a jute canvas or bitumen saturated felt paper. It is produced as plain or inlaid (where the colour is constant throughout the thickness of the material) and printed linoleum. The material is produced in standard sheet width of 1.8 and 2.0 m in lengths from 23 − 27 m except the linoleum grades of 4.5 and 6.7 mm where the length is from 11 to 14 m. The usual thicknesses used in building are 3.2 and 4.5 mm. Linoleum tiles are cut from sheet in similar thicknesses, usually 305 mm square.

Similar precautions in respect of samples should be followed as recommended for cork.

The linoleum is to be stored on site in warm conditions and laid out loose to allow material to stretch before cutting. Lay the linoleum in a suitable adhesive with close butt (or cold welded) joints, cut to design as specified, well rolled over as required to obtain complete adhesion with the subfloor and remove any air bubbles or wrinkles.
T31:Yr4.10. Yt3.10. Yu5.30. T31:1 T31:2 T31:3 T31:5

Linoleum stored in a roll becomes stiff and intractible, needing to be laid out flat to absorb natural humidity before laying. Warmth is necessary to unroll the material without damage and to keep in a condition suitable for laying. It is therefore essential that the building should be adequately heated before and after laying.

Linoleum can be laid on most subfloors as long as proper precautions are taken. With a solid concrete oversite this entails the provision of a satisfactory damp proof membrane throughout the area of the slab and a surface smooth and level such as provided by a well laid cement/sand (1:3) screed. On timber floors the problem of joints opening and boards curling can be removed by inserting a felt paper or cork underlay if the linoleum is to be laid loose. If the linoleum is to be stuck down, which is recommended for prolonging the life of the material (especially in heavy wear situations), a hardboard or plywood underlay well bradded or stapled to the boarding at 150 mm centres all over is required. The use of chipboard flooring can be an extra economy in such a situation.

Ventilation of linoleum finished timber ground floors is very important as the linoleum will exclude any passage of air through joints in the boards. Also, if the linoleum is laid loose in such a situation, rot can develop in situations such as door thresholds and in kitchens and bathrooms where moisture can penetrate through joints and become trapped between the linoleum and the boarding.

Due to its relative inflexibility and large size linoleum must be rolled out on laying to a flat and completely integral finish. This is accomplished by using a heavy steel roller to remove air bubbles and wrinkles. Joints are either close butt jointed or cold welded if a completely homogenous floor surface is required.

Thoroughly clean down the floors on completion and apply and thoroughly body in wax polish as recommended by the linoleum manufacturers.
T31: 5051 5201

Brushing down to remove loose dirt and a good application of an approved wax polish will start linoleum off on its useful life. Marks which are inevitable can usually be removed by a sparing use of white spirit and floors which require more attention than brushing can be washed down with mild soap or detergent before waxing.

Rubber Flooring:
BS 1711: 1951 Solid rubber flooring
BSCP 203: Pt. 2: 1972 Sheet and tile flooring

**Rubber flooring will be .... mm thick supplied by Messrs ....
or other equal and approved manufacturer to BS 1711: 1951. The colours
(surface texture) will be as directed and the rubber will be equal to samples
submitted and approved before the work is carried out.*
T32: Tn5.10. Tn5.50. T32: Ta0.01
Rubber flooring is basically natural plantation rubber with a proportion of
various fillers to provide texture and colour and a small proportion of sulphur.
The latter is incorporated to allow proper vulcanisation, the materials being
heated under pressure to produce a homogeneous mixture.
Rubber flooring is produced in many colours, plain, marbled or mottled and
with a wide variety of studded, ribbed and special textured surfaces.
Two types of material are produced in sheet form, a solid sheet of rubber and
a thin membrane mounted on a sponge rubber backing. Sheets are produced
0.9 to 1.8 m wide by 15 to 30 m long in thicknesses of 3.2, 4.8 and 6.4 mm.
Unless very heavy traffic is anticipated the thinner grades are generally
satisfactory. Rubber tiles are cut from sheet in a wide variety of sizes and
shapes and may be specially moulded in thicknesses from 10 to 20 mm.
Similar precautions in respect of samples should be followed as recommended
for cork.
**The rubber flooring is to be laid in a suitable adhesive with straight close
butted joints, free from all bubbles and curled edges. Clean off and wash
if so required on completion.*
T32:Yr4.10. Yt3.10. T32:1 T32:2 T32:3 T32:6
Rubber flooring is generally laid by a specialist firm. Most types of subfloor
are suitable but similar precautions in respect of rising damp and irregularities
as required for linoleum should be followed.
Adhesives are usually composed of rubber dissolved in naptha and care must
be taken to ensure that all bubbles are removed and that the edges do not
curl, by weighting or similar means.
The natural surface of rubber is dirt resisting and no further dressing or
polishing is required. Floors should be brushed clean and wiped over with a
damp cloth and soft household soap on completion.
**The rubber tiles are to be laid in wet cement and sand (1:4) bedding over a
cement and sand levelling screed. Clean off and wash if so required on
completion.*
Heavy rubber tiles can be provided with dovetail ribs on the underside and,
being laid direct into a cement/sand bedding in a similar manner to quarry

tiles, dispense with both damp proof membrane and adhesive. These tiles are mainly used in areas of heavy wear and traffic. Cleaning is effected in a similar manner to rubber sheet.

Slate paving:
Slate for paving will be best quality .... obtained from Messrs. .... (or an approved quarry) and equal to a sample to be submitted and approved before the work is carried out. S21:Se0.10

Natural slate is either blue, blue-grey, blue-green or green and produced by quarries in Wales and the Lake District. The colour is dependant on the location of the quarry and runs very true to colour samples.
Slate for internal paving is generally 6 – 13 mm in thickness and in sizes up to 450 x 225 mm. The finish is usually riven and polished.

Slate paving is to be bedded in a fine portland cement slurry with the addition of an approved vinyl adhesive and cleaned off on completion. S21:1

Slate must be provided with a rigid base of concrete and, to allow slurry bedding, the base should be finished with a smooth cement and sand screed (1:3). It is important to ensure that the slurry bedding is cleaned off properly after 48 hours by brushing or sponging the slate with a 10% solution of muriatic acid and subsequently hosing down or thoroughly washing with clean water. As the acid will attack the cement joint care must be taken with this operation.
The slate will benefit by the application of wax or a proprietory sealer on completion to intensify the colour.

Natural stone:
BSCP 202: 1972 Tile flooring and slab flooring
NOTE: Cast stone is very similar to natural stone in most respects except in the matter of size. Slabs should conform to BS 368: 1971 Precast concrete flags and their laying to BSCP 202: 1972

Stone for paving will be ...., best quality available, obtained from an approved quarry and equal to an average sample to be submitted and approved before the work is carried out. S21:Se0.10

Natural stone pavings are generally obtained from Yorkshire laminated sand-stones (York stone) some varieties of limestone and from granite. Being a natural material the quality and colour varies widely within each individual quarry and it is best to view the material in bulk in the quarry before making a selection.

The size of stones supplied for paving usually vary enormously and the thickness varies from 50 to 150 mm. There is, however, a tendency with some imported stones to produce paving in regular sizes and thicknesses and this may spread to native quarries.

The stone paving is to be bedded in .... with the joints pointed up flush in ....
S21:1

Very large slabs can be bedded in 50 — 100 mm of dry sand on a 150 mm bed of consolidated hardcore or similar thickness of concrete. Smaller paving slabs should be bedded in 1:2:6 (cement/lime/sand) internally or cement mortar (1:3) externally.

Pointing will depend on the stone used. Dense impervious mortars should only be used with impervious stones such as granite where a 1:3 (cement/ stone dust) mortar is suitable. Otherwise 1:3:12 (cement/lime putty/stone dust) or 2:5:7 (ditto) mortar should be used for internal and external work respectively.

Where any stone butts against brickwork its surface should be painted with a coat of bituminous paint to prevent staining.

Clean off and protect the stone flooring on completion

Sandstones may be cleaned with water and fine sand or carborundum if they become dirty. Limestones should be cleaned down with water and any non-corrosive cleaner while granite responds to ordinary scouring.

Oils will stain both limestone and sandstone and it is therefore most important that areas should be properly protected from any possibility of damage from this source. Natural stone floors should ideally be barred from any traffic after laying.

Thermoplastic or Asphalt tiles:
BS 2592: 1955 Thermoplastic flooring tiles
BSCP 203: 1972 Sheet and tile flooring
NOTE: Vinyl asbestos tiles are similar to thermoplastic but have a greater resistance to grease and are more resilient. Tiles should conform to BS 3260: 1969 P.V.C. asbestos floor tiles. Laying requires that the tiles are warmed to take up better any uneveness in the base which should incorporate a damp-proof membrane

Thermoplastic tiles will be ...... mm by ...... mm by ...... mm thick supplied by Messrs .... or other approved manufacturer to BS 2592: 1955. The colours will be as directed and the tiles will be equal to samples submitted and approved before the work is carried out.
T32: Tn6.85. Ta0.02

These tiles were originally called 'asphalt' tiles because they were originally manufactured from either mineral asphalt or products from the distillation of oil or coal. With the incorporation of plastic resins which enable lighter colours to be produced, they are now known as 'thermoplastic' tiles. Colours produced are generally marbled and normal sizes are 225 mm square and 3.2 mm thick.

Similar precautions in respect of samples should be followed as recommended for cork.

The thermoplastic tile flooring is to be laid in a suitable adhesive, with straight close butted joints in colours and to patterns as directed. Clean off, seal and leave perfect on completion.
T32: Yr4.10. Yt3.10. T32:1 T32:3

Thermoplastic tiles can be laid on any base, new or old. A damp proof membrane is not obligatory in solid floors, unless a head of water is present, but the surface of the concrete should have a cement/sand screed (1:3) trowelled smooth. Worn concrete, quarry tile, brick or granolithic paving, if levelled up with a filler course such as latex are also quite suitable. Wood floors are best covered with a layer of hardboard to receive the tiles. Adhesives are bituminous which act also as a damp proof membrane.

Thermoplastic tiles can be washed with warm water and soft soap or detergent and any heelmarks or similar defects removed with steel wool. A seal should always be applied on completion.

Vinyl flooring (flexible p.v.c. tiles and sheet):
BS 3261: 1960 Flexible P.V.C. Flooring
BRS Digest 33 Second Series, Sheet and tile flooring from Thermoplastic

Vinyl tiles (sheet) will be .... mm thick supplied by Messrs ....
or other approved manufacturer to BS 3261: 1960. The colours will be as directed and the material will be equal to samples submitted and approved before the work is carried out.
T32: Tn6.60. Ta0.02

Vinyl flooring incorporates a substituted proportion of plasticised P.V.C. resin which gives great flexibility to the material. This can be obtained in tiles 305 mm square by 1.6 mm thick and in sheet up to 2.4 m wide. The latter can be welded by means of a P.V.C. welding rod and hot air torch but the surface of the weld does not always perfectly match the surrounding material and being rougher picks up the dirt. Colours are varied and the surface can be printed with various designs which are then portected by the lamination of the surface by clear material. Realistic imitation of marbles, slates and terazzo and three dimensional effects can be obtained. These latter are less suitable for areas of heavy wear as the clear protective covering wears away in time. The material is quite suitable for underfloor heating.

The vinyl flooring is to be laid in a suitable adhesive with close straight butted (or welded) joints in colours and patterns as directed. Clean off, seal and leave perfect on completion.

T32: Yt3.10. T32:1 T32:2 T32: 6152 6151

Vinyl tiles can be laid on any base in a similar manner to thermoplastic tiles, but a damp proof membrane must be incorporated in any solid concrete base in contact with the ground. Adhesives are usually particular to the specialist manufacturer.

The material should be washed with warm water and soft soap or detergent and heelmarks, to which this material is prone, removed with steel wool. Any seal applied should be the product recommended by the vinyl manufacturer as some polishes are likely to break down the foundation of the plasticiser.

Wood board and strip flooring:

BS 1297: 1970 Grading and sizing of softwood flooring
BS 2604: Pt. 2 1970 Resin bonded chipboard
BSCP 201 Pt. 2: 1972 Wood flooring (board strip block and mosaic)

Provide and lay to floors of .... 16 (19, 21, 28) mm wrot softwood boarding, each board tongued and grooved on sides, end joints positioned over a supporting joist and each board fixed with 2 no. 63 mm lost head wire nails well driven and punched home. All boarding is to be well cramped up before nailing.

H42:H H42:X 4101

Timber for flooring should be quarter or rift sawn in thicknesses of 19 and 25 mm and tongued and grooved to the long sides. The widths provided are known either as battens (under 100 mm) or boards (over 100 mm).

Specimens of timber acceptable under the Building Regulations as given on page 86. Finished thicknesses of board relate to the span as follows:

Finished Thickness	Maximum Span
16 mm	505 mm
19 mm	600 mm
21 mm	635 mm
28 mm	790 mm

After kilning the moisture content should not exceed:
12 – 16% for buildings with intermittent heating, or
10 – 14% for buildings with central heating

To ensure minimum movement after laying, this should not be allowed until the glazing is complete, external doors hung and, if possible, the heating installed.

Cramping is essential to provide a tight, rigid surfaced floor and to reduce the joints opening up by placing the timber in compression. Two cramps should be used.

Two nails are required to each joist and the length must allow an adequate fixing to the joist to counteract shrinkage. Two nails also help to restrict warping or curling. See also that the heads are well punched home or damage to superimposed floor coverings will ensue.

Provide and lay to floors of .... *18 mm tongued and grooved chipboard flooring manufactured in accordance with BS 2604 Pt. 2 1970, including Clause 15 and fixed strictly in accordance with the manufacturer's recommendations.*

R53:Rj7.30. 1101 2151

Chipboard flooring is perfectly satisfactory so long as material of the correct density is employed. This occurs when flooring grade chipboard to BS 2604 Pt. 2 is used which complies with Clause 15. (Additional properties for flooring material) of a density of 750 kg/m^3.

The material should be self-tongued and grooved enabling the advantages of tongued and grooved boarding to be allied to those of chipboard, especially when the large panel size of 2440 mm by 600 mm is taken into consideration. Correct fixing is important. Generally joists at 400 mm centres should provide support with the panels laid length ways across them with ends supported on a joist and cross joists staggered. Each panel should be nailed to each joist with 3 no 63 mm lost head or annular ring nails one at 25 mm from the joint and the other two about 200 mm apart.

Flooring grade chipboard is very stable in centrally heated premises.

Provide and lay to floors of .... *wrot* .... *batten strip flooring 25 mm (19 mm) thick and 100 mm wide, all tongued and grooved on sides and ends and secret nailed to supporting joists.*

H42: Hi3.01. Hi3.10. 1251 3051 4101 4201

Strip flooring is produced in batten widths up to 100 mm wide in nominal thicknesses of 25 and 19 mm. The material is always tongued and grooved on sides and ends and usually produced by quarter sawing to produce the most decorative effect of the grain.

A large variety of woods are available, mostly imported, for strip flooring and the usual method of fixing is by secret nailing through the side of the board above the tongue at an angle of 50°. An additional nail is sometimes put in the face and stopped up.

The battens should be well cramped up before fixing and heading joints well staggered between adjacent battens and all lying over a supporting joist. The building should be weather proofed and heated in a similar manner to softwood boarding and the moisture content should be identical.

Cover up and protect the boarded floors, clean off on completion and seal (stain and polish).

H42:4451 3451

Both board and strip flooring must be protected from impact damage, plaster and cement droppings and from paint splashes. Temporary coverings of polythene or building paper or used hardboard are usually effective and the practice of well sprinkling with sawdust is a help in keeping the surface clean. Any plant such as trestles and low scaffolds must have the feet well padded to obviate abrasive or indentation damage.

On completion of general works the floors should be cleaned off and finished. Softwood floors should be lightly sanded off until the surface is flush, clean and smooth and preferably the surface sealed to protect it from further damage. Alternatively the surface may be stained to an approved colour and then wax polished.

Hardwood strip is provided for decorative purposes, the finish then being important. The surface should be scraped, planed and then sanded to a smooth finish. Open grain floors should be treated with a wood paste filler to fill any grain depressions. The surface may then be treated with a seal and wax polished.

Two coats of seal are usually applied by means of a brush. Various finishes are obtainable from matt to high gloss. Wax polishing, usually carried out by applying the wax to the floor and bodying it in with a polishing machine, assists in protecting the surface.

Wood block and mosaic flooring:
BS 1187: 1959 Wood blocks for floors
BS 4050: 1966 Wood mosaic flooring
BSCP 201: Pt. 2: 1972 Flooring of wood and wood products: Wood flooring – board, strip, blocks and mosaic

*Provide and lay to floors of .... 25 mm nominal ....
    hardwood blocks, manufactured in accordance with BS 1187: 1959, and
    supplied by Messrs .... equal to a sample submitted and approved
    before the work is carried out*
Wood blocks are produced in various sizes up to 89 mm wide and in various lengths of which 228 and 305 mm are the most common. The most common nominal thickness is 25 mm. The blocks are produced from quarter or flat

sawn timber, kiln dried to the moisture content previously indicated for boarded floors. They have a chamfer along the bottom edge to take up excessive adhesive and various interlocking devices to prevent individual blocks lifting, such as tongue and groove or dowel pegs.

Blocks require a level base and this is usually provided by a cement/sand (1:3) screeded concrete slab incorporating a damp proof membrane if in contact with the ground. The blocks are usually laid in a cold latex bitumen emulsion adhesive which obviates any priming coat required and has greater holding power than the older hot bitumen method of fixing. The blocks are laid in herringbone patterns which give a very pleasing appearance, with a two or three block margin to the perimeter of the room. Cork expansion strips are provided next to the walls and across door openings to allow movement of the flooring. The building should be weather proofed and heated in a similar manner to softwood boarding.

The finish and surface treatment should be carried out in a similar manner to hardwood strip flooring.

Similar precautions in respect of samples should be followed as recommended for cork.

*Provide and lay to floors to .... 13 mm nominal ....
hardwood mosaic manufactured in accordance with BS 11 87: 1959, and
supplied by Messrs .... equal to a sample submitted and
approved before the work is carried out*

Wood mosaic consists of small slips of wood normally arranged in groups to form blocks about 115 mm square, set alternately to one another in basket pattern mounted on either a sheet of backing material which remains in place after laying or held together by a sheet of paper which is stripped off the surface after laying.

The mosaic requires a level base idential to wood blocks but due to the great number of joints, expansion and contraction can take up in the material without causing injury to the surface. The material is usually laid in bituminous adhesive.

Weatherproofing, heating, surface treatment, are all as for wood block flooring. Sample precautions in this respect should be as recommended for cork.

17 Decorating

BS 1248: 1954 Wallpapers
BS 1336: 1971 Knotting
BS 2521, 2523: 1966 Lead based priming paints
BS 2525/7: 1969 Undercoating and finishing paints for protective purposes
(white lead based)
BS 3698: 1964 Calcium plumbate for paints
BSCP 231: 1966 Painting of buildings
BSCP 2008: 1966 Protection of iron and steel structures from corrosion
BRS Digest   55   Painting walls Pt. 1
56   Painting walls Pt. 2
57   Painting walls Pt. 3
70   Painting iron and steel
71   Painting non-ferrous materials
106 . Painting woodwork
110   Condensation

The painting of building structures is carried out for two purposes:
(a)   to protect the substrate, and
(b)   to enhance its appearance
Various factors combine to reduce the effectiveness of paints, depending on
the physical formation, degree of flexibility of the applied film and the
chemical composition of both substrate and paint film. Basically the factors
which cause deterioration and eventual failure of the finish can be summed up
as follows:
(a)   Moisture content and movement: timber with a moisture content in
excess of about 25 − 30% is dimensionally unstable. For building purposes
the moisture content should vary from 15 − 18% for exterior and 10 − 12%
for interior use. Considerable shrinkage occurs while the moisture content is
reduced to the lower limits. Thus timber to be painted should, at the time it
is decorated, approximate very closely to the optimum moisture content.
Otherwise if it is too dry the timber will swell as it equates with the atmospheric moisture content imposing stresses on the paint film which will cause
failure. On the other hand, timber with a higher moisture content than that
recommended will cause blistering of the film and opening up of mechanical
joints, thus providing further points for water penetration

(b)   Chemical reaction in the substrate: the main examples of this type of failure are the rusting of ferrous materials, efflorescence caused by leaching of salts in brickwork and cementitious backings and sulphate attack. Careful preparation is the best antidote for these problems and is discussed later in this chapter

(c)   Exudation of resinous matter etc: most timbers, both hardwoods and softwoods, exude resinous materials and oils which can interfere with the drying, hardening and adhesion of paint. Kiln drying has a considerable effect in lowering the resin content of some timbers and any which has solidified on the surface can be scraped off. In pines the exudation occurs generally at knots, pitch streaks and pockets but many other softwoods such as larches, spruces and firs have this problem to a lesser or greater extent. Some hardwoods such as oak, teak, furjun, agba and keruing (all used for cills) suffer from similar problems. All must have affected areas properly sealed and protected to ensure that the paint film does not rapidly deteriorate.

(d)   External influences: one of the principal causes of dampness in joinery and wall surfaces is internal condensation due to absence of adequate natural ventilation and the consequential increase of internal water vapour in dwellings. In serious cases, the conditon can cause saturated timber and paint failure. Water entry is usually at the joint between putty and glass or putty and wood.

Natural rainfall is an ever present source of dampness in woodwork. In addition to the places described above, entry is possible at the bottom joints of window frames and doors, the end grain of door frames and exterior boarding and contact with masonry.

Strong sunlight causes loss of colour and degredation of natural finishes which are not protected by clear finishes such as varnishes which do not filter out damaging wave lengths in the sun's rays. Painting is an effective protection against sunlight but certain pigments such as blue and dark grey are fugitive in strong sunlight and should be avoided for external use.

Micro-organisms such as fungal spores are widely present in the atmosphere. Apart from some surface growing moulds, more readily found in rural areas and which, though objectionable from appearance, do not have any effect on the durability of the timber, those which are harmful such as wet rot fungi are ineffective if the moisture content of the timber is below $20 - 22\%$ and the material is treated with a preservative.

Workmanship
To ensure a satisfactory and durable finish the paint product must be prepared and applied in accordance with certain standards and in accordance with the manufacturer's recommendations.

Mixing of paint is important, thorough integration of all ingredients prior to use should always be insisted upon. Paint which is in store must be protected from extremes of heat and cold to prevent deterioration in the container. If thinning is required, and this may be necessary in certain temperatures and on application to certain surfaces, the proportions should be those recommended by the manufacturer and never exceeded.

Application of primers should always be by brush, subsequent coats can be by brush spray or roller as appropriate. Some special primers such as quick drying wood primers may be spray applied. Each coat of paint must be hard dry before the next is applied and all surfaces must be perfectly dry before the next coat. Each coat, except the last, must be lightly rubbed down with fine glass paper to a smooth finish before the next is applied. No internal painting should be permitted until the building has been rendered free from dust and external painting should not be permitted in direct sunlight or driving rain, fog or frosty weather.

Consecutive coats should be of different shades to assist in checking the number of coats applied and the surface should be perfect and free from all brush marks on completion.

Failure to carry out the work in a proper workmanlike manner will cause certain defects to become apparent. Various defects and their likely causes are as follows:

(a)   Bittiness

Description – surface film roughened by protruding excrescences.

Cause – dirt from atmosphere, badly cleaned brushes or bits of paint skin
    stirred into paint

Cure – allow to harden, rub down to smooth finish and apply another coat
    of strained finish

(b)   Bleeding

Description – discolouration of paint coating by diffusing of underlying
    substance into or through the coating

Cause – application of decorative finish over imperfectly sealed substrate.

Cure – application of a sealer such as an aluminium primer before continuing
with further finishing coats

(c)   Blistering

Description – raised bubbles of paint

Cause – painting onto wet surfaces or painting in the direct heat of the sun

Cure – severe blistering should have the film stripped off and a new system
    applied. Scattered blisters can be burst, the edges flattened and the film
    brought forward with the appropriate primer or undercoat depending on
    the depth of the blistering

(d)   Blooming

Description – loss of gloss finish

Cause – damp (fog or mist) or contaminants in the atmosphere

Cure – light bloom can be removed by polishing with a soft rag or gentle washing Scrubbing and thorough washing should remove heavy bloom

(e)   Brush marks

Description – uneven lined film surface

Cause – uneven or careless application, brushing after set has commenced, paint too thick. Dirty or clogged brushes

Cure – allow to dry, rub down and re-finish

(f)   Cissing

Description – shrinkage or drawing away of new coating from large or small areas of work

Cause – contamination of surface by grease or oil, silicones from domestic polishes, over oily undercoat. Application of waterborne paints over oil based paints

Cure – allow to dry hard, rub down and re-finish

(g)   Crazing

Description – irregular cracking of surface coating

Cause – old age of paint film, applying hard drying finish over an undercoat not yet properly dry, applying hard drying paint to soft bituminous surface

Cure – light crazing can be rubbed down and refinished, severe cases should be stripped and new system applied

(h)   Drying troubles

Description – film is tacky or soft after an excessive time after application

Causes – application in frosty, foggy, rainy weather or in excessive humidity, application over bitumen or waxed surface, application over dirt, oil or grease or over an undercoat or primer which has not properly hardened, use of unsuitable thinner, lack of light causing drying retardation of oil based paints

Cure – strip and new system applied

(i)   Efflorescence

Description – white crystalline or amorphous deposit breaking through the paint film from the substrate and causing eruptions on the surface.

Causes – soluble salts in solution drawn to and deposited on surface of the structure

Cure – If the film is not broken the efflorescence can be wiped off, usually only with permeable paints such as distemper or emulsion. If the film has been disrupted the whole area should be stripped down, wiped and left until all efflorescence has stopped before new system is applied.

(j)   Flaking

Description — paint lifting away or peeling back from a joint or split in
    the film.

Cause — shrinkage in the substrate causing stress in the paint film, application
    over severely chalking old paint causing loss of adhesion, application over
    greasy surface causing loss of adhesion between base and undercoat.

Cure — existing flaked areas should be stripped or thoroughly rubbed down
    and cleaned before applying new paint system.

(k)   Grinning

Description — undercoat showing through finishing coat

Cause — poor workmanship and uneven application, undercoat of unsuitable
    colour, attempting too wide a colour change with too few coats

Cure — extra finishing coats

(l)   Loss of gloss

Description — finish 'flat' or loses gloss

Cause — application too greasy or waxed surface, application in fog, frost,
    humidity etc., application to porous undercoat, lack of effective
    undercoat or its omission, normal ageing or beginning of chalking

Cure — new work may be rubbed down and refinished, old work should be
    stripped and new paint system applied

(m)   Opacity (loss of)

Description — failure to obliterate previous coating

Cause — overthinning, failure to stir paint properly

Cure — apply further coat of properly prepared finish

(n)   Running (curtaining or sagging)

Description — uneven wavy lines on surface of film often incorporating
    raised defects

Cause — uneven application or over-application to particular areas, application
    of further paint to a wet edge which has commenced to set

Cure — allow to dry hard, rub down the runs and refinish

(o)   Saponification

Description — destruction of the paint film and the formation of soft sticky
    drops or runs of a brown gummy liquid

Causes — paint film attacked by a strong alkali

Cure — complete stripping and surface cleaning followed by a new paint
    system

(p)   Sheariness

Description — glossy patches and streaks on flat or eggshell finishes

Causes — uneven application, application over partially set paint

Cure — light flattening and application of further full coat of finish

(q)   Shrivelling

Description – wrinkling on parts of paint film too heavily coated

Cause – uneven application providing too thick a coat in small areas

Cure – after thorough hardening flat back to even coat and refinish

Knotting is to consist of shellac dissolved in methylated spirits and to comply with BS 1336 in all respects. Apply two coats of knotting to all knots and resinous areas of timber.

V51:Yv1.10. 5351

Shellac knotting and aluminium leaf primers are the only available seals for resinous timber areas. Knotting is génerally employed on softwoods applied to clear timber and care must be taken to see that all areas affected are properly treated. Two coats of thin knotting are preferable to a thick application and each coat must be allowed to dry and harden before any further application.

Very large knots which are exposed to strong sunlight will continue to exude resin. This is due to the use of poor quality timber rather than the failure of the knotting.

Prime all surfaces of softwood (hardwood – ferrous metals – galvanised surfaces) with an approved priming coat.

V52:Y

A good sound priming coat is the essential base for a satisfactory and lasting paint system. Subject to certain qualifications, especially as regards ferrous metal bases, the application should be in the joiner's shop or factory. Unfortunately the skimpy application of a second class material can serve to hide poor quality timbers and care must be taken to specify the exact primer which will be acceptable for the material and its potential application. Care should also be taken to ensure that the primer matches the remainder of the paint system in manufacture, otherwise, should a failure in the finish occur, it will create difficulties in obtaining remedial action if the primer is not compatible.

Any damage or the removal of any portion of the joinery exposing unprimed timber should ensure repriming of bare timber immediately and before the work is fixed to prevent water penetration. This is especially important in shooting in and adjusting the heights of external doors and the removal of horns to windows.

Softwood A satisfactory primer for softwood is 'pink primer' containing a high proportion of white lead and some red lead. The material should be formulated to BS 2521. This primer has good filling properties, a reasonably quick drying time, reasonable durability to withstand exposure before final painting and has first class water resistance. This primer is excellent for external use.

Where lead pigments are undesirable, primers with an aleo-resinous or alkyal base may be used. Qualities vary considerably, poor primers having little water resistance, chalk rapidly on exposure and provide poor adhesion for future coats. Better qualities have improved water resistance but are less durable than lead based primers. They are satisfactory for internal work. Emulsion primers, fairly recently introduced, have some advantages such as non-flammability, non-toxic and rapid drying allowing undercoats to be applied the same day. They are supplied in white, grey or cream and while satisfactory for internal use, being permeable, will not exclude moisture. Consequently external joinery built in as the work proceeds and primed in this material, will most likely be saturated by the time further paint applications are applied and this may well cause delay while the timber dries out to an acceptable moisture content. In any event the timber must be treated with a perservative if this primer is to be accepted. While these primers are often described as 'self-knotting' this must be regarded as an optimistic claim.

<u>Hardwood</u> Aluminium based primers confer, by their formulation, a degree of water resistance equal to white lead, resistance to resinous exudation and good durability. Aluminium paint is not a satisfactory material and is not to be confused with the primer material. Being good fillers they are often used for priming cills and bottom rails of external doors and windows where their resistance to water penetration is a further advantage. These primers can be used in similar situations where softwood is employed. The backs of frames, skirtings and other items in contact with the structure are particularly appropriate. The use of a suitable thinner will enable primers formulated for softwood to be used satisfactorily for hardwoods.

<u>Ferrous metals</u> As suggested before, the preparation of iron and steel and the application of the primer are best carried out under the general contractor's direct supervision to avoid division of responsibility should the preparation and priming be unsatisfactory and cause failure of the paint film.

All surfaces of iron and steel must be perfectly dry before priming and free from dirt, oil, rust, mill and weld scale. The latter can be removed by chipping and wire brushing. Proprietory rust removers can be used to neutralise any rust adhering to the surface after mechanical preparation and while expensive these, if properly applied to the manufacturer's instructions, are usually very effective. Care must generally be taken to follow up this treatment as soon as dry, with a priming coat, as protection is short lived. Special care must be taken with arrises both in preparation and priming.

A variety of primers are available, some more effective than others. Ideally the primer should have filling and rust inhibiting qualities and probably the best is red lead primer to BS 2523. This primer has a high degree of corrosion resistance and can deal with a degree of laxity in the initial preparation of the metal and the application of the primer. The material is bright orange-red in colour and should not be confused with the reddish brown/purple red oxide primer which does not chemically inhibit corrosion. Zinc chromate and other zinc rich primers, usually preferred for non-ferrous metals, are satisfactory for surfaces in good condition where exposure conditions are not severe, especially on light sheet steel fabrications. Steel base plates and stanchions below ground floor level are best provided with two coats of a good bituminous paint over the primer for extra protection. Make sure the underside of the base is properly protected.

Galvanised surfaces Where inhibition of rust is not applicable calcium plumbate primers are quite satisfactory. These light buff materials dry quickly and are used on galvanised or similar treated surfaces. Care must be taken to ensure that all surfaces are treated, especially the edges and items such as galvanised steel windows should be painted and restacked to properly dry prior to fixing. If beads are provided these should be removed and primed separately.

Alkali prone surfaces etc Certain materials such as cement/sand rendering, asbestos sheets and insulating boards must be sealed with a coat of an alkali resisting primer if to be finished in a gloss paint. With plasterboard and chipboards a proprietory primer sealer is usually satisfactory. If the finish is emulsion, these primers are unnecessary although the first coat of emulsion is best thinned.

The stopping is to consist of white lead oil paste and putty gauged in the proportions of 1 to 3.
    V51:Yv1.30 et esq. 6151 6201

Stopping and filling should follow priming of timber as holes and surface defects will then be more readily discernable. Good stoppers and fillers are difficult to obtain and internal proprietory materials should never be permitted for external work. Linseed oil putty is unsatisfactory as it shrinks and needs at least 48 hours to harden sufficiently to take paint.

Certain timbers need filling to fill the pores and fine cracks. One timber which especially needs this treatment is oak. A good filler is two full coats of white lead primer allowed to harden and well flatted with a wet abrasive.

Paint one undercoat and two coats gloss finish on all wood and metal surfaces.
    V51:5551 V52:Ya0.06 V52:1 V52:2 V52:3 V52:4

As the primer is of vital importance in determining the life of a painting system, before applying any undercoats it should be examined to determine its condition. If there has been considerable delay in applying protective coats to primed external joinery, the primer may have become powdery, brittle or peeling and must therefore be removed by scraping and sanding, and the whole reprimed. Any bare areas of wood due to the removal of bracing or wear should be touched in.

Undercoats|must be of the same manufacture as the finishing coat and the use of emulsion paint instead of undercoats for interior work should be condemned. Better protection for exterior work is provided with two finishing coats but one may be adequate for interior work. Not all gloss paints are suitable for 'gloss on gloss' application and the manufacturer's instructions should be followed. Where a very high degree of finish is required with rubbing down specified between successive coats a minimum of two undercoats should be provided.

Most gloss and flat paints are alkyd based with appropriate undercoats. One paint will cover both internal and external applications. Thixotropic paints, while possessing certain advantages in application, appear to have less durability than conventional paints. White lead paint is still available to BS 2526 – 7 but has the disadvantage of toxicity and darkening in polluted atmospheres.

Single pack polyeurethene paints are useful indoors for hard wear but externally tend to chalk and offer no exceptional durability on wood.

Prepare and paint three coats emulsion paint on all plastered walls and ceilings
    V52:2

Preparation of the wall surface is important. The plaster should be lightly rubbed down with fine sandpaper and all cracks and holes filled in with filler. If the surface is either very dry or porous a sealing coat of thinned emulsion paint should first be applied followed by two further coats.

This paint system can be employed satisfactorily on plasterboard, asbestos cement sheet and similar surfaces.

Prepare and paint all hardwood doors and frames ...... coats of exterior
    quality varnish (polyurethene)
        V51: 5301 5501 8151

The preparation of surfaces for the application of clear finishes is very important. Any fillers or stopping employed must match the timber employed and after this work has been carried out the surface should be scraped down and lightly sanded before application of any finish.

Varnish used should be interior or exterior grade as appropriate. The first coat should be thinned and this should be followed by two or three further coats unthinned, the latter being applicable for exterior work.

Polyurethene clear finishes are very similar to varnish, become tack free in about two hours and can be re-coated after six to eight. To provide proper intercoat adhesion no more than 24 hours should elapse between coats, otherwise the surface must be thoroughly sanded down before applying a further coat. Most polyurethene finishes are applied in two parts which must be mixed in equal proportions before use. The material remains stable for only about

twelve hours and should then be thrown away. Containers must be kept
stoppered as moisture in the air may cause the material to gel. Thinners
should always be added after mixing or activation.

Varnishes and polyurethene finishes should be applied by brush under dry,
warm conditions. Wet or cold may result in poor drying and lack of adhesion.

*Prepare wall surfaces of lounge and dining room, line with approved lining
paper and finish with decorative wallpapers. P.C. £   per piece. to the
satisfaction of the Architect*

   T11: Ta0.10. Tj2.10. Yt3:11 T11:1 T11:2 T11:4 T11:5 T11:6 T11:7

Wall surfaces for wallpaper must be not only sound but also properly
prepared for the paper. Walls must be structuarlly sound and free from loose
areas of plaster and structural cracks, thoroughly dry, smooth and clean. New
surfaces must have time to dry out properly and be rubbed down smooth to
remove all nibs of plaster and surface irregularities. Old plastered surfaces
must be free from dirt, grease, old distemper, loose or flaking paint, previous
wallpaper and surface irregularities.

Cracks, joints, screw and nail holes should be filled with a proprietory
crack filler and lightly rubbed down to a smooth surface.

Where surfaces have damp or mould growth they should be washed down
with a proprietory mould inhibitor before the wallpaper is hung.

Badly cracked or surfaces of varying porosity should be cross lined with a
good quality lining paper before hanging the finishing paper. The weight of
the lining paper depends on the degree of cracking or porosity. Lining papers
are hung horizontally and adjacent pieces carefully butt jointed not lapped
and allowed to dry out completely before the finishing paper is hung.

Pastes should be appropriate to the type and weight of paper to be employed
but all should incorporate a fungicide. This is especially important for impervious vinyl papers. The paste or adhesive should always be made up and
used strictly in accordance with the manufacturer's instructions.

All rolls of wallpaper should be examined before hanging to ensure matching
shades. Alternate lengths should never be reversed unless specifically required
by the manufacturer's instructions.

Finishing papers, either decorative, embossed or textured, should be hung in
one length with no horizontal joints permitted in the piece. Edges should be
neatly butted and the whole free from stains, tears, bubbles and marks on
completion of drying out. The paper should be cut neatly into extremeties
and margins and hung vertically. With strongly patterned papers or on prom-
inent features, a piece should be hung centrally and the pieces on either side
worked out to the margin. Where elements such as doors intrude strong
pattersn should take this into allowance so that the door does not break
into the pattern asymmetrically and destroy the effect. The way in which

these problems are dealt with by the paperhanger will be a test of his skill. The setting out of strong patterns and expensive papers should always be agreed before hanging to avoid subsequent disappointment.

Surface preparation for wallpaper

New bare plaster

Allow to dry out completely, remove any efflorescence with dry followed by a damp cloth and leave 48 hours. Remove any efflorescence until clear. Clean down, make good cracks, and size with thin coat of adhesive or paste

NOTE: For best results, line all surfaces to be papered

Plasterboard, paper faced baords and soft boards

Clean down, touch in nail and screw heads with metal primer, fill, apply feather edge tape to all flush joints, prime alkali resisting primer, rub down and dust off

Expanded polystyrene wall insulation

Clean down surface from dust etc., fill as required and cross line with heavy quality lining paper

Previously painted surfaces

Emulsion – clean down and dust off, make good cracks and size with thinned adhesive or paste

Non-washable distemper

Wash down and scrape to clean surface, make good cracks and size with thinned coat of adhesive or paste

Gloss, eggshell or flat oil

Wash down with soap and water and while wet rub down with medium grade · abrasive paper. Rinse off and dry and line with medium quality lining paper

After preparation and where specified priming, sizing or lining, hang the wall covering using adhesives or paste recommended by the manufacturers. The lining should be hung using the same adhesive.

Paper should be hung by applying an even coat of adhesive to the back of one piece at a time, ensuring that all edges are well pasted. The paper should be hung with butt joints and smoothed down firmly on the wall using a brush or damp sponge and taking care to remove all bubbles. Surplus paste should be removed from the face and not allowed to dry on. Light weight and washable wallpapers can be hung as soon as pasted but allow heavy papers to soak until they have become supple. Vinyl papers should not be soaked in adhesive.

18 Drainlaying

BSCP 301: 1971 Building drainage
BRS Digests 124 and 125 First Series
130 and 131 Second Series

The basic principle to be followed in the provision of drainage works is common to all materials used. This is simply to collect soil and stormwater in a suitable manner and discharge this to a public sewer or suitable outfall without causing nuisance or hazards to health. The system should be self cleansing and operate with the minimum of maintenance.

Include the Provisional Sum of £. . . . . . . for connecting the drains to the local authority sewer.

(5)11: 1251 1252

The position and depth of the outfall should be checked before any work is started on the drain runs. Information obtained from local authorities is often approximate and can, in some cases, be misleading. Notice must be served on the authority of intention to make connection and, if necessary, to open up the roads and footpath. The location work to find the sewer, details of protection to prevent any accident to the general public and reinstatement provisions will be dealt with as a separate specification clause. It is usual to bring the connection onto the site and connect to the last manhole so that this length can be tested and filled in as soon as possible. It is the contractor's responsibility to ensure that reinstatement meets the requirements of the highway authority.

The actual connection to the sewer is generally made by the staff of the local authority. The usual method is to cut a hole in the sewer pipe and attach to it a saddle branch set at the appropriate angle and position to receive the drain. The drain from the last manhole to the saddle will often be at very much steeper incline than that normally permitted for private drains, due to the considerable depths at which sewers are often constructed. In most cases it will be a requirement of the local authority and/or highway authority that the whole of the excavation be backfilled with weak concrete 1:12 to prevent subsidence, so far as is practicable. While the value of work can usually be assessed with some accuracy, the cost of the saddle connection is based on the time involved and charged accordingly. Consequently a Provisional Sum is used to meet the unknown factors in this instance.

*Drainpipes will be laid in straight runs to even and regular falls.
(5)11: 3051*

Drains must be laid in straight runs between manholes or similar access points
and with even and regular falls to reduce the risk of blockage and to regulate
the velocity of effluent to an even flow. Minimum gradients for soil drains are:

Nom. bore (mm)	Gradient	No. of living units connected or equivalent
100	1 in 80	5
150	1 in 150	10

Where flows are small or the drain is long, steeper gradients may be necessary.
These generally should be not less than 1 in 40.

The line of drains can be disturbed during backfilling, especially when the
pipes are laid on beds of compacted fill. Disturbance to line or fall can be
checked between manholes by shining a torch down from one end and the
use of a mirror at the other. Blockages, wholly or partially, of the pipe can
be located in this way.

*Construct new manholes in positions to the sizes and depths shown on
   drawings and in accordance with the following specification ....
   (or BSCP 303: 1952).
   C11:1 Y31 F11:F*

Access is required to drains for various purposes and is usually provided by
means of inspection chambers or manholes. The guiding principle should be
to provide access to allow every length of drain to be accessible for maintenance, and in any case at intervals not exceeding 90 m as follows:

At changes of direction
At changes of gradient
At junctions, unless other methods of access for cleaning are provided
Within 12 m of a junction between two drains where no chamber is provided
At the head of each length of drain (a rodding eye may suffice here)

The size of manhole depends on the angle and depth o the main run and the
number and position of branches. The size should allow any branch or drain
run to be cleared with rods operated from the surface. A guide for minimum
manhole sizes is as follows:

Invert depth (m)	Size 1 x b (m)
Up to 0.9	0.75 x 0.70
0.9 to 2.7	1.2 x 0.75

These sizes are for manholes providing access only for maintenance. The
length of manholes with branches should be calculated by allowing 300 mm
(375 mm) for each 100 mm (150 mm) nominal bore branch plus 300 mm for
the downstream end for the angle of entry and the width by allowing 600 mm
for benching plus the nominal bore of the main drain. Where no branches

occur the overall width of the benching can be reduced to 300 mm.
Branch manholes should be constructed of clay engineering bricks to BS 3921.
Pt. 2 Class B in English bond in cement mortar (1:3) using sulphate resisting
cement where applicable. Internally manholes should not be rendered. The
wall thickness should be not less than 225 mm reducing to 112 mm thick at
depths less than 0.9 mm. The manhole should be built on a concrete base
not less than 150 mm thick and provided with a similar cover perforated
and rebated for a cover and frame. The concrete should be as recommended
in BSCP 301: 1971.

Precast concrete sectional manholes to BS 556 are useful in waterlogged
ground but as their joints are difficult to make watertight in these conditions,
they should be surrounded in 150 mm of concrete, care being taken to push
this under and around incoming and outgoing connections. These manholes
are usually set on a base similar to brick manholes.

Cast iron manholes are usual in cast iron drains within buildings as these are
air and watertight with their bolted covers. A bed of concrete is usually
provided with enclosing walls similar to a normal brick manhole and a cover
and frame usually made to allow the floor finish to be laid in it and improve
appearances.

G.R.P. and unplasticised P.V.C. manholes can also be obtained and these are
fixed in accordance with their manufacturer's particular recommendations.
The channel in most brick and concrete manholes is formed from half round
vitrified clay channels with tapers or junctions as required. Some precast
manholes incorporate integral channels and branches finished smooth in
fine concrete. Otherwise side branches are formed with branch bends, three
quarter section for soil drains designed with a uniform projection of 300 mm
and bedded and pointed in cement mortar (1:3). Benching should rise vertically
off the top edge of the channel at least to the soffite of the outlet and then
be sloped back to the wall at an angle of 1:12. The finish should be floated
level and smooth in cement mortar (1:2) laid monolithic with the benching.
Where levels so dictate, a backdrop manhole may be used with the vertical
pipe placed outside the manhole. Rodding access at the upper inlet level
should be provided within the manhole and the sweeps in the junction and
at the foot of the pipe of easy radius. The whole should be cased in concrete
not less than 150 mm. all round.

Access frames should be bedded in cement and sand (1:3) and the covers in
a non hardening compound. A proprietory grease produced for this purpose
is very satisfactory.

*The whole of the drainage system shall be tested when laid and again on
    completion of the contract to the satisfaction of (Architect or Supervising
    Officer) and the local authority. Any lengths, fittings or construction*

found to be faulty will be taken up, relaid or reconstructed and re-tested until satisfactory. Testing will be by water generally as laid down in BSCP 301: 1971.
(5)11:5 (5)22:4

It is not satisfactory to accept the test carried out on the drains by the contractor for the local authority. The supervising officer should either be present at the test or arrange for his own test in conjunction with the contractor. Drains should be tested twice, once when the runs have been installed and before they have been bedded or concreted and again at the termination of the contract. The first test is to ensure that the pipes are sound and the joints watertight at a time when remedial action is cheaply and easily effected. The second test is carried out to ensure that concreting or bedding and backfilling excavated material over the drain and subsequent site traffic has not damaged the runs in any way. In addition, any rubbish or temporary plugs which may have been left in the pipes and overlooked will be found and cleared out immediately before the building is handed over.

BSCP 301: 1971 provides for both water and air testing. The tests prescribed are realistic and, providing the pipes used conform to the relevant BSS and the joints are properly and carefully made, a reliable indication of any faults or defects. The water test is preferable for site use as it more closely follows normal useage, although very few drains run full bore as tested. It must be remembered that most individual pipes contain small pores which need to be filled by absorbtion into the pipe wall when the drain is first filled with water. To counteract this problem most contractors will put the runs on test a day or two before the official test. In addition to filling the pores with water and reducing the amount of initial loss to a minimum this preliminary check will indicate whether the runs are satisfactory enabling any remedial work to be carried out prior to the official test.

Some loss of water must be permitted in a water test to allow maximum initial absorbtion normally necessary in any newly constructed drain. The permitted loss allowed in the CP for drains up to 300 mm nominal bore should not exceed 0.06 litre/hour/100 m run of drain/mm of normal bore. As the loss is, in practice measured over a period of 30 minutes the permitted loss is as follows:

Nom. bore (mm)	Permitted loss/100 m run (litres)
100	3
150	4.5

All drains, manholes and inspection chambers should be capable of withstanding the appropriate test. The tests should be carried out from manhole to manhole, short branches from the main drain being tested with the appropriate run. Long branches should be tested separately and steep gradients whose total fall exceeds the required test head of water should be tested in sections to avoid under or excessive pressure on the pipes and joints.

Before the test is carried out the drains should be inspected for obvious faults. The runs should be straight and inverts level between manholes, pipes properly supported at the collars with joints neatly and correctly made in the approved manner. Each plug inserted should be done in the presence of the supervising officer.

The water test should be carried out by inserting suitable proprietory plugs in the low end of the drain run and, if necessary, in any branch connections and filling the whole run under test with water. A test head of 1.2 m head of water above the top of the drain should be applied at the upper end but care must be taken to see that the head of water does not exceed 2.4 m at the low end of the drain under test. If it does the length should be tested in the appropriate lengths. To provide the correct head of water at the top end a bend and straight run of pipe of the same bore is temporarily jointed to the run to provide 1.2 m head. Where the manhole is deep enough this can be tested by filling with water to the depth required. After filling the drain should be left for an hour before test readings are taken.

The test should be carried out by noting the original level of the water and adding more from a measuring vessel at regular intervals of 10 minutes, noting the quantity of water required to maintain the original level of water at the standpipe. In practice, if the water level drops slowly over the initial period of the test, then remains stationary and there is no evidence of leakage from pipes or joints, for all practical purposes, the run is sound. While under test the runs and joints should be inspected for leaks and any such defects marked for remedial action. A further test will generally be required to see that this has been properly carried out.

The final test at the end of the contract is usually carried out, subject to not exceeding the prescribed heads of water, by inserting a plug in the inlet of the top manhole and filling the system up with water above this point. A continual loss will indicate a fractured or crushed pipe and need action to locate and open up the drain for remedial work. By inserting a further plug in the next section of drain, water from the upper can be re-used, saving both time and water. If the soffite of the drain is below the water table at its highest the manholes should be inspected for infiltration which would lead to pollution.

Air testing by internal air pressure is not very often used for drain testing in new work. It is used mainly for testing soil stacks, where air testing is most suitable. Both ends of the stack are plugged off and air is pumped in from a hand pump until a pressure of 100 mm head of water is measured on a U tube connected to the system. If traps are incorporated in the system, e.g. W.C.

traps and wastes, these should be filled with water and the pressure reduced to 50 mm head of water. Over a 5 minute period the air pressure should not fall below 75 mm for untrapped sealed stacks and 12.5 mm with trapped stacks. If the stack does not hold up to pressure either the pipe, the joints or the traps are faulty.

A smoke rocket or a piece of ignited bitumen felt inserted into the pipe and the plug refitted would fill the whole with smoke, which leaking from the defect would indicate its position.

Pitch Fibre drains:
BS 2760: Pt. 1: 1966 Pitch fibre pipes
*   Pt. 2: 1967 Fittings*

Soil drains will be formed from pitch fibre pipes and fittings conforming to BS 2760, laid, jointed and connected strictly in accordance with the manufacturers recommendations.
(5)11: 1n2.10 (5)11:3+ (5)11: 4401 4451 (5)11: 6101 6151

Pitch fibre pipes are made in two lengths and a variety of diameters. They are also made to incorporate two distinct jointing methods using butt or tapered joints.

Nom. bore (mm)	2.4 mm – 3.4 mm		Butt joint	Tapered joint
50	o			o
75	o		o	
100	o	o	o	
150	o		o	
200	o			o
225	o			o

Butt jointed pipes are joined together by connecting two plain end pipes or fittings with a socketed polypropylene coupling and two rubber D rings. To make the snap joint, a D ring is first fitted to a plain end and the pipe and ring pushed into the coupling. Plain ended pipes can be fitted to a socketted polypropylene fitting direct with one rubber D ring.

Tapered pipes can be connected to another tapered pipe or a pitch fibre tapered fitting with a pitch fibre or polypropylene tapered coupling, the $2°$ male and female tapered ends being complementary to each other. The joint is made by driving one pipe onto the other with a wooden dolly.

Adaptors are manufactured which allow pitch fibre pipes to be jointed to stoneware square ends (using one D ring only), the adaptor incorporating a socket to suit plain end cast iron pipes, with an internal split C coupling and outer sleeve, both using pipes of the same internal diameter. Pitch fibre

pipes of different diameters can be joined with polypropylene socketted
level invert tapers sized

100 – 75 mm

150 – 100 mm

All socketed bends, junctions (both equal and unequal), end caps and
adaptors (except pitch fibre to stoneware and cast iron spigots of the same
diameter) are made in black polypropylene. The range of pitch fibre fittings
include tapered end junctions (equal and unequal), sweep bends, half round
channels and channel bends and P trap gullies.

Pitch fibre pipes and fittings are very light and the pipes can be stored out of
doors on clean level ground by stacking in pyramid formation not more than
1200 mm high retaining the bottom layer with driven stakes.

Polypropylene fittings and D rings should be stored in frost free covered
storage until required for use as the materials lose resilience at temperatures
near freezing point.

Pipes can be cut using a coarse-toothed carpenter's hand saw and male tapers
can be turned from plain ended pipe using a field tool and pipe vice.

Care must be taken in assembly to ensure an air and watertight joint. Pipe
ends should be clean and dry and the D ring must not be twisted on the pipe.
Tapered joints should always be made by driving the wooden dolly against a
coupling, never against an unprotected male taper. Tapers should be clean
and dry before fitting on coupling, a firm backstop should be used and driving
should continue until firm resistance is reached. Temporary supports should
be provided when driving joints at junctions and bends.

Installation: trenches should be excavated 100 mm deeper than the required
pipe invert level and the bottom prepared by removing any projection stones
or dead tree roots. For bedding pea gravel, broken clinker, all-in aggregate,
quarry scapplings, ballast or shingle to pass a 19 mm screen and with less than
5% fines are suitable. Excavated material may also be used for bedding and
side fill. All materials must pass a compaction test as follows:

Fill a 250 mm length of 150 mm pipe, standing upright on a flat surface, with
a representative soil sample from the trench and strike off level with the top
without tamping. Remove the pipe, place beside collapsed soil sample, fill
the pipe with a quarter of the material at a time, well ramming with a metal
hammer with a 36 mm head until the whole sample has been used. Tamp the
material until no further compaction takes place and leave surface level.
Measure the distance between the level of the spoil and top of the pipe. If
the distance is more than 76 mm the soil is not suitable. If less than 76 mm
the material is suitable for different conditions as follows:

Distance – level of spoil/top of pipe	Suitability of material
Up to 50 mm	Suitable for back and side filling in all conditions
Up to 25 mm	For surrounding pipes jointed to structures where settlement is expected
38 to 50 mm	For waterlogged conditions
51 to 75 mm	Suitable on dry sites only, care must be taken on compacting

Pipes are laid on a 100 mm deep bed which has been well compacted by treading keeping correct gradient. Pipe lengths are jointed at ground level, fed into the excavation and laid direct onto the prepared bedding. Side filling is carried out by placing material equally on either side of the pipe and compacting by hand until the level of the pipe crown is reached. Spoil for backfilling should pass a 38 mm screen, placed to a depth of 150 mm over the crown of the pipe, compacted by treading and the process repeated with compaction by hand ramming to a depth of a further 150 mm. The rest of the fill can be placed and mechanically compacted.

Pitch fibre pipes under slab construction should have the trench formed through compacted hardcore, the pipe set 150 mm below the proposed level of the underside of the slab and surrounded with material to pass a 19 mm screen.

Pipes tightly jointed to manholes, and similar structures under buildings where settlement is likely, should be surrounded with granular material as above for at least 600 mm from the structure. Pipes through walls should have at least 50 mm clearance round the pipe.

It is not necessary to case pitch fibre pipes under buildings.

Pitch fibre drains under flexible road formations should be cased in concrete if the crown is less than 600 mm below the road surface.

Pitch fibre pipes depend on their efficiency on the care with which joints are made and in the formation of the bed. Properly and carefully made joints will stand up to air or water testing carried out in accordance with BSCP 303: 1952. If the bed is formed as suggested, problems of settlement and disruption of the pipeline will be minimised. On no account should the pipe runs be supported on bricks or blocks of wood, frozen material or vegetable matter. These materials could cause denting or failure of the pipeline when the backfill is placed.

Vitrified clayware drains:
BS 65 and 540 Pt. 1: 1971 Vitrified clayware pipes
BS 539: 1971 Dimensions of fittings for use with clay drain and sewer pipes

*Soil drains will be formed from plain end vitrified clay pipes and fittings
  with polypropylene couplings conforming strictly to BS 65 and 540 Pt. 1:
  1971, laid, jointed and connected strictly in accordance with the
  manufacturer's recommendations.*
  (5)11: 1g3.20 (5)11:3+ (5)11: 4201 (5)11: 6101 6151

Plain and vitrified clay pipes with flexible couplings are made in two sizes and
lengths as follows:

Nom. bore (mm)	Effective length (m)
100	1.25 – 1.6
150	1.6

The system comprises plain ended pipes which are connected with push fit
couplings moulded in polypropylene incorporating rubber sealing gaskets.
Adaptors are available to provide direct coupling to terminal fittings. The
pipes can be cut and trimmed to length by means of special tools to provide
jointing by the standard coupling. The action of pushing a pipe or fitting into
the coupling after applying a proprietory lubricant to the pipe end compresses
the sealing gasket to make a pressure tight flexible joint.

The system incorporates a good range of fittings including tapers, bends,
channel fittings, junctions, gullies, raising pieces, hoppers and inspection
chambers complete with channels and covers moulded in GRP. Inspection
chambers are 450 mm diameter, made in two standard depths of 610 and
915 mm. Particular requirements to suit site conditions can be provided by
cutting off the surplus with a hacksaw.

Concrete bedding and haunch is not normally required as these pipes are
within the super strength category (2800 kg/m) of BSS 65 and 540 Pt. 1:
1971, Amendment Slip No. 1 published 29th June 1973: and are suitable for
laying directly on the trimmed natural trench bottom. Granular bedding
material if required should conform to the test laid down for bedding
material under pitch fibre pipes.

Although pipes should be laid strictly to even gradients and line, displacement
laterally by 10 mm at each joint, angular movement of 5° per joint or linear
draw of 20 mm per joint will not affect the seal at a pressure of 1.4 m water
head. Care should be taken to ensure line and gradient comply with the general
requirements for drainage, joints are properly formed, the trench bottom is
free from projecting stones, rock, dead tree roots and similar obstructions and
the side and backfilling are carried out as described for pitch fibre pipes.

*Soil drains will be formed from glazed vitreous clay spigot and socketed
  pipes and fittings conforming strictly to BSS 65 and 540 Pt. 1: 1971,
  laid, jointed and connected strictly in accordance with BSCP 301, 1071.*
  (5)11: 1g3.10. (5)11: 3251 3601 (5)11: 4101 4151

Vitrified clayware pipes for drainage are produced in two classes, (i) for foul and surface water designated British Standard and (ii) for surface water only and designated British Standard Surface Water. The latter pipes can be obtained perforated for subsoil drainage. The pipes are stamped as above to certify the category into which they fall. In addition, pipes are available in 'standard' and 'extra strength', pipes conforming to the latter requirement being so marked.

BSS 65 and 540 do not insist on pipes being glazed. In fact, unglazed are acceptable as well as pipes which are glazed on the interior only or on both exterior and interior. The glaze may be salt or ceramic glaze.

Vitrified clayware pipes can be obtained in a variety of sizes and lengths to suit site requirements. Those suitable for small projects are as follows:

Nom. bore (mm)	Effective length excluding socket (mm)		
75	0.3	0.6	
100)	0.3	0.6	0.9
150)			
225)	1.0	1.2	1.5

Pipes should always be inspected before laying as they are liable to damage in transit or storage. Damage is especially prevelent to the sockets and any defective or with broken or badly chipped sockets should be set aside. The protective coating should be examined for omission and any pipes with major defects should be condemned. When stacked the bottom layer should be set on tubes to keep the sockets off the ground and the end pipes.securely chocked to prevent collapse of the stack. Pipes with factory applied jointing materials should be stacked in accordance with the maker's instructions and each pipe carefully examined before laying.

Jointing can be effected by either rigid or flexible methods. The traditional rigid joint comprises tarred gaskin caulked into the joint, the joint fully filled with cement/sand 1:2 with a bold splayed collar to seal the joint. The pipes should be wetted before jointing and the joints kept damp and protected from sun and wind until the trench is back filled. Flexible joints use sealing rings or 0 rings and care must be taken to see that whether the sealing faces of the pipes are wet or dry they are free from soil, mud, oil or grease. Sealing rings by various makers should not be mixed and only those recommended by the pipe manufacturers should be used together with lubricants supplied. In any event the correct gap should be left between the shoulder of the socket and the end of the spigot. Mechanical pulling devices which obtain their leverage on the socket of the last laid pipe may be used but levering against the pipe socket by a shovel disturbs the bed and should be discouraged. Flexible joints should always be provided close to each wall face when pipes pass through walls or are connected to manholes.

Pipe runs should be tested before placing on bedding concrete to reveal cracked or defective pipes or unsatisfactory joints. Methods of testing are described earlier in this chapter. Drains under test should be provided with support from stout raking pegs, removed before concrete or backfill is commenced.

The type of joint used will generally determine the method of bedding the pipe. Vitrified clay pipes with rigid joints are generally laid on a concrete bed. The bottom of the trench should be prepared with a blinding coat of concrete (1:12) at least 50 mm thick and the pipes supported clear of the trench bottom on blocks placed immediately behind the socket. With long pipes a second block near the spigot end is sometimes necessary. A resilient pad of bitumen impregnated felt on top fo the block will assist in permitting the barrel of the pipe to rest uniformly on its bed after the normal setting shrinkage of the concrete. The clearance under the pipe barrel should be 100 mm and the bed should extend a minimum of 100 mm on either side of the pipe.

This type of bedding is quite satisfactory for vitrified clay pipes with flexible joints but the bedding should be provided with a flexible construction joint at the face of a pipe joint at intervals not exceeding 5 m. After testing, the pipes should be flaunched up to the top of the pipe with concrete splayed off on either side from a point level with the centre point of the pipe. Vitrified clay drain runs under buildings and in similar situations should be cased in 150 mm concrete all round before backfilling. Backfilling to the trench should not commence until the concrete bed has fully developed strength, preferably seven days being allowed from the date the concrete bed was originally laid. Backfilling with selected excavated material should follow the methods described for pitch fibre drains.

Cast iron drains:
BS 437 Pt. 1: 1970 Cast iron pipes
BS 1130: 1943 Schedule of cast iron drain fittings
          Spigot and socket type for use with drain pipes to BS 437

*Soil drains under the building will be formed from cast iron spigot and socketted drain pipes and fittings conforming strictly to BS 437 Pt. 1 1970, and BS 1130: 1943, laid, jointed and connected in accordance with BSCP 301: 1971.
          (5)11: 1h1.10. (5)11: 3251 3601 (5)11: 4301
Cast iron pipes suitable for both stormwater and soil drains are spigot and socketted and made in the following diameters and lengths:-

Nom. bore (mm)	Effective length excluding socket (m)	Effective length ex. Double socket (m)
50	1.3	
75)		
100)	1.83	
150)	2.74	1.83
225)	3.66	

(Short lengths are also usually available)

As cast iron pipes are very liable to corrosion they should not be laid un-protected in soils which contain corrosive elements or be used to convey acid wastes. The pipes are coated with a mixture having a bitumen or tar base which provides a smooth hard tenacious coating. Cast iron drains are generally used under buildings and their strength and general characteristics make them suitable for this situation. Fittings comprise bolted and airtight covers in a wide variety enabling branches with sealed access to be incorporated in drain runs. Joining is by means of tarred gaskin or lead wool well caulked in with a run lead joint, or the use of a cementitious caulking compound, generally in rope form well caulked into the joint.

The bedding and support of iron pipes is generally as described for vitrified clay pipes but the flaunching is taken up tangentially from the edge of the bedding to meet the pipe. Backfilling is as previously described. Precautions for settlement should be taken by the use of cementitious joints and expansion joints through the concrete bed as described for vitrified clay drains.

Unplasticised pvc drains:
BS 4660: 1971 Unplasticised p.v.c. underground drain pipes and fittings

*Soil drains will be formed from unplasticised P.V.C. underground drain pipes and fittings conforming to BS 4660: 1971, laid and jointed in accordance with the manufacturer's recommendations and the relevant portions of BSCP 301: 1971.
(5)11: 1m6.10 (5)11: 3403 (5)11: 4501

Unplasticised PVC pipes and fittings for underground drainage are produced in one grade only suitable for both soil and stormwater use. The pipes are produced with either a ring seal socket and plain spigot or double spigot ends and one manufacturer produces pipes with solvent sockets. This enables certain ancillary fittings, which have to be jointed by the solvent cement method, to be set in the drain run without the use of special sockets otherwise wise required.

The two systems in general use are produced in distinctive colours allowing pipes and fittings to be easily identified. All pipes and fittings should be selected from the same manufacturer's range and no intermingling should be

permitted. All systems used should be manufactured in accordance with BS 4660 (and carry the Kite mark for this standard) and carry Agrement Board Certificates of Approval.
Unplasticised p.v.c. pipes can be obtained in a variety of sizes and lengths to suit site requirements. Those suitable for small projects are as follows:

Nom. bore (mm)	Effective length excluding socket (m)	
	(a) Ring seal socket	(b) Solvent socket
110	1.0, 3.0, 6.0.	1.0, 3.0.
160	3.0, 6.0.	3.0.

Plain ended pipes in both bores can be obtained in 3.0 and 6.0 lengths. Pipes should always be insepcted before laying to ensure that they have not been damaged in transit or storage. Damage is usually confined to pipe ends although damage can be caused by crushing or by abrasion. Any pipes so damaged should be cut down for use as plain ended sections and the damaged portions discarded. Pipes and fittings should preferably be stored under cover in fully supported racking. This should be divided into sections to prevent overloading or distortion of the bottom layers.·
Jointing is usually effected by means of a ring seal. This is simple, effective and allows a degree of movement to take place without joint failure. Care must be taken to see that all mating surfaces are clean and free from grease and dirt, that the spigot chamfer is properly lubricated with the manufacturer's recommended jointing lubricant and that the spigot is not inserted into the socket beyond the depth of entry mark at the edge of the socket. As pipes are generally jointed on the surface and lowered into the trench the movement joint must be checked again to see that the correct expansion gap is provided. Certain fittings have to be jointed by the solvent cement method. The mating surfaces should be clean and free from all dirt, grease and swarf. One manufacturer recommends that the surfaces should be roughened with sandpaper and cleaned with a cleaning fluid applied with a clean cloth, but this view is not universal. The mating surfaces should then be liberally applied with the correct solvent cement, the spigot inserted in the socket, turned slightly to ensure even distribution of the cement and excess cement removed. The joint should then be left to harden.
Various adaptors are manufactured to allow connection between PVC pipes and cast iron and stoneware (plain and or spigot and socketted). The joints between uPVC and these materials are formed as follows:

uPVC/stoneware socket — gaskin and 2:1 cement/sand using special adaptor
uPVC/stoneware/C.i. spigot — ditto
uPVC/c.i. socket — gaskin and lead caulking or PC4 asbestos caulking compound using special adaptor

Cutting uPVC pipes is best carried out with a fine toothed saw and the cut end must be chamfered to at least 10 mm from the end using a rasp or Surform cutter. The insertion depth should then be marked on the pipe barrel to ensure that proper allowance for movement will be made when the joint is made.

Trenches should be opened up immediately before pipe laying and should be backfilled as soon as possible after the pipework is installed. The preparation of the trench bottom, bedding material and backfilling are all as described for pitch fibre drains.

This system of drainage makes use of proprietory rodding eyes to dispense with manholes in many situations. In addition, special uPVC access pit bowls are available which replace the traditional brick or concrete manhole in many instances. The design of installations incorporating the latter are usually carried out by the specialist supplier. While the bowl can be bedded on granular backfill, it must be cased in concrete to provide rigidity protection and a base for bedding the traditional cast iron cover and frame which seals the system. Rodding eyes are usually provided with a precast concrete or cast iron frame and cover depending on manufacturer, and preformed manholes and manhole bases are also available.

Conditions of the RIBA Agreement for Minor Building Works

Contractor's Obligation 1 The Contractor shall with due diligence and in a good and workmanlike manner carry out and complete the Works to the reasonable satisfaction of the Architect/Supervising Officer.

Architect/ Supervising Officer's Instructions 2 (i) The Architect/Supervising Officer may issue written instructions which the Contractor shall forthwith carry out. If instructions are given orally they shall forthwith be confirmed in writing by the Architect/Supervising Officer.

(ii) The Architect/Supervising Officer may, without invalidating the contract, order an addition to or omission from or other change in the Works or the order or period in which they are to be carried out and any such instruction shall be valued by the Architect/Supervising Officer on a fair and reasonable basis.

Provisional or Prime Cost Sums (iii) The Architect/Supervising Officer shall issue instructions as to the expenditure of any provisional or prime cost sums and such instructions shall be valued on a fair and reasonable basis. Provided that no instruction under this sub-clause shall require the Contractor to enter into a sub-contract for work and materials which does not allow the Contractor a cash discount of 2½% if payment is made within 14 days after the date fixed for payment under the sub-contract or into a contract of sale which does not allow the contractor a cash discount of 5% if payment is made within 30 days of the end of the month during which delivery is made.

(iv) Instead of the valuation referred to in sub-clauses (ii) and (iii) hereof, an inclusive price may be agreed between the Architect/Supervising Officer and the Contractor prior to the Contractor carrying out any instruction such as referred to in those sub-clauses.

Statutory Obligations Fees and Charges 3 The Contractor shall comply with all notices required by any statute, any statutory instrument, rule or order or any regulation or byelaw applicable to the Works and shall pay all fees and charges in respect of the Works legally recoverable from him.

Contractor's Representative 4 The Contractor shall at all reasonable times keep upon the Works a competent person in charge.

Sub-Contracting 5 The Contractor shall not sub-contract the Works or any part thereof without the written consent of the Architect/Supervising Officer which consent shall not unreasonably be withheld.

Commencement, Progress and Completion 6 (i) The Works may be commenced on

....

and shall be completed by

....

(ii) If it becomes apparent that the Works will not be completed by the date for completion inserted in Sub-Clause (i) hereof (or any extended date inserted therein in accordance with the provisions of this sub-clause) for reasons beyond the control of the Contractor, then the Contractor shall so notify the Architect/Supervising Officer who shall extend the time for completion by a reasonable period.

(iii) If the Works are not completed by the completion date inserted in sub-clause (i) hereof or by any extended completion date fixed under sub-clause (ii) hereof then the Contractor shall pay to the Employer liquidated damages at the rate of £................... per week for every week or part of a week during which the Works remain uncompleted.

Injury to or Death of Persons 7 (i) The Contractor shall be liable for and shall indemnify the Employer against any liability, loss, claim or proceedings whatsoever arising under any statute or at common law in respect of personal injury to or death of any person whomsoever arising out of or in the course of or caused by the carrying out of the Works unless due to any act or neglect of the Employer, or of any person for whom the Employer is responsible. Without prejudice to his liability to indemnify the Employer the Contractor shall maintain and shall cause any sub-contractor to maintain such insurances as are necessary to cover the liability of the Contractor or, as the case may be, of such sub-contractor, in respect of personal injuries or deaths arising out of or in the course of or caused by the carrying out of the Works. Provided that nothing in this sub-clause contained shall impose any liability on the sub-contractor in respect of negligence or breach of duty on the part of the Employer, the Contractor, his other sub-contractors or their respective servants or agents.

Damage to Property (ii) The Contractor shall, subject to Clause 8, be liable for and indemnify the Employer against and insure and cause any sub-contractor to insure against any expense, liability, loss, claim or proceedings in respect of any damage whatsoever to any real or personal property to an amount of £50,000/................... for any one occurrence* insofar as such damage arises out of or in the course of or by reason of the carrying out of the Works and is due to any negligence, omission or default of the Contractor or any person for whom the Contractor is responsible or of any sub-contractor or person for whom the sub-contractor is responsible.

Insurances – Persons and Property (iii) The Contractor shall produce, and shall cause any sub-contractor to produce, such evidence as the Employer may reasonably

---

* *The cover suggested should be reviewed having regard to the nature of the Works and the place where they are to be carried out. If different cover is required delete £50,000 and substitute agreed figure.*

require that the insurances referred to in sub-clauses (i) and (ii) hereof have been taken out and are in force at all material times.

Insurance of the Works–Fire, etc.–Existing Structures

8 (i) The Works (and the existing structures together with the contents thereof owned by him and for which he is responsible)* and all unfixed materials and goods intended for, delivered to, placed on or adjacent to the Works and intended therefor (except temporary buildings, plant, tools and equipment owned or hired by the Contractor or any sub-contractor) shall be at the sole risk of the Employer as regards loss or damage by fire, lightning, explosion, storm, tempest, flood, bursting or overflowing water tanks, apparatus or pipes, earthquake, aircraft and other aerial devices or articles dropped therefrom riot and civil commotion, and the Employer shall maintain adequate insurance against that risk.

(ii) If any loss or damage as referred to in sub-clause (i) hereof occurs then the Architect/Supervising Officer shall issue instructions under Clause 2 as soon as may be practicable.

Practical Completion–Defects Liability

9 (i) The Architect Supervising Officer shall certify the date when in his opinion the Works have been practically completed.

(ii) Any defects, excessive shrinkages or other faults which appear within 3 months† of the date of practical completion and are due to materials or workmanship not in accordance with the contract or frost occurring before practical completion shall be made good by the Contractor entirely at his own cost unless the Architect/Supervising Officer shall otherwise instruct.

(iii) The Architect/Supervising Officer shall certify the date when in his opinion the Contractor's obligations under this Clause have been discharged.

Payment–Interim Payments

10 (i) If the period for completion of the Works exceeds 2 months the Architect/Supervising Officer shall if requested by the Contractor at intervals of 4 weeks calculated from the date for commencement inserted in Clause 6(i) certify interim payments to the Contractor in respect of the value of the Works executed, including any materials and goods on site for the purposes of the Works and any amounts either ascertained or agreed under Clause 2, and the Employer shall pay to the Contractor the amount so certified within 14 days of the date of the certificate.

Payment–Penultimate Certificate

(ii) Provided the Contractor shall have supplied all documentation reasonably necessary for the computation of the amount to be certified the Architect/Supervising Officer shall 10 days after the date of practical completion certified under Clause 9(i) certify payment to the Contractor of 95% of the total amount to be paid to the Contractor under the contract in-

cluding any amounts ascertained or agreed under Clause 2 less only the amount of any interim payments made under sub-clause (i) hereof and the Employer shall pay to the Contractor the amount so certified within 14 days of that certificate.

Payments–Final Certificate

(iii) Provided the Contractor shall have supplied all documentation reasonably necessary for the computation of the amount to be certified the Architect/Supervising Officer shall 10 days after the date certified under Clause 9(iii) issue a final certificate certifying the amount remaining due to the Contractor or due to the Employer as the case may be and such sum shall as from the 14th day after the date of the final certificate be a debt payable as the case may be by the Employer to the Contractor or by the Contractor to the Employer.

Fair Wages

11 The Contractor shall in respect of all persons employed by him (whether in the execution of this Agreement or otherwise) in every factory, workshop or place occupied or used by him for the execution of this Agreement comply with the conditions of the Fair Wages Resolution passed by the House of Commons on the 14th October 1946 or any amendment thereof.

Determination by Employer

12 The Employer may but not unreasonably or vexatiously by notice by registered post or recorded delivery to the Contractor forthwith determine the employment of the Contractor under this Contract if the Contractor shall make default in any one or more of the following respects that is to say:

(i) if the Contractor without reasonable cause fails to proceed diligently with the Works or wholly suspends the carrying out of the Works before completion;

(ii) if the Contractor becomes bankrupt or makes any composition or arrangement with his creditors or has a winding up order made or a resolution for voluntary winding up passed or a Receiver or Manager of his business is appointed or possession is taken by or on behalf of any creditor of any property the subject of a Charge.

Provided always that the right of determination shall be without prejudice to any other rights or remedies which the Employer may possess.

Determination by Contractor

13 The Contractor may but not unreasonably or vexatiously by notice by registered post or recorded delivery to the Employer forthwith determine the employment of the Contractor under this Contract if the Employer shall make default in any one or more of the following respects that is to say:

(i) if the Employer fails to make any interim payment due under the provisions of Clause 10 within 14 days of such payment being due;

(ii) if the Employer or any person for whom he is responsible interferes or obstructs the carrying out of the Works or fails to make the premises available for the Contractor in accordance with Clause 6;

---

* *Strike out the words in brackets in the case of new Works.*
† *If a different period is agreed, delete '3' and substitute the agreed period.*

(iii) if the Employer becomes bankrupt or makes a composition or arrangement with his creditors.

Provided always that the right of determination shall be without prejudice to any other rights or remedies which the Contractor may possess.

Prevention of Corruption **14** The Employer shall be entitled to cancel this Agreement and to recover from the Contractor the amount of any loss resulting from such cancellation, if the Contractor shall have offered or given or agreed to give to any person any gift or consideration of any kind or if the Contractor shall have committed any offence under the Prevention of Corruption Acts 1889 to 1916 or shall have given any fee or reward the receipt of which is an offence under sub-section (2) of Section 123 of the Local Government Act 1933.

Arbitration **15** If any dispute or difference concerning this contract shall arise between the Employer or the Architect Supervising Officer on his behalf and the Contractor such dispute or difference shall be and is hereby referred to the arbitration and final decision of a person to be agreed between the parties or, failing agreement within 14 days after either party has given to the other a written request to concur in the appointment of an arbitrator, a person to be appointed on the request of either party by the President or a Vice-President for the time being of the Institute of Arbitrators.

Value Added Tax **16** (i) In this Condition 'VAT' means the value added tax introduced by the Finance Act 1972 which is under the care and management of the Commissioners of Customs and Excise (hereinafter called 'the Commissioners').

(ii) The sum or sums due to the Contractor under Clause 2 of this Agreement shall be regarded as exclusive of any VAT, and the Employer shall pay to the Contractor any VAT properly chargeable by the Commissioners on the Contractor on the supply to the Employer of any goods and services by the Contractor under this Contract in the manner hereinafter set out.

(iii) (a) The Architect/Supervising Officer shall inform the Contractor of the amount certified for any interim payment under Clause 10(i) and immediately the Contractor shall give to the Employer a written provisional assessment of the respective values of those supplies of goods and services for which the certificate is being issued and which will be chargeable at the relevant time of supply on the Contractor at any rate or rates of VAT (including zero). The Contractor shall also specify the rate or rates of VAT which are chargeable on those supplies.

(b) Upon receipt of the Contractor's written provisional assessment the Employer shall calculate the amount of VAT due by applying the rate or rates of VAT specified by the Contractor to the amount of the supplies included in his assessment, and shall remit the calculated amount of such VAT to the Contractor when making payment to him of the amount of the

interim payment certified by the Architect/ Supervising Officer under Clause 10(i).

(iv) (a) After the issue by the Architect/Supervising Officer of his certificate of making good defects under Clause 9(iii) the Contractor shall, as soon as he can finally so ascertain, prepare and submit to the Employer a written final statement of the value of all supplies of goods and services for which certificates have been or will be issued which are chargeable on the Contractor at any rate or rates of VAT (including zero).

The Contractor shall also specify the rate or rates of VAT which are chargeable on those supplies and shall state the grounds on which he considers such supplies are so chargeable. He shall also state the total amount of VAT already received by him.

(b) Upon receipt of the written final statement the Employer shall calculate the amount of VAT due by applying the rate or rates of VAT specified by the Contractor to the value of the supplies included in the statement and deducting therefrom the total amount of VAT already received by the Contractor and shall pay the balance of such VAT to the Contractor within 28 days from receipt of the statement.

(c) If the Employer finds that the total amount of VAT specified in the final statement as already paid by him exceeds the amount of VAT calculated under paragraph (b) of this Sub-Clause, he shall so notify the Contractor, who shall refund such excess to the Employer within 28 days of receipt of the notification together with a receipt under Sub-Clause (v) hereof showing a correction of the amounts for which a receipt or receipts have previously been issued by the Contractor.

(v) Upon receipt of any VAT properly paid under the provisions of this Clause the Contractor shall issue to the Employer an authenticated receipt in the form of those issued by the Joint Contracts Tribunal.

(vi) (a) In calculating the amount of VAT to be paid to the Contractor under Sub-Clauses (iii) and (iv) hereof, the Employer shall disregard any sums which the Contractor may be liable to pay to the Employer as liquidated damages under Clause 6(iii).

(b) The Contractor shall likewise disregard such liquidated damages when stating the value of supplies of goods or services in his written final statement under Sub-Clause (iv)(a) hereof.

(vii) (a) If the Employer disagrees with the final statement issued by the Contractor under Sub-Clause (iv) (a) hereof he may request the Contractor to obtain the decision of the Commissioners on the VAT properly chargeable on the Contractor for all supplies of goods and services under this contract and the Contractor shall forthwith request the Commissioners for such decision.

(b) If the Employer disagrees with such decision, then, provided he secures the Contractor against all costs and other expenses, the Contractor shall in accordance with the instructions of the Employer make all such appeals against the decision of the Commissioners as the Employer may request.

(c) Within 28 days of the date of the decision of the Commissioners (or of the final adjudication of an appeal) the Employer or the Contractor as the case may be, shall pay or refund to the other any VAT underpaid or overpaid in accordance with such decision or adjudication. The Contractor shall also account to the Employer for any costs awarded in his favour. The provisions of Sub-Clause (iv) (c) shall apply in regard to the provision of authenticated receipts.

(viii) The provisions of Clause 15 shall not apply to any matters to be dealt with under Sub-Clause (vii) hereof.

(ix) If any dispute or difference between the Employer and the Contractor is referred to an Arbitrator appointed under Clause 15 or to a Court, then insofar as any payment awarded in such arbitration or court proceedings varies amounts certified for payment of goods or services supplied by the Contractor to the Employer under this contract or is an amount which ought to have been but was not so certified, then the provisions of this Clause shall so far as relevant and applicable apply to any such payments.

(x) Notwithstanding any provisions to the contrary elsewhere in these Conditions the Employer shall not be obliged to make any further payment to the Contractor if the Contractor is in default in providing the receipt referred to in Sub-Clause (v) hereof, provided that this Sub-Clause shall only apply where the Employer can show that he requires such receipt to validate any claim for credit for tax paid or payable under this Agreement which the Employer is entitled to make to the Commissioners.

These Conditions are reproduced with the kind permission of RIBA Publications Limited, the copyright holder. Full copies of the agreement may be obtained from them at 66 Portland Place, London W1N 4AD.